D0345175

"Lizzie Skurnick has been the go-to person for words for as long as I can remember. Now, she has gone even further, redefining the way we use them. This collection of breathtaking essays shows how seemingly innocuous words (and some pretty ugly ones, too) were once used to keep women down—but not anymore. Take that, mansplainers. *Pretty Bitches* is truly something."

—Marcy Dermansky, author of *Very Nice* and *The Red Car*

"Note to men: When you describe an ex-girlfriend or wife 'crazy,' all it tells me is that you're an emotional idiot. Note to women: This great new book by Lizzie Skurnick recasts the various insults directed at us for decades and centuries, breathing confident life into what it means to be an unabashed, bossy, crazy-ass bitch."

—Anna Holmes, founder of Jezebel and editor of *The Book of Jezebel: An Illustrated Encyclopedia of Lady Things* and *Hell Hath No Fury: Women's Letters from the End of the Affair*

"Funny, trenchant, moving, breathtaking—the essays here remake a language that has been used so often to trap women so that it can free them instead. A prismatic look at the state of being a woman today, from some of our best living writers."

—Alexander Chee, author of *Edinburgh*, *The Queen of the Night*, and *How to Write an Autobiographical Novel*

"This book is hilarious, amazing, and inspiring. An incredible anthology of brilliant women. Buy this book today, preferably more than one copy."

—Molly Jong-Fast, author of *The Social Climber's Handbook* and *Girl [Maladjusted]: True Stories from a Semi-Celebrity Childhood*

"Clever and potent...The book's smart premise and the incisive essays themselves are immensely relatable and should provide a great catalyst for personal introspection and thoughtful and productive discussion."

—*Booklist* (starred review)

"Sharp-witted and intimate...[An] eloquent inquiry into how language enshrines gender stereotypes."

—*Publishers Weekly*

"This uplifting collection serves as a good first step toward highlighting what's wrong with how women are talked about....A galvanizing, sharp compendium."

—*Kirkus*

PRETTY BITCHES

PRETTY BITCHES

ON BEING CALLED CRAZY, ANGRY, BOSSY,

FRUMPY, FEISTY, AND ALL THE OTHER WORDS

THAT ARE USED TO UNDERMINE WOMEN

EDITED BY LIZZIE SKURNICK

WITH AN INTRODUCTION BY REBECCA TRAISTER

SEAL

New York

Seal Press
Hachette Book Group
1290 Avenue of the Americas, New York, NY 10104
www.sealpress.com
@sealpress

Printed in the United States of America

First Edition: March 2020

Published by Seal Press, an imprint of Perseus Books, LLC, a subsidiary of Hachette Book Group, Inc. The Seal Press name and logo is a trademark of the Hachette Book Group.

The Hachette Speakers Bureau provides a wide range of authors for speaking events. To find out more, go to www .hachettespeakersbureau.com or call (866) 376-6591.

The publisher is not responsible for websites (or their content) that are not owned by the publisher.

Print book interior design by Amy Quinn

Library of Congress Cataloging-in-Publication Data
Names: Skurnick, Lizzie, editor.
Title: Pretty bitches: on being called crazy, angry, bossy, frumpy, feisty, and all the other words that are used to undermine women / edited by Lizzie Skurnick; with an introduction by Rebecca Traister.
Description: First edition. | New York: Seal Press, [2020] | Includes bibliographical references.
Identifiers: LCCN 2019038650 | ISBN 9781580059190 (hardcover) | ISBN 9781580059206 (ebook)
Subjects: LCSH: Right-wing extremists. | Hate speech. | Self-esteem. | Feminist theory.
Classification: LCC HN49.R33 P73 2020 | DDC 303.48/4—dc23
LC record available at https://lccn.loc.gov/2019038650ISBNs:
978-1-58005-919-0 (hardcover), 978-1-58005-920-6 (ebook)

LSC-C

10 9 8 7 6 5 4 3 2 1

For my teacher Lynne Vardaman,
who told me to be louder

CONTENTS

PREFACE
LIZZIE SKURNICK

A bitch is a female dog.

That was the response you gave to "bitch" in my middle school. Though I never got to use it, because no one called me a bitch. They said things like, "Don't argue with Liz!" or "She's pretty, but . . ." or "You're really intimidating." They said, "It's okay that my top is bigger, because your bottom is bigger," or "I never think of you as black," or "You have a Jewish nose," or "Flab!" Teachers told me, "Let someone else answer," and friends assured me, "You'll get into Yale because you're black." People said, "I wish I were as thin as you," or "You're twice as big as she is." They said, "Liz will be so pretty when she grows up, with her looks and her figure," and "Liz is *ugly*."

All of which is to say, they said—as we all did—numerous contradictory things, some compliments, some torments, many subject to opinion, many sheer sexism or racism. But none of it mattered because the world changed, we grew up, and we turned out to agree, or disagree, or laugh about them in therapy, or never think of them at all.

Or did we?

When the term *mansplaining* was invented, I was confused. No one ever mansplained to me—did they? *Manspreading*, on the other hand, I understood. Every day on the subway, I smashed down between two men whose thighs were taking up three seats, terrified of being yelled at, doing it anyway. When #MeToo started, I wrote down all the times I had actually been sexually harassed. Two strangers had seriously attempted to rape me, I realized. Bosses had massaged my shoulders—and fired me when I told them to stop. I had moved after a Con Ed man exposed himself and masturbated in my living room, then claimed I had met him the night before at a club. I had physically hidden from men—men hitting on me, following me, even chasing me. Men had snidely said, "Oh, *girl's* books" when I talked about my work in young adult literature. Not one but two boys routinely tackled me after I made a touchdown—in touch football. And yes, when my boss opined, "There are no real women writers," that was mansplaining. I had just been tuning it out.

There was something so freeing about this new language, a language invented to describe women's experiences we had never had words for. Jezebel's brilliant construction: "Crap Emails from a Dude." That was the term for those lengthy self-justifying, self-pitying, oddly formal emails you got after a breakup! #YesAllWomen—that was what you said when men said not all men were sexual predators! Those men commenting on my articles who said I needed to be taken out in a car and fucked—that wasn't because I was a bad writer. That was called *toxic masculinity*. The colleague who repeatedly harassed and accosted me in the halls after I declined coffee? I was not "unprofessional" for saying no. That was *workplace harassment*.

All this time, I had thought I was being a good feminist, pushing myself, not letting men take advantage of me or drag me down. But it was now clear I was staggering under a huge load of guilt, shame, and dread. All of these experiences: I had thought they were something I could have prevented or had brought on— that they were my fault. But now I had words for all of them.

And it *wasn't*.

When Hillary lost, buried in an avalanche of *flawed* and *shrill* and *ambitious*, I started to think back on those small words again.

How I was *loud*, or *argumentative*, or *bossy*, or *demanding*. How I was *tiny*, or *stocky*, or *confused*, or *sort of stupid*. How I was *too nice*, a *huge bitch*, kind of *nasty*. How I was *intense*. I was *psycho*. I was *irrational*. I was *lazy*. I was *dramatic*. I was so, so *smart*.

I had always felt words like *loud* or *crazy* were mere pinpricks, irritants you brushed off on your way to someplace bigger. But these small words, I was starting to realize, had had real consequences, in my life and in others'.

A single mom at forty, I found myself particularly outraged by the financial cost. I had lost a two-thirds 401(k) match when I was fired from the pervy boss. ("Lazy.") It had cost me $1,200 to move after the Con Ed masturbator. ("Slut.") I had lost access to cheap health care from Mr. Unprofessional. (A million dollars.) This was just the short list. Those dollars were a down payment on a house, a gymnastics class for my son, taxes. Those people who had mansplained, shut me down, shut me up, had not only called me names. They had hit me in the wallet. Which took away my power.

And I was one of the lucky ones.

I began to realize these words weren't pinpricks. They weren't the punishment. They were the justification *for* the punishment: the jobs we lost, the promotions, the houses, the money, our respect, our bodies, our voices. Because, yes, it wasn't 1952. You could no longer outright say you weren't giving someone the position because she was a woman. But what if she was shrill? Ambitious? Difficult?

As women, our problem wasn't that we needed to be more forceful, more self-assured, to make our way in the herd of confident, self-assured men currently ruling the world. It was that when we spoke up, they told us to sit down. And shut the fuck up.

Our voices were hurting their ears.

The day I sold this book, a man called me a yappy bitch. He was not a stranger. He was a fellow dad, a member of the PTA, a man I'd done after-school programs with, whom I always waved to on the street.

I was at the park with this fellow dad and my friend, and he wanted to talk to us about race. It was actually a tedious argument, the one black people have to have about race with white people all the time. (Guess what: he didn't see it!) But my friend and I both had biracial kids. I was biracial myself. He was a fellow dad. He did a lot for the school. We could have the talk.

As we watched our children run up and down the slide—my friend's son and mine, kinky haired and many hued, and his daughter, like him, a redhead with milk-white skin—I braced myself.

"It's talking about race that causes racism," he began.

I was polite during the "I don't check race on the sheets!" part and even the "It's racist for you to call me a white man" section.

But when he said that the only difference between him and black people was that he burned more easily in the sun, I spoke up.

"Actually, black people have to be a lot more careful about the sun, because it's not as visible when the burn is happening," I said. My friend nodded.

His face clouded. "But black people have more melanin," he explained to the two ladies with the mixed-race children.

"We're all aware of that," I said, because friends help friends stop mansplaining. "But black skin is actually quite a bit more sensitive than white skin. It can scar and keloid more easily. It was a big problem when dermatologists didn't know. And they didn't know because they didn't care." I paused. "Your not marking 'white' doesn't really do anything about that."

Fellow Dad had removed his iPhone from his case to clean it with his keys. As he scraped at the edges, his face reddened, and his hands began to shake.

"You're quite a yapper, aren't you?" he said.

My friend and I looked at each other and laughed. We had been containing ourselves, but it was enough. "You do know you're not supposed to call women *yappy*, right?" I said.

"I mean, you're kind of a bitch," he said, scraping his keys across the case faster.

I knew he wouldn't hit me, but suddenly I could feel how much he wanted to. I tried to think what I would do if he did. Duck? Call the police? Contact the PTA?

But before I needed to do any of that, he called his daughter. He stalked off the playground without saying goodbye. But I didn't feel relief. I felt terror about seeing him at the next PTA meeting.

"I wasn't sure what I was going to do if he hit you!" my friend said.

"I know!" I said. "And we were being *nice*."

I did not, on the playground, use that opportunity to say, "A bitch is a female dog." (Or "A dog is yappy," for that matter.) But that day, I realized what the actual problem was. I *am* yappy, of course. I can (sometimes with joy!) be a bitch. But on that playground, I was being neither. I was trying to be polite. I was trying to be a friend. We were just having an argument.

But I was winning.

INTRODUCTION
REBECCA TRAISTER

Oh my god, my mom was talking about fucking and I wanted to melt into the seat of the car, on an afternoon trip to the dentist during which my brother and I—probably then about ten and thirteen—had made the grave error of getting into an argument in which one of us had, experimentally, probably humorously, told the other "Fuck you" within her hearing.

My mother had not reacted with anger—there was a high tolerance for profanity in our home—but rather with something far, far worse: sadness. Our use of *fuck* as an expression of animus, even in jest, had led her down some sort of private rabbit hole, and she was meditating wistfully about the word's origins.

"It means *sex*," she was telling us as we suffered horribly, me in the front seat and Aaron in the back. "And you know, that should be a *good* thing, a *warm* thing; it can be a *loving* thing. In fact, fucking should be about people who like each other or want to be with each other, not about hating each other or expressing a desire to hurt each other." We both stared straight ahead, un-moving, waiting for it to end.

"It's too bad, because I used to love the word *fuck*; it was a fun and intimate word," she went on, and my barely teenaged brain may or may not have briefly clocked that my mother was saying that the word *fuck* had once been appealingly dirty, before seizing in horror and moving on. "But now I mostly hear it as an aggres-sive word, a mean word, a word that suggests that the act of fuck-ing itself is mean and aggressive and often *particularly* aggressive toward women. . . . It's really a shame."

It was a wretched car ride.

But three decades later, decades I spent as a woman who cares deeply about language and its uses and abuses, a woman who had been used and abused by some of the words she loves best, I now understand my mother's dejection better. It's not that I feel that way about *fuck*, a word with which I joyously oversalt my expres-sions of frustration and aggression, even as I also enjoy it as dirty and intimate.

But more broadly, I understand how she feels about the ease with which so many beautiful words, loamy with meaning and nuance—some sharp and specific, some pliable—have been ru-ined, made flaccid and lackluster by the simple, monotonous constancy of bias. Their negative implications have become ordi-nary, part of the daily landscape of racism, sexism, diminution, that undergird not only our politics and our popular culture but the world in which we live our lives, and in which the relentless-ness of diminishment and insult can take fluid and descriptive elements of our lexicon and turn them mean and cramped.

Reading the essays that follow makes me think of all the words I mourn. Words I loved fiercely and had to abandon, and those I never even managed to appreciate on their own before absorbing the ways they'd become tools of containment or degradation. Some that I have relied on as sturdy and useful, some gendered and some unsexed—*ambitious, mature, lucky, victim, disciplined, intimidating, exotic, loud, zaftig, nurturing, aloof, crazy*—I have come to understand as undermining. Here are the ordinaries, the ones I never thought twice about: *mom, funny, small, loud, effortless.* And then of course there were the prepoisoned ones I knew never (or rarely) to touch: *princess, ugly, pretty, bossy.*

In my case, and perhaps ironically, the words I am saddest about are the bad ones. The curse words. The slurs: *cunt, bitch, harpy, virago, termagant.*

Yes, I love *cunt*: crisp and vicious, acidic and eviscerating when used (oh so rarely, saved up for when it is truly earned) about a woman and more regularly about men, when describing a kind of tight meanness that gets its negativity from its association with denigrated female sexuality, yes, but which so very often applies to men who behave like, well, cunts. I try not to use it anymore about women—because it has become so violent and cheap, not sharp and damning—or about men, because its power seems to me increasingly to stem from the wearisome assertion that the worst thing you can say about a man is that he is, somehow, female.

And *harpy*! Oh, how I used to love the word *harpy*, evocative and mythical and old, such a useful way to describe a particular, specific kind of person, a malevolent bird of prey with a woman's face. Yes! There are people who are like that, very specifically like that, and how fine to have a word to say so.

I like these words in part because in a perfect world, deploying them would mean, necessarily, taking responsibility for having used them, and I like taking the use of language seriously. I like thinking about words and treating them as powerful, direct conveyances of meaning, including when what you intend to convey is that a person—sometimes a woman—is bad. Or cruel. Or difficult. Because sometimes women, who are people, are bad and cruel and difficult.

But no, now it is simply a word to describe a woman who threatens you—by talking, or competing, or being ambitious, or existing when you would prefer she didn't. And it is boring and mean and sexist and watery and no longer fun and powerful and descriptive and pointed, not just for those of us who want to call people harpies, but for the harpies themselves!

Someone recently pointed out to me how remarkable it was that some words used to describe furious or threatening women assume their passion and aggression are forces so strong that they overtake them, transforming them into literal monsters—along with *harpy*, there are *virago, termagant*—rendering them inhuman. This is endlessly interesting, but now I think of how using words to dehumanize women isn't really that surprising or dramatic; it reflects only that it is Wednesday or Monday, in April or January, in Ashtabula or Shanghai.

I have a particular fondness, one that often has seemed at odds with the feminism that guides so much of my work and thinking, for words that are especially negative about femininity—not just the above, but *bitch* and *pussy* and *slag* and *whinge* and *hysteria* and *scold*—words that derived their nasty implications from their very associations with femininity. I find their origins fascinating, telling, and every so often, useful.

Because of course it's not just the big bad words that derive from vaginas or patriarchal mythologies, but also the words that are the ordinary conveyors of elucidating information about people, the words designed simply to differentiate human beings from each other, to flesh out personalities, quirks, talents, traits, and shortcomings: *big, small, ambitious, brainy, eager, talkative, competitive, professional, nice.*

So many of the stories in this volume wind up being about the crumpling up and ruination of these small words, the ones that should be meaningful or useful or just reliable guides to the people around us, but instead have been deployed against us, so steadily and exhaustingly, as part of an effort to define and diminish and distract us from life as we might be living it were we not saddled with having to prove our rights to participate equally in it.

So that *small* stands in for *Vietnamese* and *professional* for *white*, and *effortless* for the lie that women are not asked to spend their lives and energies conforming to standards set for them by men, and *shrill* is a way to point out that a woman is talking when she would ideally be silent.

Utterances that might otherwise be communicative tools become blunt and dull, pedestrian instruments used to chip away at the dignity of non-male, non-white existence. These words don't always deliver mere insult: they may also carry the weight of dishonesty, heightened expectations, double standards, celebrations of reduced power, and affirmations of other kinds of femininity to which we do not measure up (or down).

Perhaps the most heartbreaking of the pieces that you'll read in this volume is the first one, Adaora Udoji's meditation on the word *too* and how it has been used to censure and shame her since childhood. She points out, with a pain immediately recognizable to so many of us, that *too*, when in reference to women's traits—from kindness to intelligence—is always a signal of opprobrium.

Her point is underscored again and again in the volume that follows her essay, as writer after writer points out how many of the ways in which the words they have come to rear back from have, in one way or another, been associated with having "too" much of some quality.

Afua Hirsch is told that her legs are "too muscular" for TV and that her Afro takes up "too much of the screen"; Amy Choi describes the quandary of having "too much eyebrow"; Dahlia Lithwick remembers that her first evaluations in high school debate included the observations that she spoke "too fast" and was "too nervous"; and Jillian Medoff remembers boys telling her that she was "too mature" and notes that in adulthood, the eventual implications of the word *mature* stand in for "too old," "too slow," and "too twentieth century." Julianna Baggott understands, in her meditation on ambition, that as soon as she begins winning awards and getting a reputation as a writer, she is seen as having "achieved too much" and as being "too prolific." Tanzila Ahmed includes the classic warning, coming from an auntie, that the reason she is not married is because she is "too successful," "too educated," and "too intimidating" for men.

The grievous revelation of Udoji's piece, followed by so much evidence backing it up, weighed on me so much that I internally struggled to push back against it: considering that the very meaning of the word *too* is of course about an excess of some quality, surely when it's used about the most powerful—the white, the male—it's also critical, demeaning, diminishing. But the reality, I realized as I wrestled with this possibility, is that white men are rarely told they possess too much of anything. That all the things women do *too* much of—talk, think, desire, aspire, smile, yell, take up space—we cannot get enough of in men.

The horror of Udoji's examination of this simple, three-letter adverb in daily use is simply gutting: that *too*—the description of overabundance used to deplete so many of us, so easily— telegraphs the grim reality of how so many women are deplored because we are understood to have, simply, an excess of humanity itself, so irritating when we insist on possessing it.

And that is how so many of these words that could be fun to use, useful to weave together to create meaning and increase understanding and make written connection more fluid and frank, have instead been turned into little stinging darts, a thousand pinches to our personhood. Because part of the pleasure of language is using it to describe and sort out people, and women aren't really supposed to be people.

As I have aged, been slowly boiled in this world, I have become ambivalent or antagonistic toward my former pleasures: the deployment of intentional and weighty insults, now mucked up by the understanding that most of them are heard as common diminutions. I no longer revel in the pungent intimacy of filthy oaths, because they are too often used as implements of boring disdain. I think twice and three times about using certain adjectives and adverbs that might otherwise bloom or bite but that have now simply ground us to tired dust.

Like my mom, I mourn the loss of—my ability to easily and briskly use—words that were once beautiful and electric but that have been perverted by the very forces to which I'd like to use them to say: *Fuck you, fuck you, fuck you.*

Note this realization—that what I want to do is scream—is itself revealing of the imperative: to keep using these words, keep screaming them, writing them, saying them aloud to each other and the world. Because when the tools of expression are turned against you—from the extraordinary *cunts* to the ordinary *toos*, the intimate *fucks* to the bruising *bitches*, the basic *nice* to the glorious *ambitious*—what becomes clear is that thing they want is for us to stop opening our mouths at all.

PRETTY BITCHES

TOO

ADAORA UDOJI

Craig was a tad taller than me. Let's say a quarter of an inch. Thin, with brown hair, a little too long in front. Brown eyes. He was funny. Smart. White. Slightly awkward—or, as I would learn later, extremely awkward.

It was first grade circa 1973, and we were a class of a dozen kids in a magnet school in Boston's Roxbury neighborhood—lab rats of a sort in a radical integration experiment. The class was roughly one-third white, one-third black, and one-third "Other." Then, Roxbury was the heart of Boston's black community. I, half Nigerian and half Irish leprechaun, lived in the all-white neighborhood of Brighton many miles away. Ironically, I was bused to Roxbury when, all by myself, I could have integrated the school down the street.

I had a crush on Craig. Perhaps *crush* is too strong a word. But I liked him, and I wanted him to like me back. Craig asked interesting questions, like, How big is the ocean? Can you count all the fish in the sea? If we got on a motorcycle and kept driving, could we make it around the world, and if so, how long would that take? He illustrated his name tag with endless loops of Nordic comic book characters.

I angled to sit next to Craig in art and assemblies. I asked his opinion on the world map I had made, on which I'd spent endless hours, marveling at the expanse of Earth. I listened closely to what he said and considered his opinions even when they ran afoul of my deeply held beliefs. For some unknown reasons, he liked the color yellow. Though it was not my favorite, I tried really hard to appreciate its finer points.

But not only did he not show interest in me, he apparently felt stalked. One unusually hot day in late spring, on the vast black concrete lot known as the Trotter Elementary playground, Craig's friend followed me as I followed Craig.

Craig's henchman was a verbose, ten-year-old African American boy. He approached me like a person with a life-or-death mission and proceeded to curse at me like a grown-ass man. "You talk TOO much," he unloaded in a raspy adult voice. "Stay the fuck away from Craig."

It was the first time I had ever been stunned into silence. It took my brain a minute to catch up. Who talked to anyone that way, especially at ten years old? He could have slapped me and I would have been less surprised. I was sure my eyes bugged out of my face, cartoon style. My stomach dropped to the floor, and I felt a blast of light-headedness that is seared into my memory.

I can still see him, short and stubby, round. I don't remember his name. I do remember his head bobbing atop his round body like one of those Mickey Mouse toys you buy from sidewalk vendors at street fairs. I had clearly stepped over a line I didn't know existed—which, for the rule-following daughter of a former

Catholic nun, was excruciating. This was a world I knew nothing about and was unprepared for, like walking into a summer downpour to find it was really a tornado.

To make sure I'd heard him, he spoke again: "You talk too much, TOOOOOOO much. You are TOO loud. TOOOOOO loud. Do you understand? Stay the fuck away from Craig."

It never occurred to me I could yell, or curse back, or square my shoulders and tell him to mind his own business. I felt powerless, like he had it and I had none. I wanted to disappear so badly I felt the concrete transform into an ocean and swallow me up.

I turned on my heel, said nothing, and walked away.

I could not know then that it wasn't the harsh *fuck* but the *too* that would linger and loom large. I didn't yet know how easily that word could be weaponized against me as a woman, used against any woman, pulled from the ever-ready "stay in your place" toolbox. *Too* would follow me through my academic life and ensuing career, trailing with permanence, delivering daily doses of feeling like I'd done something wrong, that there was something in me that needed fixing. That word, more than any curse, would haunt me in ways I could not have imagined.

According to Merriam-Webster, *too* has two primary applications: It modifies or qualifies a verb. Its benign use means *beside* or *also*, as in, "Sell the house and the furniture too." But it can also indicate judgment—negative judgment. *Too* can mean *excessive*, as in, "The house is too large for us." It can be a rebuttal: "I didn't do it!" "You did too!"

But when was the last time you heard *too* used as a compliment? Think about that for a second. When was the last time you heard someone say "too healthy," "too smart," or "too pretty"?

Betcha something else came to mind, like slightly veiled criticism. Too loud. Too intense. Too ambitious. Too black. Too white. Too fat. Too cutting. Curse too much. Too domineering. Too abrasive. Too much of a know-it-all. Too anything but something good.

Too often seems as if it were especially created for women. Too emotional. Too curt. Too obnoxious. Too rude. Too pale. Too pushy. Too nice. Wait, is it really possible to be too nice? Apparently it is if you are female. A quick Google search for "Women are too nice" kicks back 1,100,000,070 results, the first one titled "Quit Being So Nice." "Men are taught to be right," the article begins. "Women are taught to be nice. And the need to be nice can be a downfall."

You read that right, a downfall. We, women, are too nice—apparently so nice that we nice our way out of promotions, roles, and responsibilities. *She's nice.* That's a compliment. *She's too nice.* That means she's not tough enough, not single-minded or a go-getter, not someone who can successfully manage people, build a business, be relied upon, make money. When was the last time you heard someone say a man was too nice? Um, probably never.

I didn't want to seem too ambitious, so I only applied to two colleges and got into one. That was good enough. When I got to law school, my property professor told me I asked *too* many questions. He told me to "relax my brain" when I challenged the genesis of property laws in the United States that radically favor the wealthiest landowners into eternity. He point-blank told me that talking too much and digging too deep wouldn't get me anywhere.

Those supposed personality failings were unconsciously added to that list of deficiencies noted by Craig and his pal. It was a classic compounding scenario; that I was too loud, talked too much, and asked too many questions was a potent trifecta. I spent a lot of time trying to figure out how to "relax my brain," how to talk less, ask fewer questions, and be quieter.

This is dogma woven into our culture: that girls and women should stay in our lane, the quiet lane, where we speak softly and demurely and tread lightly, where we are deferential to the status quo. Being told I was too loud and too talkative on too many occasions to count was peer pressure, a form of herding that shut me down and encouraged me not to engage. I obliged this idea that I needed to change, convinced that there was something wrong with me and that I could fix it by participating in my own life a lot less.

I stopped raising my hand in class, answering only if called on. I can only guess as to whether it affected my grades. Law school graduation? Didn't go. Why bother if I didn't graduate in the top 10 percent of my class? Not good enough.

Early in my career, I didn't speak up when I was offered a job that I knew for a fact paid men $25,000 more a year, afraid that if I pushed back, they would rescind the offer. Compound the smaller wages I took again and again, and it translates to an enormous amount. But I saw that employer and many employers after them as doing me a favor, overlooking my defects to give me a chance. I told myself, "Play it small; don't be too visible; you are not there yet; keep your head down and work toward perfection."

This head-down approach blossomed into a habit at work and in my personal relationships. Rather than correct the president of the media company that the idea to increase efficiency in assignments was mine, not John's, I kept quiet. My boyfriends were radically self-involved people—narcissists, my therapist would say—who never asked me much about myself. There were minimal opportunities to be too loud, to upset the balance of things. It's hard to breathe, never mind talk too much and be too loud, when you're trapped in a box.

Too shook my sense of self and my sense of self-confidence. It made it less likely I would speak out on my own behalf. When I didn't, I was busy doubting myself, busy not pointing out that the award the team got was a result also of the work I contributed though somehow my name was not on the trophy, busy explaining away why I didn't get the promotion, the position, the role, the job.

Too is used to launch uncertainty, throw you off your game, make you second-guess, take your eye off the ball, to subtly let you know there is something wrong with you when you start coloring outside the lines—and goodness, don't let it be with a neon crayon. It tells you that *you* are the problem, and that the solution is to stop your behavior, right now. It shames you and justifies why they are not listening to your ideas, why you are not in charge and they are.

───

The cherished feminist poet, thinker, and writer Audre Lorde says, "I have come to believe over and over again that what is most important to me must be spoken, made verbal and shared, even at the risk of having it bruised or misunderstood." Thankfully, standing up for myself runs deep in every cell in my body. My Nigerian grandmother, Mercy Adaora Udoji, whom I was named after, was a revered chief in our Igbo hierarchy. She was a commanding, witty woman and not to be trifled with. I am also the proud granddaughter of a hardy and wise farmer's daughter from County Clare, Ireland, Elizabeth Mary Browne Callanan. She passed on an optimistic resistance: "Always remember, nothing and no one is ever as it is or as they seem."

The beginning of the end of believing the *too*-much-of-everything version of myself came in 1996, when I was working as a producer in broadcast reporting. When a TWA flight went down off the coast of Long Island, another producer and I split the white pages and called dozens of businesses, asking questions over and over, looking for witnesses for what was at the time thought to be a terrorist attack. It wasn't, but that persistence, asking endless questions, led to my first video exclusive, and we got some of the first wreckage on camera.

Then in 2000, just hours after the legendary Concorde plane exploded and crashed in a rural area outside of Paris, my producer and I slipped through a hole in the fence in the middle of a rainy summer night to get closer to the site. Cutting through shoulder-high grass, we were stopped by the barrels of many guns. We'd run afoul of the French special forces, who walked us out and told us we were too pushy and asking too many questions. We were lucky. They could have shot us; they didn't. And pushing got us more information to report, faster.

Being inquisitive is a bonus for a reporter. After all, what do journalists do? They ask way too many questions, they do it often, and they do it loudly. I was and am driven by relentless curiosity. I wonder about everything, all the time. I ask endless questions because the world fascinates me, and this has made me very, very good at my job.

And I've been rewarded. I rose rapidly from a producer to an on-air correspondent to an anchor and ultimately the cohost of my own show, the holy grail in broadcast news. I covered some of the most critical international and domestic stories in modern history, reporting on the wars in Iraq and Afghanistan for ABC News, four presidential elections between 1995 and 2007, the Israeli-Palestinian conflict, global sporting events like Wimbledon and the Tour de France, and the Oscars, the world's defining accolades in film.

As a reporter, I saw the world, from the Isle of Islay off the coast of Scotland to the dunes of Doha; from the streets of Geneva to the flatlands of Baghdad; from the mountains of Islamabad to the swamps of Louisiana to the big sky in Montana. The sights were majestic, barren, flat, swampy, and bumpy. I met people surviving war, running for president, or just winning the local lottery.

How could I possibly have known all those years ago in Roxbury that Craig's loud friend had actually identified my superpower: the ability to be persistent, to connect, to ask questions loudly? When you're a reporter, you have to talk too much and do it over the din of helicopters, bombs, cheering crowds, hurricanes, election results, holiday cheer, school board meetings, and everything in between. (I wish I had a dime for every time a producer thanked me for talking live through technical difficulties. I would be really rich.) The universe has a great sense of humor, right? What I was routinely lambasted or punished for were the very things that created and fueled my successes.

This rapid rise culminated in a tremendous opportunity, to cohost a new radio show. But the dream job turned into a desperate nightmare. My cohost was a bully, and he bullied me off the show, as he did the two cohosts who followed me. He sexually harassed young women on staff and even guests. Ten years later, at the crest of the #MeToo movement, it became one of the most reported examples of sexism and harassment.

My experience on that show felt worse than my experience with Craig and henchboy. But even all those years later, my reaction was the same. I took off. Retired. Left journalism altogether. It took a while to regain my voice, my platform, my place in the world. But I did, talking too much the entire way.

Words matter. They tell a story. They leave an imprint. I encourage you to look out and listen for that sneaky and tricky little *too*. I hope you think about how you use it and how perhaps it's been used against you, 'cause chances are, if you are of the female persuasion, it has. Most important, I hope that next time you hear it, you question the intent. Give the speaker the side-eye and ask for clarification. In fact, turn it around, and feel free to agree that you are *too* whatever. Chances are it's taking you to a damn good place.

Because really, truly, life is too short.

PROFESSIONAL
AFUA HIRSCH

The first time I went to Ghana, the West African country of my mother's birth, I was struck by the names we were taught to use for our adult relatives. An auntie who lived in the village, named Irene at birth, was now known to everyone as "Teacher." In the city, the family friend whose house we stayed in was simply "Doctor," and an uncle was "Lawyer James."

It dawned on me then that to have a profession was so prized, it became the bedrock of a person's identity—even more so than a given name. With this heritage on one side of my family and that of Jewish refugees on the other, there was no way I was ever not going to become a professional.

So a professional is what I became. This is a statement of fact. After an attempt at a career doing serious and important work for NGOs across West Africa—which I overheard my mother describe to family members as my "gap year"—I fell in line and trained as a barrister in London. But could I become someone to whom the adjective *professional* truly applied? This was a far more complicated question.

At twenty-three years old, I was a young black woman of mixed heritage, with brown skin and black hair, which I wore in its natural state of Afro curls. I tended to adorn my wrists with wooden bangles and hoop earrings I'd picked up from the Mali market in the Senegalese capital of Dakar, where I had moved when I was twenty-one and from which I'd only recently returned. I favored bright colors—I still do—alternating sometimes with a toned-down palette of muted brown, dark red, beige, or green. It was the early aughts, after all, the apex of boho chic. My partner used to joke, when I first met him, that I looked like an "eco-warrior"—which, in my head, I replaced with "earthy." As he was an aspirational barrister himself, this was not necessarily a compliment.

The setting for this and other conversations was the Inns of Court, four expansive medieval campuses located in the beating heart of central London yet cloistered away behind majestic Tudor walls.

My first encounter with Lincoln's Inn—the one I joined—took my breath away. I remember the first time I saw it, hidden away as it is behind obscure brick portholes—its Great Lawn a manicured expanse of striped green, with a grand redbrick library that looked like a palace on the other side.

That building, constructed in 1843, holds Lincoln's Inn's New Hall. Its Old Hall was begun in 1490, before Christopher Columbus set sail, during the reign of King Henry VII. Lincoln's Inn itself was founded long before that, around 1320. I was fortunate enough to gain a scholarship from the Inn that helped pay for the cost of my legal education and allowed me to live in the Inn.

It was a great privilege. But it was also an immersion course in what it really means to become a "professional" and the baggage of that concept's history—a history neither explained nor etched into the Inn's ancient stone walls.

The "oldest profession in the world" is not prostitution, as Rudyard Kipling would have had us believe when he coined that phrase in his 1888 story "On the City Wall." It is membership in a religious order, and the term *profession* derives from the Latin *profiteor*: "to acknowledge, promise, confess." Chaucer was one of the first to use it in English: in his *Shipman's Tale*, a monk declares, "This swere I yow on my profession." The word soon began to apply to all three vocations requiring the swearing of an oath: medicine, theology, and law.

The practitioners of these professions were not just men but men of the elite ruling class. Lincoln's Inn, one of the first professional centers, was reserved, said Sir John Fortescue, the famous jurist and ally of King Henry VI, for "sons of persons of quality, those of an inferior rank not being able to bear the expenses."[1] That I got a scholarship from Lincoln's Inn was evidence of how much had changed. That I needed one was evidence of how much had not.

When it came around to interviewing for that scholarship, I ditched the "earthy" look, straightened my hair, and put on a white shirt and black suit: the only acceptable attire for barristers. When I later became a qualified barrister, I continued straightening my hair so that I would be able to position the white horsehair wig on top of my head. (The wig, along with a black gown, was my compulsory work uniform.) Soon I learned that things could have been worse: the "skirts only" rule had just been abolished in 1995.[2] Women had only been allowed to wear trouser suits in court for a decade.

A female QC—Queen's Counsel, the most senior and respected of barristers—whom I hugely admired told me a story of how she'd appeared before a judge in London's High Court in the 1990s. In spite of her articulate and audible representations, he boomed "I can't hear you" at her. Mystified, she repeated herself with her already-impressive volume at full pelt. Again, the judge, who wasn't known to have any hearing problems, boomed, "I CAN'T HEAR YOU." A male barrister sitting beside her took pity and pointed at her light-brown hair, which fell loosely around her shoulders. "He's referring to your hair," he whispered. "He won't take representations from a woman unless she has her hair tied back."

The female QC with the shoulder-length hair was one of the first women to even enter the legal profession. If a white woman, and a highly respected one at that, had endured this kind of behavior from the bench, I dreaded to think what a black girl with natural hair might go through.

British history is rich with examples of women either being relegated to subservience or, when leadership has been required of them, having to disassociate themselves from their gender altogether. In mid-Victorian Britain, professions like accounting were deemed unsuitable for women because the skills "contrasted markedly with the image of the weak, dependent, emotional 'married' woman."[3] Schoolchildren are taught to this day about Queen Elizabeth I's fabled and apocryphal speech at Tilbury, in which she rouses the troops by declaring, "I may have the body of a weak and feeble woman, but I have the heart and stomach of a king."

The law, where much of this started, remains a study in point. Women were overtly prohibited from legal careers by a system academics now describe as "exclusionary closure through credentialising."[4] The professor Minna Kotkin describes the imposter syndrome she still feels after twenty years of teaching and practicing law: "When lawyers, particularly adversaries, begin to talk about professionalism around me, I sometimes still get anxious," she writes. "My reaction has nothing to do with doubts about my ethical behavior but, rather, it relates to my gender: I wonder whether others think I am acting like a woman instead of like a lawyer."[5]

In the last few decades, social change has meant that women are allowed to join the professions—and do, often in numbers equal to men. But it's a path that is still overlaid with gender exclusion.[6] A study of two professions—law and accounting—found that women were leaving professional services early in their career, not only because of sexual discrimination and the burden of balancing professional and family commitments, but because they did not fit a prevailing masculine model of performance or success.[7] And within the professions, women remain crowded into less professional, more maternal, more caring areas of practice—"feminine, community orientated and relatively underpaid specialisms on the one side as opposed to the male dominated, corporate oriented and highly remunerative practice areas on the other."[8]

Women are disadvantaged by ideas of the "professional" before we even walk through the door, because to be truly *professional* is to conform to the ideal on which it is based: an elite, white man.

───

With the white man as the ideal and everyone else positioned somewhere along the spectrum, we must meet the standards of attractiveness applied uniquely—or disproportionately—to women.

The study of law and accounting professionals also found that women were penalized for dressing too "trendily" on the one hand and for having unattractive footwear on the other. When one female applicant turned up to an interview at a law firm, one partner reflected, "Okay, you were almost there honey, I almost would have taken you seriously," but he didn't because of her "gigantic shoes."[9]

Conscious of the need, women were more likely than men to go to great lengths to look well dressed. "I sort of think that if you go to a meeting and you are the only women [*sic*] in the room you better be the best dressed one there," one said.[10] The lawyers and accountants also displayed a preference for thinness as a more "professional" look, something that was presented as an objective, gender-neutral question of health and self-control.[11] But it was clear the perceived failure to exercise such "self-control" was a greater problem for women. One lawyer described his female colleague as "heavy" and said, "I have seen her struggle throughout her career with . . . being taken seriously, and unfortunately I think some of it has to do with her weight, and . . . she had all her own issues about it already and then I think on top of it she was being judged for it."[12]

My experience was the same. One woman I worked with in TV was told she was "eating herself off the telly"—an unsubtle suggestion that weight gain would not be acceptable—in spite of the fact that some of the most popular and famous male broadcasters were notoriously wide of girth and habitually unkempt.

The pressure on women to conform to the ideal of the professional by abandoning their preferred jewelry, footwear, or fashion sense is problematic enough. But what about the characteristics that can't be changed? What about the inherent threat to their own masculine standards of professional behavior that men perceive from the simple sound of a woman's voice?

The historian Mary Beard, who has traced ideas about the male desire to decapitate and silence vocal women from ancient times, reminds us that Medusa—the classic tale of male dominance removing the illegitimate and depraved power of a woman through ultimate violence, leaving nothing but a decapitated head—was resuscitated in America's 2016 election campaign as a response to Hillary Clinton. In one particularly unsettling image, Trump is cast as Perseus, the disembodied head of Hillary Clinton held high in his triumphant hand. The comment made repeatedly about Clinton was not about her policy platform but about the unbearable shrillness of her voice.

To be shrill is a fatal flaw for the authoritative female—an ultimate failure to conform to the masculine professional ideal. In the study of lawyers and accountants, one man described a woman's voice as "so strident [that] he felt attacked," while a partner commented that, for a woman, there is a "very fine line between assertive and shrill and you can't go over the shrill line."

Voice is a damning symptom of femininity, and for a woman to be "professional," she is expected to adapt hers. At the beginning of my own TV career in broadcast journalism, a well-meaning male manager told me, "You might want to try lowering the tone of your voice—a lot of women find it helps them to be taken more seriously." The failure to do so has potentially commercial implications, since women are expected to protect the fragile egos of not just their male colleagues but their male listeners and viewers as well.

These experiences are no accident. The concept of professionalism is, at its root, embedded in a patriarchal system that depends on mobilizing and managing male power.

Take the very foundations of bureaucracy, deconstructed by German sociologist Max Weber as the most efficient and rational way to structure human activity within organizations. When I read Weber as an undergraduate, his ideas were presented as an ungendered system for augmenting efficiency and eliminating nepotism. Subsequent work has revealed they are anything but. One theory is that the way we organize our workplaces is premised on the presumption that they are populated by men who will inevitably regard each other as hostile strangers.[13] This male aggression needs to be organized into a stable and predictable order, keeping intimacy and the exercise of emotion to a bare minimum, so that a dynamic of functional strangers can be preserved.

The irony is that, while this "professional" workplace may have been constructed to drive out the feminine, it cannot exist without it. The secretary who is excluded from the professional status of her male colleagues is the one on whose support they depend. The stay-at-home wife, who is often as well educated or even better educated than her husband, in many cases a fully trained professional herself, is guided into supporting the professional man from the home by our complex web of social conventions and pressures.

Like many women at work, I was conscious of my voice, of the shape, size, and contours of my body. But most of all, I was conscious of my race. Black people often describe instinctively understanding that they cannot speak in the workplace as they would to people within their own community; instead, code-switching is necessary in order to sound closer to the white ideal. When it comes to our hair, there are also standards black women instinctively know. As an aspiring barrister, without the confidence, knowledge, or vocabulary to articulate what I was doing, I was in no doubt that I needed hair straighteners to do it.

As a woman, from the very beginning of my career, the concept of what looked "professional" was an oppressive wall of convention. If you run a Google image search for "professional hair for work," the results are hundreds of images of white women with straight, sleek hair. Switch that for "unprofessional hair for work," and the results are a similar number of black women with natural hair textures.[14] Black women's professionalism, beauty, and disability are measured against Eurocentric ideals, which dooms them to be measured against white norms only to always fall short.[15]

When I was applying for my pupillage—the apprenticeship aspiring barristers must complete in the English Inns of Court— an American lawyer around the same age named Ría Tabacco Mar was applying for legal internships in the United States. "I wore my only interview outfit, a conservative navy skirt suit and a cream blouse," Tabacco Mar recalled. "A classmate complimented me on the look. Then she added, 'But you'll never look really professional with your hair in dreadlocks.'"[16]

Mar went on to become a successful lawyer at the ACLU, where she last year represented a woman named Chastity Jones.

Jones was suing a company called Catastrophe Management Systems because, when she interviewed for a customer support job with them in Mobile, Alabama, she was told the company would not hire her so long as she wore her hair in dreadlocks. They "tend to get messy," a human resources manager claimed, although she admitted that Jones's were not. The decision hinged on a company policy that required an employee's hairstyle to "reflect a business/professional image," an image that it interpreted as not capable of including dreadlocks. Jones refused to cut off her hair, and she was denied the job.

Jones's case is the only one to have advanced all the way to the appeals court, where it was unsuccessful because, although it is illegal to discriminate against racial characteristics under the Civil Rights Act of 1964, judges mistakenly regarded dreadlocks as a race-neutral hairstyle. But they are being replicated across the world. In the United Kingdom, a woman who wore her hair in braids to a job interview was told that it was not a suitable hairstyle for selling "high-end" products.[17] In London, a boy was refused entry to a school because it claimed his cornrows amounted to a "gang-related" hairstyle.[18] In Australia, two girls of Sudanese heritage were told to remove their braids, while a boy was told to cut off his dreadlocks or face expulsion because his school's uniform policy prohibited "extreme styles."[19]

But the real tragedy is, it does not take an all-white panel of judges to reinforce these ideas—we have so successfully internalized them, we police them all by ourselves. In my case, straightening my hair, thinking I was proudly entering a profession having successfully completed my legal training, I didn't know that what I had really completed was my "structural apprenticeship"—the process by which the society I grew up in had already taught me to mimic the behaviors, norms, and ideals of whiteness.

I was playing my predetermined part in this dialectical relationship, where that world informed my body, and my body—these cultures and rules inscribed onto it—was reflecting them right back.[20]

As a woman attempting to excel in a space that was not designed for me, being measured by standards that were designed as oppositional to me, and being presented with an aesthetic that is about as far away as possible from how I actually look, I let the world inscribe its culture and rules on my body. There was no room for the expression of my African heritage or Afrocentric beliefs.

Ironically, it was the realization that I was destined to be an inherently "unprofessional"-looking human being from the very moment nature assigned my DNA that liberated me. As an on-air TV journalist, I had middle-aged white men whose job it was to monitor my appearance. When one such person told me, authoritatively, of his concern that my legs were "too muscular" for TV, this scrutiny sent me over the edge. It was another failure repeatedly lobbed at black women, and, after years as a lawyer and then a newspaper journalist, I realized that the simple act of being black whilst on news television was, apparently, controversial enough.

If I was going to be disruptive by simply existing, I sure wasn't going to spend hours straightening my hair for the privilege. At this point, I had nothing to lose except years of conditioning that had made me believe myself inadequate by virtue of my gender, race, and appearance. Still, it would be a full decade before I would have the confidence—indeed the audacity—to wear my hair in its natural state at work. First came the curls. There were a few disapproving sounds here and there. Another of the male image police told me that my "Afro" took up "too much of the screen." I solved that with braids, crochet locs, cornrows, and then back to the old Afro anyway.

Reclaiming how we wear our hair, and how we dress and adorn our bodies, does change what it is to be "professional." But what it is really about is reclaiming ourselves.

Notes

1. Walter Thornbury, "Lincoln's Inn," in *Old and New London*, vol. 3 (London: Cassell, Petter and Galpin, 1878), 51–58, www.british-history.ac.uk /old-new-london/vol3/pp51-58.

2. "In Brief: Women Get Go-Ahead for Trousers in Court," The Lawyer, May 23, 1995, www.thelawyer.com/issues/22-may-1995/in-brief-women-get-go -ahead-for-trousers-in-court/.

3. L. Kirkham and A. Loft, "Gender and the Construction of the Professional Accountant," *Accounting, Organizations and Society* 18 (1993): 516.

4. Rosemary Crompton and Kay Sanderson, "Credentials and Careers: Some Implications of the Increase in Professional Qualifications Amongst Women," *Sociology* 20, no. 1 (1986): 25–42.

5. Minna J. Kotkin, "Professionalism, Gender and the Public Interest: The Advocacy of Protection," *St. Thomas Law Review* 8 (fall 1995): 157–173.

6. Crompton and Sanderson, "Credentials and Careers."

7. Kathryn Haynes, "Body Beautiful? Gender, Identity and the Body in Professional Services Firms," in "Researching Gender, Inclusion and Diversity in Contemporary Professions and Professional Organizations," special issue, *Gender, Work, and Organization* 19, no. 5 (2012): 489–507.

8. Haynes, "Body Beautiful?," 4.

9. Haynes, "Body Beautiful?," 8.

10. Haynes, "Body Beautiful?," 10.

11. Haynes, "Body Beautiful?," 10.

12. Haynes, "Body Beautiful?," 10–11.

13. Celia Davies, "The Sociology of Professions and the Profession of Gender," *Sociology* 30, no. 4 (November 1996): 661–678.

14. Leigh Alexander, "Do Google's 'Unprofessional Hair' Results Show It Is Racist?," *Guardian*, April 8, 2016, www.theguardian.com/technology/2016 /apr/08/does-google-unprofessional-hair-results-prove-algorithms-racist-.

15. Ingrid Banks, *Hair Matters: Beauty, Power, and Black Women's Consciousness* (New York: New York University Press, 2000); Althea Prince, *The Politics of Black Women's Hair* (Toronto: Insomniac Press, 2010); Emma Dabiri, *Don't Touch My Hair* (New York: Penguin, forthcoming).

16. Ría Tabacco Mar, "Why Are Black People Still Punished for Their Hair?," *New York Times*, August 29, 2019, www.nytimes.com/2018/08/29/opinion/black-hair-girls-shaming.html.

17. "Woman 'Lost Job Chance' over Hairstyle," BBC London News, March 16, 2015, www.bbc.co.uk/news/uk-england-london-31914177.

18. Matthew Taylor, "School's Ban on Boy's Cornrows Is 'Indirect Racial Discrimination,'" *Guardian*, June 17, 2011, www.theguardian.com/uk/2011/jun/17/school-ban-cornrows-indirect-discrimination.

19. Kathomi Gatwiri, "The Politics of Black Hair: An Australian Perspective," The Conversation, March 18, 2018, https://theconversation.com/the-politics-of-black-hair-an-australian-perspective-93270.

20. Haynes, "Body Beautiful?," 343.

EFFORTLESS

AMY S. CHOI

Twice a year I have a ritual. I go up to Thirty-Second Street in Manhattan's Koreatown and head into an anonymous building where I am greeted by a tiny, beautiful Russian woman who leads me to a stack of mesh disposable undies, the likes of which I hadn't seen since slipping on some of those bad boys in the maternity ward after giving birth. No loaf-sized pad to layer in, though, or mewling baby to squish onto a nipple. No, these days, in my sheer (what is the point) water-repellent undies, I am directed into an igloo-shaped hot dry sauna, then a hot tub full of lemons, then a cold tub full of cucumbers, then a hot wet sauna.

The spa is not so much relaxing as it is a march of boobs-out, crotch-masked efficiency. Everything around me is busy. Small Asian women bustle about, directing customers here and there, guiding dripping, naked bodies to and fro. After emerging, dripping sweat, from the steam room, I am led by the elbow to my penultimate destination, a vinyl-topped massage table that recalls a combo of your great-aunt's plastic-covered floral love seat and Hannibal Lecter's dissection room. Here, my clinician instructs me to remove the mesh and lay down on my belly on the slippery plastic.

I am naked, ass-side up on the plastic-coated table, when she starts tossing buckets of hot water on me from an industrial-size drum. There's a pause as she straps on her tools of the trade: sandpapery gloves with which she will scour every inch of my body, including within my butt crack and under my boobs and in between my toes. The whole thing takes an hour; I will shed at least three pounds worth of dead skin, endure countless buckets of hot water, and be manipulated this way and that on the plastic butcher block. This is BEFORE I get passed off to a sadist dressed as a facialist to extract six months' worth of goo from the pores on my nose and chin and get layered up in algae and kelp—I pay extra for that—and scolded for letting my face absorb so much filth.

This is just the beginning. This is so I can then go to the multitude of beauty stores on Thirty-Second Street and literally buy snail smegma to smear on my face every night, after washing my face twice with two different kinds of rice oils, toning, then adding some sort of ginseng brightening serum, then slapping on a collagen cream.

Right now, my bathroom shelves include the following:

- Oil cleansers
- Face oils
- Moisturizing body oils
- Anti-cellulite oils
- De-oiling mattifiers for all the oils I've added on

- My fucking RETAINERS, to hold in place the work done when I got ADULT BRACES, to "fix" my smile
- Teeth whiteners, which I use with frightening regularity (seriously, there's a schedule that aligns with my birthday and the holidays)
- Seventy-three thousand millionty bazillion NEUTRAL lipsticks and glosses, because the point of slathering chemicals on your face is to look NATURAL
- An equal number of "barely there" blushes and bronzers
- Concealers for the scars that I sometimes like to show when the rest of my skin is flawless but that I like to cover up when it's not (my level of imperfection is closely calibrated)

Why? The key is to be only imperfect enough to be charming, so that I can say, "Oh, I don't really wear makeup. I'm pretty low maintenance." So I can be the kind of lady that is *effortless*.

In 2018, when Google did that brilliant data-mining scam and asked us all to upload our personal information and FACES to the damn internet to find ourselves in their global database of portraiture (liars; I was matched with some French lady because obviously Asians don't make art), I posted a #makeupless selfie on Instagram with my art match and felt smug about that photo for days. Because #nofilter, my skin looked fucking great. Just enough freckles and my bright scar, so people knew I was being *authentic* and I looked *real*, but glowy and smooth and lovely, like the kind of lady who has an IV of collagen and turmeric juice. I looked *effortless*.

Why the cloak-and-dagger routine? Why not say, *Hey, this shit is hard*? Nobody actually has perfectly groomed eyebrows. If you don't have enough, you fill them in. Pencil? Brushes? How many shades do you use? Maybe you microblade, even, to save yourself the time every morning of filling them in. You literally slice pigment into your face WITH SHARP METAL OBJECTS to SAVE YOURSELF BEAUTY TIME. If you have too much eyebrow, you wax and you pluck and you thread and you groom the remaining brow with pomade and comb it with tiny little eyebrow brushes. If you have just enough—wait, are they the right shape? Right angle? Right shade? Did you know you can dye your eyebrows? If your eyes are the windows to your soul, the eyebrows are—well, goddamn if I know. But it's *boring* to talk about this stuff. Right? Like, smart women aren't supposed to care.

But I do.

I was never the Pretty One in my family. I was not light skinned, or petite, or doe eyed enough. My sister was the Pretty One, and also the Straight-A Smart One. I was the Fun One, and the Popular One, and the Smart One Whose Parents Still Worried About Her Because She Had Rebellious Tendencies.

Those tendencies were programmed at an early age. I am not Gen X, I am not a millennial, but I *am* part of the female American microgeneration that grew up on *Sassy* magazine, riot grrrls, Courtney Love's band Hole, Claire Danes in *My So-Called Life*, and every other cultural touchstone that dictated that you must be grungily and rebelliously imperfect and maybe even a little bit outcast, but only in just such a way that actually made you *cool*.

Early on, it was very clear to me there was a Right Way to have a perfectly messy ponytail or slightly disheveled T-shirt or a lean, loungy body. Somewhere in the very narrowly defined gray area between outcast and edgy, nonchalant and within the accepted standards of beauty, was the effortlessness I so wanted to achieve.

But to be effortless, you couldn't talk about it. It's not that all effort was uncool. It was cool to play sports and go to practice every day. It was cool to be a musician and need to rehearse. It was cool to be a pretty, thin girl who could hang and take big, messy bites of burger. It was NOT cool to tell people that in order to maintain your weight you only ate lettuce and Laughing Cow cheese squares and that to throw your hair up in a cute ponytail actually required twenty minutes of teasing at the crown. Feminism Lite (my preferred brand of feminism as an adolescent) required keeping your damn mouth shut about the desire to be something as superficial as pretty, so I did. Being pretty had to be something you just *were*, not something that you tried to *achieve*, and if I wasn't it, I had to be quiet about wanting it and what I did to get it.

I am also Korean American. I grew up living in a vale of silence and not some small amount of shame. That is, I was primed to take up the mantle of silent effort in the pursuit of effortlessness.

In my eighties childhood, in the verrrry white Midwest, my parents owned a convenience store within Oasis Mobile Home Park, a massive trailer park in a then-industrial suburb that felt a million miles from the fancy suburb we lived in. They made an excellent living as small-business owners, but as an engineer and a nurse by training (immigration does things to a person's job prospects), they were ashamed of their jobs among the doctors and lawyers and executives in our community. We ate kimchi and broiled fish every day, but we never unleashed the smell in front of white people, because, you know, *foreign*. My parents occasionally struggled with English but insisted that their children's was perfect.

I absorbed it all: the need to succeed and the internalized judgment of how we did so; the love of who we were and the not-wanting-to-be-weird-in-front-of-white-people; the need for the linguistic cues of my Americanness to appear *effortless*, to show that it was *natural to me*, even though English was my second language. Internalized white supremacy is a real trip, lemme tell you.

So here we are. I am basically programmed to be wildly, savagely proud, and also always a little bit ashamed. I am groomed to always cultivate the appearance that I belong here, that I am beautiful, and that this is how I was born to be. That this is all effortless.

I AM LIVING A LIE AND I AM SO TIRED.

Because, of course, I am relaxed about literally nothing. I am effortful about everything, and it extends far, far beyond trying to be pretty. Wait—I was relaxed about potty training my kids, maybe? No, my husband and I were just too overwhelmed with having two kids under three years old that we essentially forgot to potty train, and they did it themselves. The truth is, we were drowning. If you are nearly killing yourself with effort in other arenas, turns out, not putting forth any effort and somehow getting a good result can turn into actual #effortlessness! But oh, the temptation TO LIE! To blithely say to other parents, "Don't worry so much about potty training! It'll happen when it happens. We hardly had to do anything and it was so easy!"

The things I could do if I weren't carrying around the mental burden of the need-to-find-the-perfect-blend-of-sheer-lip-plumper-slash-gloss-and-maybe-it-would-make-me-feel-better-about-my-mommy-pooch-which-makes-me-feel-weirdly-regretful-about-my-C-section-because-maybe-my-pooch-would-be-smaller-if-I'd-had-vaginal-births-but-we'll-never-know-but-thanks-for-the-lifelong-question-that-I'm-too-embarrassed-to-talk-about-because-women-are-only-supposed-to-be-grateful-for-healthy-babies-and-a-feminist-shouldn't-care-so-much-about-a-round-belly! The sheer SPACE I could clear in my brain! The loneliness I could let go of!

The mental gymnastics—Jesus. What a waste of goddamn effort. How much more useful, how much more joyful, how much *easier* to actually be truthful, to celebrate our efforts, to create communities around our desires and not fucking live with the shame that the desire for effortlessness brings, for women, and for immigrants, and for people of color who may never fit into a white, Westernized standard of beauty. Maybe all the effort that goes into being effortless could be used, I don't know, in loving ourselves and loving each other better. How transformative being honest could be.

The lie doesn't just exhaust me; it hurts us all. When we lie about the basic values of our culture (that women must be beautiful) and yet do everything in our power to adhere to that value (we kill ourselves to make ourselves beautiful) and lie about the labor women must put into adhering to the unspoken value of our culture (we have to be *effortless*), we ensure that nothing will ever change. We can't change our culture when we lie about what the culture is. We can't accept ourselves until we stop pretending that we already do. And we can't value our work until we acknowledge that this is work—this, THIS (please imagine me gesturing expansively at the world)—that existing in a body as a woman in this world is work.

Nothing is effortless.

PRINCESS
CARINA CHOCANO

When I was in the first grade, my best friend, Sally, and I dressed up as princesses for Halloween. This was in the seventies, back when there was no shame in your mom buying you a cheap plastic costume at the drugstore to wear over your clothes. But Sally and I wanted more. We wanted the authentic princess experience. So our moms took us fabric shopping and made us matching skirts out of glittery gold-and-silver polyester, which we wore with turtlenecks and parkas and molded plastic masks. Because you couldn't be a princess without the mask. The mask was beauty.

Never mind that the masks were actually hideous. I have a vague memory of a photo of the two of us standing together in our costumes that looked like a still from a horror film. Pale, frozen in fake, red smiles, with arched black eyebrows over gaping holes where the eyes should have been, framed by mustard-yellow hair and topped with gold crowns, the frozen princess faces didn't transform us into monsters or animals or even masked humans. They didn't even turn us into Cinderella or Snow White or Stephanie of Monaco. Instead, solemnly setting out into the chilly evening, trailed by our superhero brothers, our dark hair peeking out from behind the faces we'd strapped to our actual faces, Sally and I understood we were representing the archetypal feminine ideal.

From today's vantage point, it seems hard to fathom—the missed branding opportunities alone! But merchandising and marketing hadn't quite overtaken storytelling in those days. We had yet to encounter synergy or sponsored content. We had Little Golden Books and lunch boxes, coloring books and stickers, but Sally and I spent our formative years in a relative princess void, culturally speaking. I mean, we'd been to Disney World. We'd grown up with *Snow White*, *Cinderella*, and *Sleeping Beauty*. But *Snow White* came out in 1938, *Cinderella* in 1950, and *Sleeping Beauty* in 1959. Part of their appeal was historical. They seemed old-fashioned because they were.

It's hard to picture that long-ago moment in the 1970s anymore, with its weird contradictions and extremes. The era was so sexist and hidebound, and at the same time so progressive and free. The nameless uniformity of the princess mask seems innocent now, but it's also sinister. Back then, when we had no nylon gowns for dressing up in, no countless iterations of actual characters, we could dwell for a bit longer in the abstract realm of ideas. We had no clue that Princess Diana was right around the corner, or that *The Little Mermaid* would come out in 1989 and unleash a corporate fantasy princess hegemony like the world had never seen. The masks were just uncanny face replacements for our actual faces. The standard sublimated us, made us fungible. The masks didn't so much provide us with new identities as erase the ones we had.

A couple of years ago, I wrote a book about how stories enculturate us into "playing the girl." I wrote it as a way to understand the confusing mixed messages I'd grown up with, as a way to try to make sense of the crazy-making rules, prohibitions, and prescriptions that seemed to govern girls' lives. When I started working on the book, my daughter was a preschooler and obsessed with *Sleeping Beauty*—just as I'd been at her age. Still, when I asked her what she thought a princess was, she said: "It's a very fancy lady who always gets her own way."

It was not, I think, how I would have described a princess when I was her age. And in some ways, this seemed like an improvement. The princesses I was raised on didn't get their own way—not remotely. On the contrary, it was precisely not getting their own way, pretty much never getting their own way, until that one time, at the end, that made them noble. A princess was nothing if not a pretty doormat, a machine that suffered abuse and exploitation nobly and exquisitely, not to mention without complaint. It was this quality—more than her hotness or her duets with songbirds—that caught the prince's attention: how gracefully she endured abuse. Then he married her, turning her nobility of spirit into the other kind. Making her status official.

Girls of my daughter's generation are growing up with a different model. In our materialistic age, nobody cares about nobility in the spiritual sense. They care about status and the items that confer it. In the current iteration of the princess dream, the prize isn't love; it's luxurious, well-funded, highly publicized leisure. The archetype has shifted from a girl who is rewarded for having and expecting nothing to a girl who gets everything in return for doing nothing. This new princess—the pop culture princess who populates reality TV shows, Disney Channel shows for teens, Instagram—is not technically a princess but feels like one, and this feeling of entitlement is her principal, maybe even only, feeling. This girl, we're encouraged to think, has it all figured out. This girl has gotten away with it.

The more I delved into the parallels between the stories the culture tells us—in myths and fairy tales, comedies and commercials, pop songs and dramas—the more I realized that the princess and "the girl" were one and the same. Just like the princess, "the girl" is a performance of femininity born of renunciation. What you give up in exchange for status and safety in a patriarchal culture are your needs, desires, and feelings. This, I think, was the version of the princess represented by the masks Sally and I wore. She was, and still is, a smooth surface for men (a.k.a. "the hero") to project their needs and anxieties onto, or for women to perceive their anxieties about how they are seen by men—what they are worth, where their worth resides. She swaps subjectivity for self-objectification, removes everything that makes her a person, assumes a new identity that is no identity at all. The ideal, archetypal princess is a piece of plastic you literally strap to your face to keep your human qualities hidden from view.

I didn't intend to watch the royal wedding—I'm talking specifically about Meghan Markle and Prince Harry's, the weird mash-up between a coronation and a rom-com. But I woke up at 5 a.m. and fell into a Twitter hole, and before I knew it, I'd let myself get sucked into the regular-girl-becomes-a-princess show in the name of staying up to date.

By the time I dropped my daughter off at school, I was in the blackest of moods. What had sent me over the edge was the sight of two American journalists—both women—losing their shit as La Markle passed by them in a pumpkin-shaped carriage. (At least, that's the shape it is in my memory.) Not long after that, I got a call from my friend Jeanne, who was just as bothered as I was and wanted to know what it was with grown women and the princess hysteria.

People have gushed about what Markle's absorption into the royal family means for the royal family—about how she's brought them into the modern age. Nobody talks about what it means for a modern, independent woman to be absorbed into the royal family like a vanishing twin. That this is framed as a "fairy tale" tells you all you need to know about the stories women are told or the ways in which the culture grooms us to equate total sublimation to the patriarchy with the only true happiness a woman can have.

This is reflected in the fact that, for a girl protagonist to matter—see every Disney movie aimed at girls save for one—she has to code as a "princess," as an emblem of the feminine ideal, whatever fashion dictates that is at the moment. It's reflected in the lives of our reality show princesses, like the Kardashians or *The Bachelor* winners, in Meghan Markle's decision to leave behind her life and career in exchange for tenured celebrity and a lifelong sinecure. A woman's happiness, these stories tell us, resides in not having to do anything anymore, in forsaking all future adventures, in ceasing to exist as a desiring subject unless those desires can be easily gratified by her bottomless access to cash.

This contemporary princess feels different from the princess we know from every story we're ever told as children. Nor is she the updated version of that princess—the one who rides a motorcycle, rescues frogs, and has something to prove. (Her humanity, tendentiously.) But no matter how many times she's updated, or reinvented, or supposedly subverted, her function remains the same. She is the irreducible unit of femininity in the story our culture tells itself and, more importantly, tells us. What she is and signifies has only adapted to current conditions.

The message we get is this: Out in the world, all is peril and suffering. Then a prince comes along and recognizes your innate qualities and whisks you off to the castle, where you'll be safe, and do nothing, and never be heard from again. (What else does "happily ever after" mean?) But your function doesn't change. This is what the princess has always been: in real life, a political pawn; in stories, propaganda. In stories, a tool for indoctrination.

The princess is the girl the patriarchy wants you to be. The girl with her life all mapped out for her, her interests narrowed, her sights trained squarely on herself. She's the girl who sleepwalks through life, dreaming of being no one.

Why else do you think she's always unconscious?

UGLY
DAGMARA DOMIŃCZYK

On a warm (cold?) weekend (weekday?) afternoon, I am standing with some neighborhood kids in front of Agnes's building. I am ten (eleven?) and the neighborhood is in East Brooklyn, a stone's throw away from Flatbush Avenue, from Kings Plaza mall. The buildings are five (six?) stories high, and they cluster together like identical brown stalks. These are the Glenwood Houses, where I've lived for a few years now and where I will remain till the summer I start college. The kids are a mixed lot—mostly Polish and Russian, some Puerto Rican, some black, some white. I am friends with all of them. Or, more importantly, I want (need?) to be friends with all of them.

Agnes just moved here from Poland. Or maybe she's already been here a year. Agnes is tall and skinny and has perfectly straight hair that hangs like a mysterious curtain in front of half her face. Her hair looks like velvet. Her face is heart shaped. She is statuesque. She is twelve (thirteen?), and I kind of think her nose is too wide and her eyes are somewhat beady, but all the boys think she's amazing, and they're right. Agnes *is* amazing. Because Agnes commands attention.

I command the opposite. Meaning, I command nothing. The only attention I get comes from my own scrutiny. On the first page of the diary I start that year, I write in fat, neat cursive, "Life has been hard for me. Starting with my looks. Double yuck." I describe in detail all the flaws I have registered and stockpiled—zits, glasses, buck teeth, oily hair. I write that Patricia has a better waist and Caroline has better skin. I write a note to a boy I met at the community pool, a boy named Robert. It is a note I never give him. "Why don't you like me? I'm really not that ugly."

Back by Agnes's, we are standing around doing nothing. Usually "nothing" is wonderful. I get lost in this nothingness—I forget what I look like, forget what I feel like. We hang off monkey bars, or play hide and seek, or sit on green benches, peeling the paint, whispering about crushes. I have a crush too. His name is Sasha, but of course Sasha only has eyes for Agnes.

And then, out of nowhere, a boy gets in my face. I know this boy. His name is Ronnie, he's American, and he once chased a group of us all around the complex threatening that he would thrash us if he ever caught us.

I see him in front of me. (I see him now, thirty years later.) He's a bit greasy. Tall, with a gut, as if he spent his free time chugging beer, when really he's our age, thirteen (fourteen?). He has a swath of thick, blunt bangs that cut across his forehead, so that the effect is both ridiculous and menacing.

He puffs his chest, leans over me, into me.

"Hey. Hey! You're so ugly . . . your name should be *Dog*mara."

I start laughing (crying?). I want to punch Ronnie. I walk away. I walk home.

Maybe.

So much I don't remember. But I remember that moment, that word, and I will remember it forever and ever, and how pointedly, publicly, and casually it was hurled in my face.

The word for ugly in Polish is *brzydka*—which sounds eerily close to the word for razor blade, which is *brzytwa*. And for most of my formative life, *ugly* cut me. Quick and to the bone.

I've been looking through all my journals lately. They're peppered with typical adolescent musings: longing, anxiety, diatribes about late periods, and, sometimes, prayers to Jesus. They're also peppered with sentences—nay, paragraphs and pages—about what I could do to become less ugly. Tallies of diets, workouts, of Dexatrim pills swallowed. Notes about potions, lotions, lipsticks, foundations, piled on, layers of armor, when all I yearned for was to be *seen*. I revealed so much of who I was by writing about how desperately I wanted to cover myself up. Smothered by my own insecurity, for years it was hard to breathe. When I flip through those diaries, when I think good and hard, here's what I realize.

Ugly owned me. It tossed me about as I clung on for dear life. How did it arrive? And why? When did ugly happen to me?

Ugly happened *all the time*.

It happened at the age of almost-seven when I moved to a foreign country. When I couldn't speak the language and the language had no rhyme or reason, nothing I could take a stab at, and the only thing that saved me was television and memorizing dictionaries. Ugly happened when I had parents who had no time to parent because they were too busy surviving. Ugly happened when a girl on my block slapped me because I didn't understand that she was asking to play with my doll. It happened when the clothes I wore were bought by the pound, fished out of giant, grimy laundry baskets from a warehouse called Domsey's. Ugly was *immigrant, secondhand, Polack, project kid.* Ugly happened when my accent emerged—a mix of Brooklyn and Polish—a strange, breathy, grating sound. Ugly was a large nose, pointy chin, features that took forever to settle down and settle in. It was teeth that were yellow, sticking out when they should have been in hiding. It was nails bitten down to pulp. *It was my entire name.* It happened when my father told me I was a coward, when he yelled at me to stop being a pussy. It was a distant uncle asking fourteen-year-old me how it felt to be the smart sister. It happened when I started eating my feelings, book in one hand, a bag of chips in another. It happened in Budapest, on vacation, near some bridge, when my sisters took me aside and gently told me I'd gained too much weight. Ugly happened when I had no say. It happened when pimples happened. It happened when my mother looked past me. It happened when I realized I wanted to be an actress despite the fact that I looked nothing like the actresses I saw on TV. It happened on March 23, 1996, when I wrote a poem in my journal. The poem was titled, "What I See When I Look in the Mirror." The poem was one line long and the line was:

An ugly old thing.

I grew up aware of the fact that my parents, for a long time, did not think of me as their beautiful daughter. When I was fifteen, my mother, unbeknownst to me, entered my name in a local beauty pageant. I wept at the news. It was a cruel shot in the dark, and I wonder now if the thought entered her head—if the judges believed I was pretty, maybe she would too.

I won first place. Not because of my face—photos reveal an unfortunate perm, buck teeth, and pudgy cheeks. I won because I was articulate. Because I read a poem I'd written about what it meant to be an immigrant. I read it proudly, my voice shaking with emotion. I stood tall, sharing something more interesting than a pretty face. It was quite a coup, my title, and my mother reeled from both pride and surprise.

And that's when ugly gave way. It lost some of its footing. My pageant crown was won not because I looked like a pageant girl but because I acted like one. A lightbulb went off, its light dim and flickering, but suddenly there it was, piercing through the dark.

We yearn to go through life—us ugly ducklings—not wanting to give a shit about validation, and yet we constantly seek it out. We are desperate for stamps of approval, and when they don't come, we carve out other selves—we find something else and dig our heels in. We become the funny girl. The smart girl. The girl with a talent, a story, a sport, a poem.

My voice had somehow defeated conventional beauty. So I turned up its volume. I showed up to acting class in clogs I'd painted like a rainbow and ragged overalls, no bra. I cut all my hair off. I wore a row of silver studs on my earlobe. I inhabited other people, characters who spoke to me through their desires, fears, accents, their otherness. I kissed boys; I broke their hearts. I dabbled in promiscuity, in romance, in high-brow literature, in traveling, and, senior year at college, in anorexia. I was afraid but open, an egg whose shell I managed to crack without smashing it entirely. So when a prospective agent told me that I needed to lose weight and that my eyes were slightly lopsided and, boy, would the camera pick that up, I nodded my head and walked out of the room, and I kept walking. I stopped focusing on what the world saw when they first saw me. I started wanting to show them the rest. It wasn't easy. It was changing my mind-set before that trendy word even existed. It was looking beyond the mirror.

And here I am now. I'm not ten anymore. I'm forty-two. I've left ugly behind, but if I turn my head in a certain direction, if I squint hard enough, it's there, sitting quietly. Except now, it doesn't say a word unless I give it permission.

Almost every day, I sit down at my vanity and I look at myself. The house is quiet: the kids are in school; the dogs are sleeping downstairs. My husband is in his office, or at the gym, or somewhere on a set far, far away. At noon or something like it, it's just me and my face.

This is what I see. Lines like brackets around my lips, from years of smoking or genetics, who knows. Creases like the one in the middle of my brow, a faint white line, a millimeter in length, invisible to all but me. Large pores, a few blackheads, a somewhat dull complexion. An Eastern European nose that keeps growing because fucking cartilage. Dark circles under my eyes. I see the imperfections; I greet them casually, as one would greet an acquaintance walking their dog. I smile. I widen my eyes. I bat my eyelashes—oh yes, I do—which have remained steadfast, as black and thick as they were decades ago. I see everything I would change or could change. And I feel pretty anyway. *I feel pretty.* It is an adolescent thought, but when it's taken me years to get here and when it's been so long since anyone, including myself, has called me ugly, *I feel pretty* is a battle hard won.

Over time, I learned the secret to ugly: it can only hurt a girl who is already hurting. Otherwise, it's powerless. But in the beginning, *I* was powerless.

What we *think* we look like matters more than anything else. It matters more than science or symmetry. What we think we look like is how we allow ourselves to be perceived. Ugly means nothing to me now. When people call you ugly, they're lying; that is not the word they mean. They mean *garbage, worthless, inconsequential*. But they use *ugly* because they think ugly is easy. Except they're wrong. Ugly is complicated, unapologetic, wild, brusque, difficult. Ugly is unladylike; it is what we don't want to talk about or admit.

And ugly is mine all mine, to do with as I please.

When I slam doors: ugly. Ugly is when I'm tired, wearing a shirt I wore the previous day and slept in, showing up in it when I drop my kids off, not smiling at the other moms because rough mornings happen and I won't pretend otherwise. I am ugly when I spit out words like *fuck off, shut the fuck up, can I help you?* I get ugly when my period is coming and I am bloated and I spend seven days wiping blood that sometimes gets on my fingers. I am ugly when I yell at my sons. When I roll my eyes at certain women because they look too perfect, because they cook dinner every night. When I'm the one looking past my mother now. This is my ugliness. When I lie awake watching *Real Housewives*, wondering about my demise, farting, and eating an apple at midnight. I am ugly when I can't be bothered. I get ugly when I fight dirty, and I fight real dirty sometimes.

The difference is that I finally own my ugliness. I explore it. I let it lead me down dark tunnels, and when I'm done, I let go of its hand and find my way back toward the light.

And then I am beautiful. Beautiful, capable, unstoppable. I wear lipstick when I am beautiful. Or when I step out of the shower, and just as it happens in movies, I stare at my naked body—scarred, strong, large—and run my hands over it kindly.

Or when I climb off my stationary bike, sweat dripping, and I catch my reflection in the framed poster of *Little Children* that hangs in the basement and think, *This is beautiful.* I'm beautiful during sex, right after I come. When my husband tells me he loves me. When I radically allow myself to love in return. I am beautiful when I finish a chapter I've been working on, when my own words turn me on, ignite me, give me reason and hope. When I walk down Ninth Avenue, boldly staring down the skyscrapers that used to scare me when I first arrived in America. I am beautiful when my girlfriends and I exchange intimate stories, replete with softness, ballsiness, in awe of what we hold inside and how easily we are able to share it. How easily we break bread with one another, in a way that most men can't, and the value in that, in the willingness to unravel before one another. I am beautiful when I rewatch myself on a screen; when I catch every gesture, each genuine smile, the way I've widened my eyes, or stuck out my tongue, or leaned my head into my palm. *You look pretty*, I think. *You look like yourself.*

I am beautiful when I want to be. How did *that* happen?

It happened slowly (suddenly?), in increments (all at once?), like a trickle (like a flood?). I don't remember how it happened. I think of a tree, or the sky. How and when did they get so big, become so evident, as if they were always there, since the beginning? Same with a woman's beauty. You might be able to plot the course, connect the dots, if you go back far enough. Or it just happens when you drown out the noise.

It doesn't matter, does it. It's yours. You hold on to it. You cup it in your hands and slip it in your pocket. Nobody can touch your beautiful now . . . even when they call you ugly.

SHRILL
DAHLIA LITHWICK

The first time I was ever called shrill, it was on the judge's ballot at a high school debate tournament. It was one in a list of adjectives that may or may not have included "speaks too fast," "funny," "too nervous," "great promise," and there, nestled among all of those complicated scrawled notes about my "style," was "shrill"—rhymes with *harridan*, rhymes with *fishwife*, rhymes with *the woman in Chaucer who never gets the guy*. Whatever it meant, it wasn't about my voice—even in high school I didn't have a high-pitched voice. It was some comment on how I argued. Grating, emotional, nails on chalkboard. I was mortified.

The dictionary definition of *shrill* doesn't seem gendered until you realize that having a voice "too high, too loud, and painful to listen to" won't ever be directed at even pubescent high school boys debating euthanasia, but it sure as hell can include the bulk of the girls. It seemed not even to be about pitch or tone so much as about showing any kind of passion during debating and while in possession of an ovary. It was a few years before I learned that no woman in parliamentary debate history has ever *not* been called shrill, as the women in high school and later college debate came to compare judge's ballots, and that no man in parliamentary debate history has ever been called it. Ever.

In 1973, when Ruth Bader Ginsburg argued her first case before an all-male Supreme Court, none of the justices asked her a single question. Justice Harry Blackmun gave Ginsburg's oral performance, in which she attempted to soften her sharp Brooklyn accent, a C+ for eloquence—adding "Very precise female" in his notebook but also too "emotional." Once she was herself on the bench, she occasionally interrupted other Supreme Court justices, as is common on the bench, and was labeled "Rude Ruth" for a time, though statistical analysis shows she interrupted no more often than the men. She was not the only one to be thus critiqued. Justice William O. Douglas, who retired from the court in 1975 and died in 1980, wrote in his autobiography, "I remember four women in one case who droned on and on in whining voices that said, 'Pay special attention to our arguments, for this is the day of women's liberation.'"

Shrill, the writer and memoirist Lindy West tells us, is not about whether you speak in dulcet tones. It's about whether you are beautiful enough, skinny enough, youthful enough, to be admitted into the public conversation. It is also, as Douglas's snide aside about "women's liberation" makes clear, about authority. We criticize female voices in the public sphere chiefly because we aren't certain that women have the authority to lead public thinking. And, perhaps not coincidentally, *shrill* is also the word we direct at women in authority who have more than proven they have the wherewithal to lead public thinking. In a sense it's the perfect double-edged sword: you're shrill if you try to speak too soon, and you're also shrill if you have earned the right to speak. Shrill is much less about what the speaker is saying, as it turns out, and more about the listener's capacity to cede ground. *Shrill*, in other words, is the word people use to signal they aren't ready to listen—not to your voice, but to what you're actually saying.

Shrill was the word men in the media would regularly and unerringly level at Hillary Clinton, most notably in her 2016 Democratic National Convention acceptance speech, which was denounced as shrill by BBC's James Naughtie and NBC's Tom Brokaw, who said, "She's often quite shrill and hectoring people." Earlier that year Bob Woodward had complained "She shouts" around the time former Republican National Committee chair Michael Steele had claimed she was "going up every octave with every word." This critique was sometimes conflated with judgments about her coolness, her artificiality, and her likability, but often it served as a way to avoid engaging meaningfully with her policies and ideas.

And it wasn't just "Shrillary." *Shrill* and her ugly stepsisters *harpy* and *scold* were the words leveled at young women who debated with me as an undergraduate, and at my law school classmates trying out their oral argument voices in moot court competitions and later in courtrooms. The handful of female advocates who have succeeded in the years I have covered the courts have learned to pitch their voices as low as possible, to eschew emotion, and to mostly channel some version of James Earl Jones. Shrill is the polar opposite of persuasive. It is importuning and nagging and small.

Even though I now only write about the law, I have found that print is no escape. Though men and women share the same keyboard, the act of typing while female can trigger furious backlash about shrillness on the page. A judge once called me a harpy in print. Shrill, harpy, harridan, shrew, scold—all the ways Chaucer implies the female voice sounds whiny and clutching. And so much of the pushback on the women of #MeToo has been about reducing accusers to attention-seekers, money-grubbers, cast-asides pushing into public spaces at the expense of male authority. Brett Kavanaugh shouted and was somehow not shrill but powerful. Dr. Christine Blasey Ford barely whispered and was swallowed up in the noise.

Social science theorizes that accusations of shrillness in the human voice are less about tone or volume than about accusations of "otherness." Musicologist William Cheng has written that "in ancient Greece, public female vocality often bore associations with prostitution, madness, witchcraft and androgyny." My friend the musicologist Bonnie Gordon has similarly written about opera's anxiety about the "dangers of music exuding from the wrong mouths." Music, in other words, is also about who *doesn't get to sing,* and what happens when outsiders make the attempt. *Shrill,* in music, includes the charge that when women sing, men lose something. Perhaps that explains why Justice Ginsburg fell in love with the opera long before she fell in love with constitutional law. For decades, in her early career as a civil rights litigator on behalf of women, Ginsburg had to use her voice to implore male judges to imagine what the life of a woman was like—what it was to be paid unequally or denied government benefits—and she had to do so without appearing to be shrill, or whiny, or pushy. It wasn't enough that she was correct on the legal merits; she had to use her voice to soothe and mollify powerful men, in courtrooms and in court papers. How alluring the full-throated female voice in opera—a voice of urgency and power and passion—must have seemed to Ginsburg, in contrast to the voice required, in those early years, to cajole and persuade male power. Her career was about making women's voices palatable to men, just as opera creates parameters for female voices in music. Both are attempts to pry authority from reluctant arbiters of who matters, who counts.

To make our arguments heard, in debate and in public discourse, our voices must first and foremost give *comfort* to men. The way we've learned to combat being called a harpy is by having gummy smiles and shiny hair and a general aura of being ever eager to please, as if we were golden retrievers, not equals. As a young attorney, Ruth Bader Ginsburg taught herself to speak more slowly and less New York-y, and she described her own role arguing her early cases as an oral advocate at the Supreme Court in terms that sound more like a kindergarten teacher dragging the naughty boys around to the park on a long rope.

In my writing life, I have used different tricks, including humor, to make male readers comfortable, to elicit laughter, to discomfit and destabilize through the quick joke, the sly aside. But even humor can't counteract the charge of shrillness. Clinton's critics hated her laughter—they called it a cackle—even more than they hated her shrill humorlessness. And think of Joan Rivers, Sarah Silverman, Michelle Wolf—there is nothing more shrill than the woman who uses humor and a public platform to tell the truth. (Michelle Wolf famously offered this apology: "I'm sorry my shrill voice offends your man-head.")

There is an astonishing conversation America is having about the power and utility of female anger. Only if you aren't angry can you escape the stabbing forefinger of *shrill*. For decades, as an appellate lawyer and later as a judge and a Supreme Court justice, Ginsburg never allowed herself to write or speak angry. That changed around the time she became the only woman on the Supreme Court—after Sandra Day O'Connor retired, when Ginsburg began to write about women's work and women's reproductive freedom in increasingly furious terms. Long before Trump, but for years after Justice Ginsburg had begun to allow herself to "write angry," I was still a get-along gal—more bees with honey and all that. In the middle patch between college debate and 2016, nobody called me shrill for a while, in part because I gave comfort and in part because I wasn't terribly angry.

But perhaps we have reached a point in national public discourse where assuring that one's voice doesn't threaten or discomfit or seize power from men has become the problem as opposed to the solution. When Trump was elected, I abandoned my rule about never writing angry, because you can't make injustice ingratiating or solicitous and because public gaslighting (#fakenews, #alternativefacts, #maybehedidmaybehedidn't) felt very, very dangerous to women. Women who have seen themselves insulted, berated, humiliated, and shamed by the president, who have disappeared from government office and who have been erased from the federal bench, are not all prepared to go quietly back to their corners and their rooms. It cannot possibly be an accident that for the first time in our lifetimes, we have a first lady who is breathtakingly beautiful and whose voice is barely heard.

Men, even men who are superb allies in their work, often tell me they really wish I would start to be funny again, that I'm not as jolly as I used to be. But at public events, women often fall wordlessly into my arms. So here I am, just on the sunny side of fifty, gazing down a long, inexorable slide toward a voice that will never be as youthful, honeyed, charming, and witty as it was. I am no longer particularly gentle or patient, and I have two teenaged sons who associate my voice with something about as dulcet and pleasing as the fan over the stove. I worry that I am poised to soon meet, nose to nose, that shrill harpy I was accused of being at debate tournaments, back when I was only fourteen and made of taut flesh stretched over bone and muscle, when I ended each and every sentence with a pleading smile.

But I've also been reading about the original harpies—the mythical Greek creatures who were part bird, part woman, part wind. I have begun to think that perhaps we could appropriate *harpy* and *shrill* as less about begging to be allowed into the discourse and more about something piercing and true, something supersonic that the ear must strain to hear, not an irritant but something authentic.

When I coach middle school debaters, I tell the girls that the day they receive a judge's ballot with the word *shrill* on it, they should count it as a badge of honor, then tear it up and forget it ever happened. That it will continue to happen, throughout high school, then college, and then law school, and then life. That they needn't try to make their voices nicer to please men, and that they needn't change the pitch and the register and the volume. Whether we choose to be angry, or sad, or loud or quiet or fat or thin or importuning or imploring, when we speak urgently and unapologetically as women, we will be called shrill. Perhaps we really need to invent a word to describe the problem as being with their hearing as opposed to with our throats.

Someday, I hope, one of these young women will run for president and not a single person will comment on the tone of her voice or the sound of her laughter, on whether she used every single tool in her rhetorical toolbox to soften and buff down the threat contained in a woman's unfiltered thoughts and point of view. I am hoping that by the time my sons read female voices, *shrill* will be associated less with high ranges and loud volumes and more with injustice and compassion and human pain. I am hoping that soon *shrill* will either be a compliment or disappear from the public vernacular.

In the meantime, there's nothing wrong with my voice or the way I write. I'm not shrill. I'm supersonic.

LUCKY
GLYNNIS MACNICOL

Not long after my fortieth birthday, people began telling me I was lucky. Actually, not people. Women. (In my experience, men actually don't care much about what women are doing unless they are related to them or speaking about them en faceless masse as a group they'd like to control.)

I was, to put it mildly, unprepared for this. I was single. I was childless. I had approached this culturally recognized milestone (gravestone?) with the dread of a person being marched to the executioner's blade. My luck had run out. My number was up. That number, depending on how you looked at it, was forty (my age), zero (the number of children I had birthed or was ever likely to, according to nearly every fertility article), or one (the number of people in my household, the number of people I grocery shopped for, the number of tickets I bought to anything). Whatever awaited me, I was sure, was bad.

But it was not bad, I quickly discovered. Quite the opposite. After burning out terribly in my late thirties, I'd constructed a life for myself that was reasonably under my control. In fact, I spent much of my fortieth year rather delighted by the life I had built for myself. I had acquired some financial stability and was able to travel. Once I stopped seeing men as permanent decisions, they started to appear everywhere, multiplying like gremlins (though mostly fun and easily contained). Unlike female characters in the movies (or magazines, or centuries of novels), I was not being herded off onto the sidelines, forever expected to be an audience member to other people's main storylines. At forty, I was on the stage, a fully fleshed-out character, leading a fully fleshed-out life. It was, I discovered, possible to live a notable life as a woman who had never achieved either of the two things women were noted for: being a wife and giving birth.

So when the "You're so lucky!" comments began to trickle in—initially on a Facebook post about an assignment to Iceland I was able to take on short notice precisely because I was directly in control of so much of my time—I greeted them with a sense of relief. I had, in the few months since my birthday, grown increasingly furious at the bill of goods I'd been sold about women and age, equal parts astounded and gleeful that so much of what I'd been taught—that to age as a woman is an act of shame best hid from the world at all costs, even apologized for—had turned out to be a lie.

But one woman feeling satisfied with her life is far from a culture recognizing that said life could be satisfying. After all, when you're a single woman of forty, there are no shows about women like you to binge, no movies to attend. Though I wasn't lonely, I did long for my life to be recognized in a way that would make me feel less alone in the world. And there in my comments section was some small recognition of the life I had chosen. Other people were seeing my life, and seeing it as worthwhile too. Not just worthwhile, but covetable!

And then my luck changed. In my late thirties, my mother had been diagnosed with Parkinson's. During the year I turned forty, it progressed to dementia, and my sister, my father, and I had been scrambling for the better part of a year to find my mother full-time care. I'd been doing the ninety-minute flight from New York to Toronto every few weeks as I frantically tried to get the necessary paperwork done, all the while rushing my mother to the ER when her symptoms got extreme. Two days before Christmas, the call came that there was a bed available for her, and the holidays quickly became a blur of forms and check-ins, explaining to my mother she was going to a new home, and then explaining it to her again, followed by packing and unpacking, and the terrible moment of leaving her there.

It was a whole other kind of last-minute traveling, and not the sort one posts about on Facebook. When I finally returned to New York shortly after New Year's, I felt like I was crawling out of the scene of an accident: exhausted, numb, and bruised. My studio apartment was still in the same frantic mess I'd left it in two weeks before. The dishes unwashed. Dirty laundry piled on the bed. The refrigerator empty. The next morning, I woke up and went for a massage. I wanted to be still and be cared for. Even briefly. Even if I had to pay for it.

On the way home, I ran into a woman I knew. She remarked on the indentation on my forehead from lying on the massage table, and I told her where I'd been, though not the reason.

"I would love to have the time to get a massage," she said with the familiar exasperated smile of a woman with small children. "You're so lucky."

It felt like an accusation. I don't doubt she *did* wish she had the time to get a massage (small children are hard; I know this because I am often filling in for friends who need childcare!), just as I often wish there was someone at home to touch me, or at least cork the wine bottle or unload the dishwasher. America hates women, and we are all fucking tired.

I also knew the responsibilities I was shouldering at the time, though equally overwhelming, were not the ones made visible by motherhood or marriage. Yet the tone of her remark suggested there'd been a random draw, and I'd pulled the right card and she the wrong one. As if neither of us had had a hand in creating our own lives—ones filled with challenges, joys, and hardships—and that mine let me do decadent things like get massages. *Unearned.*

Also unearned was a (working) trip to Paris I took after I'd sold two books in thirteen months. A friend connected me with a breathtakingly cheap sublet; I looked at my finances, budgeted carefully, and bought a plane ticket, hoping that getting away would give me the time to focus on the deadlines.

"Lucky duck" was the first Facebook comment. The next: "Jealz!" Further along: "SOOO lucky." And then again, like the woman following the massage: "I wish!"

The model Suzy Parker, who inspired Audrey Hepburn's character in *Funny Face*, famously said of her career, "I was lucky to have been born with cheekbones." Here are the ways in which I am lucky: I was born in a first-world country into a family of educated people, who made sure I was also educated. I am white, which affords me innumerable advantages in a world that continues to privilege whiteness. I was born after both birth control and abortion were legalized, not to mention after the invention of antibiotics. None of these were available for my grandmother, who was born before women could vote.

I don't think that is the sort of luck people are referring to, however, when they tell me I'm lucky. What they are saying, even if they would never phrase it this way, even if they would never admit it out loud, is that I don't deserve the life I lead. That I have somehow cheated. I've skipped out on responsibility. Life has handed me nice things. I bear no responsibility for my own good fortune.

I bear a great deal of responsibility for my own good fortune. Before I became "lucky," I was a writer for years, often barely making my rent, rarely able to afford health insurance. I spent years working eighteen-hour days, seven-day weeks. I took a gamble on this life and then *toiled*. In the words of Emily Dickinson, "Fortune's expensive smile" was *earned*.

I try to imagine a forty-year-old single man, having acquired two book deals in the space of thirteen months, leaving for Paris to write and being told he was lucky. I suspect that instead he'd be told "Congratulations!" Or "You deserve it!" Or "Nice to see all your hard work paying off." This is the language we're comfortable with when it comes to men doing what they want. Men get the benefit of the doubt. Why wouldn't they? They have been cast as the hero in nearly every story we've been told.

Me, on the other hand? How do we value a woman who's willingly rejected all the things she's supposed to want, built a life without them, and now appears to be enjoying herself? What would it mean to credit her for doing it on purpose? How much of the way the world works, and how we value our places in it, would be diminished by that admission? So much easier, and less scary, just to say I'm lucky.

We do not like the idea of women determining their own lives. (Has anyone ever used the phrase "woman driver" as a compliment?) We don't like women on their own. A woman on her own is either in peril or a source of shame. "How do you eat by yourself?" was the question I was asked most frequently on book tour, followed closely by "How do you travel by yourself?" We like to keep the things that benefit women the most in our culture—beauty, motherhood (the idea of it, anyway), women's bodies, satisfying relationships—out of women's control. We like to keep women in their place. Some get off on the idea of locking women up entirely.

What do we reward women for? Staying put. (In the stories we tell ourselves, I mean—in real life, we don't reward women at all.) For tying themselves to others. For not having time for themselves. For not doing as they choose. I'm not suggesting, obviously, that women who are married and have children have not made their own choices—simply that the aspects of those roles they are most rewarded for often involve them depriving themselves. Anything else is decadent. Like a massage.

The writer Alice Sebold, best known for her novel *The Lovely Bones*, titled her memoir about being violently raped as a college student *Lucky* because so many people told her she'd been lucky she hadn't been killed. It's in keeping with the female experience: luck for so long was having things *not be worse*. If a woman was lucky, she wouldn't get pregnant before she was married. If a woman was lucky, the man she was married off to would be good to her. If she was lucky, she would get pregnant with a baby of the right sex (hello, Anne Boleyn) and, as the marriage progressed, not get pregnant with more kids than she could afford (emotionally and/or financially). If a woman was lucky, the person in charge of her finances—by law, because it wasn't until 1974 that women were allowed to have credit cards in their own names or sign leases on their own apartments—would be responsible and she would be well fed, well housed. If she had to go out into the workforce, perhaps she'd be lucky enough to work at a place where the doors weren't locked in case of fire. If she was lucky, the men in her life from birth onward could be trusted with her safety. Could be trusted with the care of her physical well-being. If she was lucky, if those men proved untrustworthy, the other members of her family, of law enforcement, of the judicial system, would believe her. If she was lucky, she could leave home alone and expect to make it back safely.

So much depended on luck! "Luck" being men.

Chris Noth, the actor who played Mr. Big in the series *Sex and the City*, confessed he found it "disturbing" when women told him they found Big attractive because he was so unattainable. To me, this seemed to be the most understandable thing in the world! From puberty on, women are taught to pursue the unattainable—beginning with thinking their periods are going to be the equivalent of a free-spirited dance through a flowery field and not a monthly exercise in blood clots and heating pads. Life is something that happens to us, in which the unattainable is attained only if we are lucky enough to be born beautiful. And then we get old, which is the unluckiest thing of all. (And even with her famous cheekbones, Suzy Parker was married three times. Her first husband demanded she pay for a nose job in the divorce settlement, and her second denied they were ever married and left her when she became pregnant.)

We tend to think of luck as something that happens to us if the timing is right, if the numbers align, if the car swerves one inch to the right, if the sliding doors open and the right person walks through. It's infused with magic and otherworldliness. Going to get lucky tonight. Playing our lucky numbers. Luck is a force over which we have no control, that we have no role in creating, that we can take no credit for. Which, not for nothing, bears some similarity to how women are conditioned to think of their own lives. Men talk about how they make their own luck. Women talk about being unlucky in love.

I am a member of the first generation of women who can make their own luck, by way of bank accounts we directly control, leases we can sign on our own, and abortion laws that (theoretically) give us control over our own bodies. I can eat alone (as recently as the 1970s, some NYC restaurants would not seat a solitary woman at the bar for fear she was soliciting). All of which essentially just means that, unlike all the women who toiled for most of history, I have the ability to directly benefit from all my hard work, on my own, no permission needed, cheekbones or not.

Luck be a lady, indeed.

MOM

IRINA REYN

Let's get it out there right off the bat: you're probably the least qualified person to be writing this essay. What do you know about the word *mom*? If someone else tackled it, they would get it right, create the definitive guide to the word. You would actually love to read it so you could take comprehensive notes, learn a thing or two. You might forward it to one of your mom friends to parse the essay's blind spots together, and you would ultimately commiserate and identify with so many moments depicted within it.

It might even make you cry, because any text with the word *mom* in it seems to trigger that these days. Because somewhere, deeply ensconced, is a certainty that your momness is not enough, not quite up to par, and always on the precipice of failure.

The separation between the word and the person happens immediately after birth, a simultaneous severing of body and language. "Checking Mom's blood pressure," they say to you in the hospital moments after your daughter is born. "What's your daughter's birth date, Mom?" they ask in the pediatrician's office. It is a kind way to ease you into a new identity and you appreciate this, answering them as if it is a perfectly normal way to be addressed. Now it is Mom's turn to speak!

But inside you don't feel like this "Mom" they keep referring to. It is a heavy word reserved for worthier women. You are winging the mom thing even by the standards of a culture that really has no idea what a mom should be anymore. Who are you to write about moms, the very word that connotes mom, when the world is filled with actual, authentic moms, moms who have nurtured and suffered and worried more, who have felt guiltier than you, who are more competent than you, who have sacrificed more, stretched themselves thinner than you. They take possession of the word *mom* in a way you never will. But here you are, writing about them as if you're some authority on the subject. It's almost comical.

Your daughter's school wants parents to volunteer to cut fruit at lunchtime. When you first toured the school, the fruit cutting was emphasized so much, you wondered if the job was designed as metaphor.

"Sure," the head of the school said agreeably, "if that's how you want to think about it."

So one afternoon, there you stand behind the cafeteria glass in a hairnet, slicing apples into browning moons. "Whose mom is that?" a few kids ask. Their friends lob around some names. Who do you belong to?

The upper classes have filed into the cafeteria, and a debate ensues about to whom you belong. The middle school and junior high school kids hope it's not their mom. They would be mortified if you were attached to them. They do a quick scan of you for recognition and are relieved you are not theirs. But they take the apple slices you offer them, and the polite ones even thank you. You realize that the moment will come for you when your daughter will prefer if you didn't cut fruit. The very idea of you cutting fruit at her school will fill her with horror. Not too long from now, she will sit with her friends, her back turned to your hairnet and blunt chef's knife chopping slice after slice.

The word *mom* is a foreign word to you anyway. It is a word reserved for Americans. You grew up with a "mama" in the Soviet Union who stayed a mama after you emigrated, who is a mama to this day. Your American friends call their own mothers "Mom," while for a Russian, a "mama" is always a "mama." Your mama calls you every day to make sure you're still alive, that you've survived the day without incurring bodily harm, and, if you don't pick up, she will call you three more times because a part of her is convinced some catastrophe has befallen you. That's the kind of mama you have. Your mama is the real deal, while you're just some middling student of future momness.

Because you emigrated at an age of some cognition, you became an amateur linguist, a Ferdinand de Saussure of sorts, scrutinizing signs and their signifiers. Foreign words were scrawled onto index cards to be memorized; your parents were wringing their hands that you wouldn't speak English, but only you knew each word was an impostor and there was a better word elsewhere. Meanings were expendable, exchangeable depending on where you lived, what language you spoke, and there was no reason to commit to any one definition. In the Soviet Union, a mama never permits her child to drink beverages with ice. In

America, this is considered harmless, even desirable. You saw the disconnect early on and you vowed to pick no side, to tag yourself as nothing. Eventually, the word *mom* must be questioned as well, the impossibility of stepping into a definition designed by others.

According to linguist Roman Jakobson, the reason *ma* is a root of the word for "mother" in so many global languages is that this is what babies are capable of saying first. These particular letters, these stops and nasals, fall into the phonetic reach of toothless, weak-tongued babies and quickly come to be associated with need. But can you be trusted to be the dispenser of need?

You could handle *mommy*. At least a mommy has valences, is implanted with affection and intrigue. You were younger when you were Mommy, you had a waist and long, soft hair and sharper ambitions. You had a high laugh, you were a laid-back traveler, and you didn't need under-eye concealer. You didn't feel like a mommy either, but at least you were a character in a rollicking game with audience participation, and it was cute, a little whisper between you and a pudgy creature with a soft protruding tummy and huge brown eyes. It felt like you still had time to fix some fatal flaw, steer the ship into the right port, just as soon as you got your bearings, sleep, and mental health back. But a mom conceals no mysteries; the word is closed and complete, the *o* tucked away, protected by the same bulbous *m*. You exist because you are easy for babies to say.

The word *mom* is injected with furious, flowing time. You know how old you will be when your daughter is ten and twenty and thirty. When you think of survival or your own death, you gauge how old your daughter will be when you are alive or dead. You now exist in relation to the age of the child. Her timeline has been set to zero and yours to negative [insert age]. You are no longer at the center of any timeline, and there is a relief and a sadness to that unseating. The minute you are contextualized as mom, you are shepherded right back to negative [insert age].

And now it pains you to realize that nothing will be fixed, not in your head anyway. You are almost Mom, like a day away from being Mom, and you still feel a fraud, a pretender, a simulacrum of the real mom. Perhaps it takes longer than you think to embody the thing. Maybe you need to be patient.

Your daughter flows into the cafeteria with her friends, and she is quickly informed that you belong to her. "Your mommy's working fruit," her friends say, and this fills her with such excitement that she screams and insists you join her at the table. You're still wearing the hairnet, and your hands are slick with apple juice. You're enveloped by chatter, a closed network of children's language.

This is the payoff of the fruit, you understand. You're now encouraged to leave your station and join your child. You have taken part in the ritual, and now you know what's on the other side.

"That's your mom." Her friends point. Of course. You see the world has shifted. It has turned to your daughter. She's the "you" and you're the "mom." She—still, but not for long—wants to sit on your lap, and you hold her with apple hands right there in front of her friends, and you see in this moment that *mom* is not as solid as you thought but always shifting, evading capture. You will spend the rest of your life pinning down the word, pushing against it, stepping in and out of it.

Dammit, you knew this fruit-cutting thing was a metaphor.

MATURE
JILLIAN MEDOFF

I have a Pavlovian response when a man—any man, any age—calls me mature: I cross my arms, like a protective shield, over my chest. This is not only to express disgust; it's also to encourage respect. *Eyes up high, pal,* I'm signaling. *Say it to my face.* Mostly, though, I'm hiding my breasts.

My feelings about the word *mature* are as twisted as my feelings about my breasts—and just as old. I first realized that *mature* had a double meaning way back in early adolescence, when I went from flat to va-va-voom seemingly overnight. My loathing for the word ignited in my early twenties when, stacked like a Hooters waitress, I entered the workforce; went dormant in my thirties after a successful breast reduction; and was retriggered in my forties when it became clear that, having aged from office ingenue to office mom, it was time to swap my tight blouses and skimpy lingerie for relaxed-fit turtlenecks and full-support Spanx.

Now, as I enter the black hole of midlife, my reaction to *mature* is mixed. On one hand, I can't deny that I am, in fact, a mature woman. I'm on the far side of fifty; I've been working for thirty-odd years; and day by harrowing day, I can feel my face, neck, and breasts yielding to the forces of gravity. On the other hand, many people consider *mature* a compliment. Mature females are reliable and relied upon. We're knowledgeable. We're level-headed and calm. But in my experience, when a man, particularly a corporate man, describes me as mature, he isn't referring to my actual maturity; that is, my business acumen and achievements. He's referring directly to my advanced age and indirectly to my ever-diminishing value—not only to the organization but to the human race. *You're done,* he's saying. *Die already.*

On the third hand, maybe I'm just being dramatic; maybe I'm letting my girlish sensitivity cloud my perspective. After all, there's nothing wrong with *mature* in theory, particularly when it's equating my decades at the office with my accumulated wisdom. And yet, my fraught relationship to *mature* is based entirely on my body, specifically to all the ways that men have reacted to my breasts—their size, weight, and what I suggest we call *uplift*—over the course of my life. Some women's faces write their fates; for me, it's my breasts, once glorious, now humbled.

These are their stories.

34C

Fifth grade was when I first understood that my breasts mattered to the world. On an otherwise unremarkable morning in 1973, my mother pointed to my chest. "Bra time." In my memory, she sounds appalled, as if my budding breasts were an offense.

At three o'clock, I found her waiting for me at a prearranged spot. She was chatting with a man I recognized. He was balding, he had a soft belly, he was around my dad's age, and he was familiar; in other words, the man on the sidewalk posed no threat whatsoever. So, for the sake of this story, let's call him Fuck Face.

Spotting me, my mom waved. I wasn't difficult to pick out of a crowd. At ten, I was tall for my age and husky, with a sweet smile and thick thighs. I towered over all the girls and most of the boys in my class, so I was often mistaken for a teenager. Plus, my breasts. But while I was aware that my body was changing, I wasn't yet enslaved by it. I wore shorts that were too small and too tight and rode up my ass. My new round, red nipples were visible through a clingy tank top. I was still a child, unformed and ungraceful; I moved through the world like a big floppy Muppet, unconcerned about how much space I occupied or—this sounds unfathomable now—how I might look.

My mother turned to Fuck Face. "You know Jill, right? She's my eldest."

"How old is Jill?" Though he asked my mother the question, he was staring at my shirt.

I was a messy kid (I'm a messy adult), forever staining my clothes. I glanced down. Was there something on my— And then, just like that, I understood. Suddenly I wasn't a girl anymore; I wasn't a person. I wasn't even a Muppet. Instead I was a body—just a body—and I was out in the wild, alone and exposed. I crossed my arms to hide my breasts, but they'd grown to circus proportions, and I couldn't contain them.

"She's ten," my mother told him, oblivious. "But people usually think she's older."

"Well, Naomi." Chuckling, Fuck Face let his eyes go from my breasts to my face then back to my breasts. He stared at me with intent, as if we were sharing a sleazy secret. "Jill sure is *mature*, isn't she?"

34DD

When I was growing up, my dad was in sales, and we moved a lot (I mean, *a lot*; I went to seven elementary schools, two junior highs, and two high schools). So my childhood, especially my teenage years, was characterized by chaos. But I was a disciplined and methodical student as well as a can-do kind of girl—eager to please, happy to help—so I was able to keep the madness at bay. I was also desperate to be good. This meant following the rules— any rules, didn't matter whose. You asked, I jumped. The simple reason was that I craved approval; the darker, more complex reason was that it never occurred to me not to. Honestly, I didn't even realize *no* was an option.

In my early teens, I was a solid citizen and loyal soldier. My parents and teachers frequently called me mature, which I reveled in. If I was acting maturely, I was acting grown-up, like a lady, and a lady puts everyone else's needs and desires ahead of her own. The code, then, was simple: *mature* meant *helpful* and *helpful* meant *good* and *good* meant *selfless* and *selfless* meant *pure*. At the same time, I couldn't ignore my breasts, which had continued to grow (and grow). Depending on who you spoke to, by age thirteen, I was *fully developed* (Mom), *healthy* (Dad), *buxom* (Grandma), *voluptuous* (Fuck Face), or I had *titanic tits* (male classmates). I was so big busted, when I walked into a room, my breasts announced themselves. *Forget her face,* they demanded. *Look at us.*

Here's something else about me. I'm naturally introverted and painfully self-conscious, so having "titanic tits" made me want to die a thousand deaths. Desperate to disappear, I wore oversize sweaters, harness-style bras, layers of T-shirts. Unfortunately, my breasts would not be defeated. And you know who noticed?

"Jill's *too mature*," said the boys in my school. "She won't hang out with us."

Feigning deafness, I shut my locker as quietly as I could. If I made no noise, I told myself, they wouldn't see me, and if they didn't see me, I wasn't there.

"She's so *grown up*. Jill, don't walk away. Jill, Jill, Jill—"

Oh my God, those fucking boys, they were everywhere. They traveled in packs, like feral dogs on the hunt. While I'm sure they were typical teenagers—foulmouthed, insecure, and horny, horny, horny—they terrorized me. Those boys were forever trailing behind me, making comments—about my breasts, about my ass, about parts of my body I'd never heard of. They slipped hand-drawn pictures of hairy pussies into my books and love notes into my backpack: "JILL HAZ THE BIGGEST BOOBZ." "If I had tits like yours," they surmised, "I'd be feeling myself up all day long." It was a confusing paradox, to be so shy as to feel unnoticed and yet so visible as to feel unprotected.

The worst of it, though, wasn't their loud jokes about my big breasts but their whispered insinuations about what my big breasts represented. To the boys (and, I suppose, to men like Fuck Face), my big breasts signaled that I was fast, loose, and dirty; I lacked morals and boundaries. You asked, I opened wide. My big breasts meant I was the sluttiest slut of all the sluts (a *nympho*, in the parlance of the times), therefore I wanted to fuck you, therefore I wanted to fuck all your friends. And go ahead—tell everyone! Girls with big breasts can't get enough attention because girls with big breasts have no shame.

Of course, I thought. *This must be true.*

Because I was too young and naive to know otherwise, because I was happy to help and eager to please, I believed what the boys said about me. And because I was a young lady, I put their needs and desires ahead of my own. When they felt like touching me, they didn't have to ask. They just reached out; they grabbed me. But I never said no; I never said "Don't." Instead, I stayed very, very quiet, so very quiet I wasn't even there.

34DDD

"Well, I can see why they hired *you.*" Gray-haired and distinguished, the plastic surgeon (my customer) wore a crisp white coat over a dark navy suit. (To protect his identity, let's refer to him as Dr. Jeremy Veague III of 343 Beverly Drive, Beverly Hills, California.) "I wish I could offer you a job myself." His office was lavish, with plush carpeting, rich leather furniture, and original art on the walls. Seated across from him, wearing my own tailored suit, I perked up.

Because of my smarts? My can-do attitude? A recent college graduate, I was eager to hear what made me unique.

"*You,* my dear, are a walking, talking product advertisement!"

Oh my God. Realization set in. *He's talking about my boobs.*

I was twenty-five years old and selling mammary (breast) implants. A year before, I'd been hired by the marketing department of a medical device supplier. The company was small, so our sales force was lean and forever in flux. Six months after I started, my boss asked if I'd lend a hand. "We need new blood in the field, and you need the experience." *Oh boy, did you come to the right girl!* Eager to please, happy to help, I soon found myself traveling to doctors' offices at appointed times, persuading them to buy our products: in this case, silicone implants ranging in size from 175cc to 775cc. Most of the people I worked with were men (the surgeons, my colleagues, our managers). So I figured being a young, female breast saleswoman would make me a novelty—and it did—but where I was focused on *female*, everyone else was focused on *breast*.

"Any chance I can get my hands on a sample?" Grinning mischievously, Dr. Veague turned to Bart, my colleague. "Bet they feel *great!*"

Too stunned to reply, I hunched my shoulders and tried to disappear behind my product case. Bart studied the art on the walls. I was used to men pointing out my still very large breasts. But this was the first time my very large breasts had been discussed *at my job, in front of a coworker, by a medical professional* who was *old enough to be my grandfather*. Mumbling a nonresponse, I resumed my sales pitch.

Dr. Veague wasn't interested—but he did invite me out for a drink. "Bring your friends." He eyed my chest. "I'm sure we'll all get along just fine."

This time, when I ignored him, he got annoyed. Again, he turned to Bart. "What's her problem? She can't take a joke?"

"She's new," Bart replied with a laugh. "Young, fresh out of school. You know the type: too mature for dirty old men like us." And then he opened his own sample case and took over the meeting.

Normally, this is the part of the story where I describe my Norma Rae moment, how I filed a lawsuit and testified before

Congress. But that's not what happened. Instead, I learned a valuable lesson: not playing along meant losing business; it meant risking my job; it meant *shut the fuck up.* I also began to understand the rules. I had chosen to work in a male-dominated industry, one whose stated purpose was to objectify, scrutinize, and alter the female form. Plus, I was a young girl with a pretty face and enormous assets. You could almost say I had it coming.

"Yeah, okay," I told Dr. Veague. "One drink."

Next time, I told myself. Next time, I'll speak up.

32C

I had a breast reduction at thirty-three. The result was perfect breasts, round, firm, and proud, like a pair of high beams cutting through a dark night. I lost ten pounds; my body was slamming. No one called me mature, though if they had, I wouldn't have cared. But you know what they did say?

"You have great tits."

Honestly; I'm not kidding. Random men, strangers of every age, nationality, income bracket, religion, and creed, would approach me on the street and say, not to my face (because of course) but to my chest, "You have great tits."

What did I say? What could I say? Really, tell me, what is an appropriate response? When I gave birth to my daughter, my body would betray me all over again, but for one brief, shining moment, I could agree, if not aloud, then at least privately.

You're right, Fuck Face; my tits are *magnificent.*

34C

I work with a young, ambitious tech guy named Larry who thinks I'm a dope. Granted, I'm sure other men in my office feel similarly, but Larry can't hide it. On the phone, he's rude and belligerent; when I ask for his help, he'll say no; his emails are terse and aggressive: "This is wrong. L."

I am fifty-five years old. During my career, which has spanned three decades, I've worked for brand-name companies like Revlon, Merck, Deloitte, and Aon. At this point, I can close deals, solve client problems, supervise project teams, and meet deadlines. Compared to my junior colleagues, I can do all this faster and far more efficiently. Recently, however, Larry let me know that he prefers to work with Brittany: "She's so . . . I don't know, she just *gets it*." Brittany is twenty-five. During her corporate career, which has spanned maybe eleven months, she's worked for one company. But I am a lot older than Brittany and therefore I am a pain in Larry's ass: "Hey Larry, I'm not sure what you mean by 'wrong.' Please advise in detail. Thank you, Jillian."

The workplace is a microcosm of the larger world, and in business, just like in life, as a woman advances in age, she loses valuable currency her younger self once possessed. In this way, I've become invisible—not as a worker (for now) but as a woman. My breasts no longer matter because no one is looking at them— or at me. While it's a relief (albeit bittersweet) to stop being a target of attention, as an older female, with ten, maybe fifteen years of working life still ahead, I now face the real possibility that having lost my youth, I could also lose my job. Worse still: given my age and current salary, it would be difficult, even impossible, to find another one.

It's a fact: in the corporate world, when a man matures, he moves into a desired/final state, but a woman moves into obsolescence. To describe a businesswoman as mature is to evoke images of beehive hairdos, extreme bosoms, and thick compression stockings; to be a mature businesswoman is to be too old, too slow, too twentieth century. While *mature* may sound less harsh than other words men use to describe women like me— *aggressive, bossy, uncompromising*—it's actually more lethal. If you're perceived as old, slow, and out of touch, you can't properly service clients, which means people start talking, which means your days are numbered—regardless of whether or not it's true. In this way, you become worthless sooner than a man who is described as a *respected elder statesman—patrician, learned, distinguished.* In the porn industry, female performers are considered mature at *age twenty-eight.* At fifty-five, I'm even too old to play the horny granny.

And so we've come to the end—of my story, of my glory, of my patience. Yet news from the front isn't all bleak. While it's true that, for me, *mature* is a heat-seeking missile that sneaks up, catches me off guard, and detonates on impact, rendering me speechless, it's also true that after fifty-five years on this earth, I have weapons of my own. After carrying the sin of my big breasts for almost half a century, I'm finally ready to fight back. To wit: this essay, my very first attempt to express the horror and shame of simply being me. By finding my voice, not only as a novelist (which I am) but also as a real woman in real time, it occurs to me that men like Larry, Dr. Veague, the boys, and Fuck Face are not the final authorities on who I am and what I'm worth. On the contrary, by calling attention to my breasts (in public! on my own volition!), I realize that the cumulative power of my stories defines me beyond the sum of my parts: I am more than my body; I am more than my breasts.

Listen, I know that the next time you see me in person, you'll feel compelled to stare at my breasts, but that's okay: I can protect myself. More to the point, the next time some man calls me mature, maybe I won't respond with injured silence and damn myself. Instead, maybe I'll speak up in the moment; maybe I will roar.

AMBITIOUS

JULIANNA BAGGOTT

In my twenties, I used to blank on the word *ambition*. It's the only word I've ever blanked on, and it happened so persistently I created a mnemonic device for it. The drug Ambien was new to the market at the time, and I was haunted by the story of a woman who'd sleepwalked out of her house in her nightgown and was found peeing in the middle of the street. For the sake of memorization, it wasn't only that *Ambien* and *ambition* sound the same. Both words brought up the notion of humiliating self-sabotage and my own sleeplessness, both of which felt tied to the complexity of my own ambition.

Once I'd made the association, I never blanked on the word again.

Female ambition is really a field of study, but I'll keep this personal. Here's the message that I received early on: male ambition is good and necessary. People assume that any man who's gotten far in his career has a lot of it.

Female ambition, on the other hand, is dirty. It's selfish. It's ugly. Female ambition is suspicious. It comes at a cost. It's necessary to get ahead—we're told—but if a woman uses it to get ahead then she's sacrificed her soul. And she's going against society's virtuous goal for her: motherhood. And motherhood—so sainted and holy—has no room for personal ambition. Women are to sacrifice themselves, wholly and completely, for their children.

This notion of women sacrificing themselves completely for their children didn't come from within my family. The women who came before me worked. My paternal grandmother was a single mother who did bookkeeping. My maternal grandmother worked in the family bar, was a secretary to a bishop, opened her own children's clothing store. My great-grandmother was a madam of a house of prostitution. My great-great-grandmother hoed cotton and eventually ran a store. To the best of my knowledge, my mother marked the first homemaker in our ancestral line, but she also was a trained pianist and taught lessons in our house. The notion of the dark side of female ambition has been so pervasive in our culture, like some odorless gas. It didn't need to come from within my own family.

So what to do with a woman like me? Early on, I knew that I wanted to have kids *and* write. I was bullheaded. My late-college plan was to get my MFA, move back into my parents' attic, and have kids, raising them with my parents' help. This was a weird, vague plan that I was smart enough not to say out loud. There would be no husband. Men were fun, but I couldn't imagine finding one worth spending my entire life with.

My plan hit a snag. I fell in love. Halfway through my MFA I got married to my husband, a poet I met in graduate school, and

I was pregnant soon after graduating. By then, I'd already started publishing short stories. By the time my husband and I had our second child, I was publishing essays and poetry. By the time we had our third, I was writing my first novel. Now we have four children, and I've published over twenty books.

Throughout my career, the word *ambition* has appeared and reappeared. When it was applied simply to my literary work, it felt good. I'm a writer. I write. *It's not ambition,* I can hear myself scrambling. *It's artistic drive.* Ambitious creative impulses are healthy. But when it attached itself to me, it felt awful. Being a great (ambitionless) mother felt like a basic expectation for me as a woman.

If you'd asked me over the years whether I was ambitious, you'd have found a woman trying to disconnect herself from the word. Long before I published my first book, I wore motherhood like a floppy hat and sunglasses to disguise it. It was easy. Our neighbors saw a young stay-at-home mom, and that was completely comfortable for them, easy.

I was complicit. I only brought up my writing with people I was very close to. I was protecting myself. I knew well enough by then that our culture is hard on aspiring artists. I'd already learned that talking about my writerly ambitions would be countered by well-intentioned warnings from people who knew nothing about publishing. They usually began with "Do you know how hard it is to get published?" but the litany could be long, and it was always punishing. Instead, I talked about weird rashes, first words, croup. Don't get me wrong. I wasn't taking motherhood lightly. I was in deep, emotionally and intellectually fascinated by birthing and raising children—the psychosocial aspect, the brain development. These are how characters are forged, so there was something transferrable, as there are in all aspects of a writer's life.

But if I'd only been raising children, I'd have been gutted by the boredom. Parenting is like air traffic control. For long stretches, you keep constant watch when very little is happening, and yet it's always high stakes. To put it simply, if I'd abandoned my writing for my children, I'd have resented my children. If I'd forgone children for the sake of my writing, I'd have resented my writing. In order to try a resentment-free (or resentment-reduced) life, I had to do both.

But when that first book sold, I finally had to come out. It was like a baby that had appeared out of nowhere. And because I'd hidden my ambition, I had to spend a lot of time convincing my nursing mothers' group, the neighbors, my husband's work friends that the book was legitimate.

Because I was a mommy, they would ask, "Is it a children's book?"

"No, it's for adults."

They would nod with understanding. "So it's romance?"

"No, it's a literary novel."

This baffled them. "How will it get published?" It seemed likely that I would be stapling it together myself.

I learned to say, "My agent sold it to a publishing house." With the word *agent* my book made sense to them, perhaps because it sounded like a man had taken over.

Still, sometimes they had one more question. "But where will I be able to get a copy?"

And I would tell them, "Wherever books are sold." Granted, that was strangely satisfying.

In those early days of the internet, I joined a writing mothers discussion board. I was there to be inspired and to try to inspire other mothers who were balancing motherhood and the craft. I talked about how I would bring notebooks with me to parks and playgrounds. I would sit in the driveway while the kids were on tricycles and jot my ideas.

One mother attacked me. She said that I was a terrible mother and that my children were going to wander into the street and get hit by a car. Whereas I think it would have been okay to read a book while my children played, it was not okay for me to write. Ambition would kill my children. Got it.

When my husband and I swapped roles and he became the stay-at-home dad, it became harder to call me a danger to my children. When Dave and I first got together, we both were jockeying for housewife. We loved kids. We wanted to write. Dave's need to write, over time, simply wasn't as fevered as mine. He was very happy to quit his nine-to-five job and stay at home with the kids. He started writing down *homemaker* on forms.

At the time, he was a rarity; he probably still is. (It remains very difficult to find hard numbers on how many men are stay-at-home parents.) We braced ourselves for criticism. Dave was giving up his ambition—seemingly, from the outside perspective—to take on a traditionally female role. Certainly, he'd take a hit.

Nope. Dave, as a stay-at-home dad, was worthy of sainthood. The sacrifice of his ambition was divine. And he was beloved and celebrated by everyone, but especially by the women who did the same things that he did—for which they received no fanfare. Over the years, I've gotten used to the term "Saint Dave."

He wasn't only our homemaker. As my partner, Dave supported my ambition. He was my editor, negotiator, organizer, creative director—the one who, at a crossroads, would stop me and say, "What would a straight white six-foot-three guy ask for in this scenario?" When I was blind to sexism because I'd become used to it, he saw it for what it was.

This was good, because it wasn't just my motherhood that was supposedly at risk because of my ambition. It was my writing.

I was in the final interview with a search committee for a professor job. By then, I'd published six novels, three collections of poetry, and seven books for younger readers. I was thirty-eight. I was sitting at the head of a boardroom-style table. The committee of six or so were asking final questions.

A female professor who didn't have any children asked me, point-blank, how I intended to do the job while balancing the demands of motherhood.

I paused, glancing around the table at the other professors, giving them a chance to intervene. It's an illegal question, after all.

No one did, so I answered it.

I was already a tenured professor handling the demands of motherhood, I said. In fact, having had my first child at twenty-five, everything I'd accomplished in my career had been done *as a mother*, so one could assume that my entire career so far was an example of how I'd do it—the way I always had, the only way I knew how.

After this experience, the innocent question "How do you do so much?"—which had started popping up at every Q and A—felt so charged to me that I fantasized about just answering the question with the question, "How do you do so little?"

Once it became impossible to ignore my success, for me to downplay it, both men and women found new ways to diminish my career. And it became clear why I had disguised my ambition for so long.

When I took my first job in academe, a few colleagues asked me if I'd met a certain high-profile writer yet. When I told them I hadn't, they warned me that he'd make a pass at me, but also that I'd really like him.

He did not make a pass at me. I met him at a party and he questioned my parenting by comparing me to another woman writer who had it much harder than I did—she was single and had adopted a child. I already knew I had it pretty good. When I was unmoved, he drove home his point: I was successful because I was self-promotional. How else could my review coverage and interviews be explained? I was out there begging for it, pimping myself. I got attention that I didn't deserve. Subtext: it was attention that he did, in fact, deserve.

Luck was another thing used again and again to explain my success. After a talk that I gave to a Hadassah group on Long Island, an older male writer got up to speak. His first line was this: "You might learn what it is to be young and lucky from Julianna Baggott, but from me you'll learn . . ." To be honest, I forget what they were supposed to learn from him. I learned that luck was a way to put my career into a tiny little box.

Or somehow, it was my looks that had done the trick. Shortly after I'd landed one of my academic positions, a female colleague commented that it hadn't hurt that I was easy on the eyes. I'd published more than most of the professors two ranks above me. If anything, I was overqualified for the assistant professorship.

I got used to these gibes and got better at using them as fuel. However, just when I thought maybe people had exhausted ways to diminish my career, there was the perfect one. It was clean, precise, and impossible to fight.

Once I was in *The Best American Poetry* and winning an American Library Association award and having books listed as *New York Times* Notables, people started saying things like, "You sure can crank it out." That was it: I'd achieved too much. The greatest sign of my weakness as a writer was that I was too prolific.

This particular dismissal is airtight. I can't write my way out of it. It puts my career in a box designed for my ultimate suffocation.

I kept writing.

But before I go on, I want to pause a moment. I am lucky—and I never forget how lucky—to do the work that I do. Amid all of these stories, there were champions of me as a writer, an academic, a mother-artist—from family, from fellow writers, men and women, from arts organizations, and eventually from the publishing industry itself, which has a strong women-centric presence.

Yet still, now that my career means I'm the sole breadwinner for a family of six, I sometimes use motherhood to disguise my ambition. That statement shifts all of the selfishness implied by female ambition and repositions it back under the umbrella of maternal love. Me? Ambitious? No, I'm doing all of this for the kids. This is my job. This is how I make a living, and I have to make a living because I'm . . . *the sole breadwinner for a family of six.* Why do I still feel compelled to make these kinds of statements? If Dave gets to be sainted, I guess I like to feel a little holier-than-thou too. After all, it's hard work.

This is the part of the essay in which I'm supposed to embrace the word *ambition*, to reclaim it for women and celebrate it. I don't feel like it.

As an artist, it's my job to actively shed how I'm perceived and, on a certain level, to shed who I am. As toughened as I am in my career, I have to remain completely vulnerable as an artist. All these years, throughout all the stages of social commentary, it has become my primary task not simply to write or to support my family but to protect my relationship with the page. This realization has happened slowly over time. I've needed to learn how to create this kind of insulation when things are going badly— through rejection and rough reviews and disappointing book sales—and, just as importantly, when things are going really well. Success can be just as disruptive to the creative process for me as all the various forms of failure.

Protecting my relationship with the page doesn't require ambition. Ambition alone is nothingness. It didn't make me a writer or a mother. Ambition is something I never should have worried about to begin with. It's desire without a name. It's anxiety without a fear. Ambition wants to achieve. I want to make and keep making.

As for my children, they've grown up with a stay-at-home father and a mother who makes a living in the arts. The oldest is a sculptor; the second is studying film production; the third is a business major; the fourth is only eleven, but her favorite documentary is *The September Issue*, featuring the life of powerhouse Anna Wintour.

And for all I've said about not needing ambition, I see ambition in my children—the various forms it takes, all those beautiful, dangerous pistons—and I'm happy they're pounding away. It's healthy, after all, to want something for yourself. On a very primal level, I see it as my children figuring out what they love to do and desiring to do it well. And I also teach them to be ever watchful for those who try to chip away at that love.

VICTIM

KATE HARDING

I don't recall who first told me that I wasn't a victim, but it happened soon after someone told me I was raped.

I was seventeen and shit-faced. I was a nerd who had been drunk maybe three times in my life, surrounded by the safety of giggling girlfriends and a childhood home free of vacationing parents. I had never been to an actual party where everyone was drinking, and a boy seemed to like me, and I had no curfew or responsible adults to report to. I was a virgin who didn't want to be one much longer.

Several strains of the impossible became possible all at once. There was nothing but the present moment, walking out of a party that was too loud and too crowded, holding a guy's hand, like I was the kind of girl who got to do that.

Well, what did you expect to happen?

I knew this: a man I had some vague sexual interest in,

mostly because he showed interest in me, had brought me drinks all night, and then I left a party with him.

I knew this: I kissed him outside that party, on purpose, standing between two white, green-shuttered colonial-style dorms, the thumping heartbeat of De La Soul or Deee-Lite pouring out open windows.

And I knew this: whatever I expected when I left a party with a guy whose name I had not committed to memory, I did not expect to end up on damp, patchy grass, floppily trying to convince him to stop fucking me. I did not expect to stumble toward three identical white dormitories, crying and hoping I was right about which one was mine. I did not expect my roommate to react to the very sight of me with shock, or insist that I tell our RA in the morning. I did not expect to end up at the hospital, where a very kind man examined my genitals, prescribed the morning-after pill, gently scolded me for smoking, asked if I wanted the police to do a rape kit—I declined, not wanting my parents to know anything about it—and told me to do follow-up STD testing with a campus doctor in six months. I did not expect to see my rapist in the dining hall a day or two later and suddenly understand how tiny our five-hundred-student campus was. I did not expect the campus doctor who did the follow-up testing, another strange man penetrating me, to treat me with naked contempt for having unprotected sex during the window when there was no longer any excuse for ignorance about HIV but the good drugs hadn't arrived yet. I did not expect to become a feminist. I did not expect to write a book about rape culture. I did not expect to write this essay more than twenty-five years later.

After the rape, I didn't blame myself. It was 1992, and feminism had gotten through to me enough that when I said something like, "I just had sex on the lawn with a guy I don't know and he wouldn't stop" and heard "That's called rape" in response, I thought, *Yes, I suppose it is.*

This made it weird when well-meaning people—my RA, an ER doctor, a counselor—reminded me, again and again, that it wasn't my fault. These people were beautiful, compassionate angels who only wanted to help, as long as helping meant giving the same canned speeches to every victim who came along. "It's not your fault" is a Thing You Are Supposed to Say, a theoretically healing benediction, but I never felt the kind of shame that that reassurance is meant to ameliorate.

The angels told me with the same earnest vehemence that the preferred alternative to *victim* was *survivor.*

I get the "survivor" thing, in theory. Rape is fundamentally a crime of power, and whether the mechanism is gunpoint or incapacitation by alcohol, the very essence of it is to remind the [victim] [survivor] [person being raped] [check all that apply] that they are not in control of what happens to their own body. Death is the ultimate loss of bodily control, and every lesser instance is on some level its harbinger. This is how rape becomes a weapon of war and the threat of it an element of women's systemic oppression. All very Women's Studies 101, thanks to Susan Brownmiller's work in the 1970s.

By 1992, that theory had traveled as far as my RA's training at my small liberal arts college in New England. *Survivor* was, she said, my word and identity to claim.

However, in practice, I did not feel I had *survived* anything in particular. I felt that a strange guy had done things I didn't want him to do to my body, and I understood that the simplest word for that was *rape*. But I had never doubted there would be an end-point. I had *endured* a thing, but to say I *survived* it was no more meaningful than saying I'd survived every moment of my life until then. To call myself a "survivor" felt somewhere between putting on airs and appropriating a visceral pain that wasn't mine.

This is the part where the angels would say, "Here's some literature and let me remind you once more that it's not your fault." They'd say that violation is violation, that survivors often underplay their own experiences and deny the gravity of rape, usually as a means of self-protection.

Listen, I am a person who minimizes the gravity of *everything* as a means of self-protection. On the morning of my mother's funeral, I came upon my sisters sobbing and hugging and, unable to tolerate the depth and earnestness of their despair, cut it short with a snarky, "God, *who died?*" To be fair to the angels, what they were describing sounds a lot like me.

But I don't minimize the violation of my rape. I draw a sharp distinction between what a man did to me on the lawn outside a house party and a near-death experience, but let's be clear: I became a mouthy public feminist largely because of that man doing things I didn't want him to do to my body. I'm still telling the story almost two decades into a different century, a different millennium. The scarred and stiffened muscle of my heart would love to finish telling the story, believe me, but, having passed our silver anniversary, the story and I have grown so fucking enmeshed, we're probably going to die in the same bed.

But the question that first struck me at seventeen and continues to haunt me at forty-three is this: What's wrong with being a victim?

What's wrong with being a victim?

Obviously, *becoming* a victim is undesirable. We don't wish for bad things beyond our control to come along and interfere with our plans. But once the bad thing has happened, why are we so allergic to using the simplest, most accurate language to describe the condition of being post–bad thing?

I had been violated without being in fear for my life, ergo I was far more accurately termed a "victim" than a "survivor." That part was simple enough. The complicated part was that many other people who had been raped preferred *survivor* and found *victim* actively insulting.

It wasn't clear to me why the plain truth should be insulting, based on my understanding of *victim* as "a person to whom something bad has happened, through no fault of their own." Even the most thorough and thin-sliced definition available, from the Oxford English Dictionary, didn't offer any more persuasive reasons. The original meaning of *victim*, from the Latin *victima*, referred specifically to religious sacrifices. Something lived and then, at the hands of believers in a morbidly greedy god or gods, it died. A small animal, a child, a virgin, Jesus Christ.

In the seventeenth century, we begin to see it used metaphorically, for, as the OED puts it, "one who suffers severely in body or property through cruel or oppressive treatment." Scrolling down through the layers of nuance, we find a definition that includes a judgment of how seriously we should take it: "In weaker sense: One who suffers some injury, hardship, or loss, is badly treated or taken advantage of, etc."

But pick up a thesaurus, or type "victim" into an online one, and you begin to get the picture: *butt, clown, dupe, fool, gopher, gudgeon, gull, mark, patsy, pawn, pigeon, prey, pushover, stooge, sucker.* These are the words that begin rewriting your story as soon as you utter the word *victim.* These are the synonyms and judgments that cling like burrs to your helpless body. *Well, what did you expect to happen?*

In 2015, Susan Brownmiller herself gave an interview to *New York* magazine in which she called the campus-based anti-rape movement "a very limited movement that doesn't accept reality," adding: "Culture may tell you, 'You can drink as much as men,' but you can't. People think they can have it all ways. The slut marches bothered me, too, when they said you can wear whatever you want. Well sure, but you look like a hooker. They say, 'That doesn't matter,' but it matters to the man who wants to rape. It's unrealistic. I don't know what happened to the understanding people had in the 1970s."

Never mind that it's just as illegal and immoral to rape sex workers as young editorial assistants or retail clerks or ice cream scoopers who wish to express their sexuality without being assaulted. To a great many people, apparently including the mother of the anti-rape movement, victims are people who weren't smart enough to avoid becoming victims.

What's wrong with being a victim?

Another strain of anti-victim sentiment seems based on the premise that there *is* something intrinsically appealing about becoming a victim. Like people who hear *victim* and think *patsy, pawn, pigeon,* those who complain about "victimhood culture" don't accept the "through no fault of their own" part.

Consider the anti-feminist usage of phrases such as "playing the victim" and "professional victim." Consider that "Refuse to Be a Victim" is the name of a National Rifle Association training program for women. Consider that if one enters "victimhood" into the search bar of a large online bookseller that made victims of an entire industry, the top results are titles like these: *The Rise of Victimhood Culture: Microaggressions, Safe Spaces, and the New Culture Wars*; *The Coddling of the American Mind: How Good Intentions and Bad Ideas Are Setting Up a Generation for Failure*; *The Great Blame Game Escape: Breaking Free from Victimhood and Claiming Your Independence with Personal Responsibility*.

No, wait, it's worse than that. In an article titled "The Rape Epidemic Is a Fiction," right-wing pundit Kevin Williamson argues that anti-rape activists' real goal is not preventing sexual violence but "making opposition to feminist political priorities a quasi-criminal offense and using the horrific crime of rape as a cultural and political cudgel."

I don't want to make too much of the violent metaphor, lest I be called to account for my own bloodthirsty rhetorical flourishes, but the image he's created—victimhood as weapon—illustrates how some people come to regard victim status as a type of power, rather than its opposite. *That's* what's ostensibly appealing about it: the perceived ability to pull emotional rank over non-victims when discussing contentious cultural issues.

What's wrong with being a victim?

Being a reasonably polite person who doesn't like hurting people, I am happy to use the word *survivor* for those who prefer it.

But when you're part of a group that prefers one word and you prefer another, politeness to others comes into conflict with your very identity—or at least with how you articulate it. And there are times—early in the process of reclamation, or soon after the introduction of a neologism—when members of a group face off over the acceptability of a word.

Whether I should call myself a "victim" or a "survivor" is a relatively simple question—I'm a grown woman who can call herself whatever she wants—that pops the lid on a much more difficult one: How precisely should I tell the truth about my own life, if increased precision edges us closer to damaging anti-woman stereotypes and bad-faith arguments stretching all the way back to Eve in the garden? At what point does my need to break everything down to its most literal, straightforward definition make me vulnerable to criticism that quietly indicts every other person who has been raped?

In other words, is it my story to tell or not? Is this a thing that happened to me, or a thing that happens to one in six American women? Even if I prefer not to be called a "survivor," what do I owe to those already traumatized people who might be harmed by the implication that they, too, are "victims"?

Thinking seriously about pejorative language as a tool of oppression, a mechanism by which we reinforce cultural disdain for entire groups of people, begets frequent internal conflicts of this nature. Do I, as a woman, have a right to call other women "cunts" if I can make a cogent argument that it should rightly be a term of endearment? What about "bitches"? As someone who suffers from depression, am I allowed to roll my eyes at disability activists who discourage the colloquial use of *crazy* and *insane*? Is a mood disorder technically the same as a mental illness? Was that year I spent lying on my side in front of the TV a disorder, a disability, an unfortunate choice? What about the period while I was writing my book on rape culture, when my husband sat me down and said, "I will write a check to return the advance right now if you'll stop doing this to yourself"?

What's wrong with being a victim?

What's wrong is that using the word makes you a palimpsest on which people will write whatever they happen to think it means. Ultimately, I suspect this is what people who identify as survivors (or something else entirely) are getting at when they refuse the label "victim." It is not merely that they don't wish to be seen by aging feminists and other purveyors of smug "common sense" as *pushovers, stooges,* or *suckers.* Or that they don't wish to be accused of exploiting some (always hypothetical) *innocent victim*'s genuine pain to garner sympathy for what should rightly be their own shame. Or that they don't wish to hurt other [your word of choice]. It's not even that they don't wish to be seen as weak, or broken, or permanently traumatized. It's that they want to speak for themselves. They want their stories to be *theirs.*

Speaking only for myself, if such a thing is possible, I'm just trying to tell you what is true.

It is true that one cannot desire or invite an act defined by non-consent.

It is true that I borrowed a tight black dress; that I loved the way alcohol helped me slide out of my inhibitions like a used-up skin; that I wanted the raw new me underneath to touch and be touched, up to a certain point.

It is true that only rapists deserve the blame for rape; that clothing choices, drinking, and kissing do not indicate consent to sex; that rape and sex are distant cousins, not twins; that predators often use alcohol to control their victims.

It is true that seventeen is so goddamned young.

It is true that I went on to become a happy and settled adult. Mostly.

It is true that I have been spiraling around the same story for twenty-five years.

And it is true that any attempt to sort human beings into categories necessarily shaves off some of our humanity, replacing each unique individual with a type. Would you rather be the victim type, who courts and marinates in adversity, or the survivor type, who triumphs over it? Are you *pawn, pigeon, prey* or a strong, capable woman who courageously saved her own life? There's no option for "Would prefer not to confront adversity, as a rule, but it's not always up to me."

Or maybe there is. A quarter century after I became a victim who wasn't supposed to call myself one, the preferred terminology is shifting to *victim-survivor*, in recognition of differing preferences on the matter. Instead of jettisoning one term or inventing a new one, today's feminist hive mind in its wisdom has saddled us all with an unwieldy label that doesn't quite fit. And yet, over time I've come to love how *victim-survivor* solves the problem by *not* solving it, by openly flouting the social justice commandment to call people only what they wish to be called. It is a term that looks over its glasses at you, absolutely finished with your nonsense, and dares you to answer: *What's wrong with being a victim-survivor?*

In truth, I am both and I am neither. Like every victim-survivor, I am one human being with a particular story about a life-shaping act of violence that, no matter how many times I tell it, only I will ever know by heart. Call me whatever you like.

DISCIPLINED

LAURA LIPPMAN

When I was in my thirties and working full-time at the *Baltimore Sun*, I decided I wanted to write a novel, a mystery. At the time, successful crime writers were expected to write a book a year, so I set that goal for myself—finish a novel in less than twelve months. Besides, my husband would not "allow" me to buy a computer unless I promised to meet this schedule. (Related: he is no longer my husband.)

But that husband was there for me over the next seven years when I woke up at 6 a.m. and wrote for two hours before going to work. Because once I finished that first book, I was advised to start the second even as I searched for an agent, who then put me through a tough revision before showing the first novel to editors. It took so long to land an agent and sell the first book that the second was almost done when I signed a two-book contract. A year later, I signed another two-book contract, then a three-book contract, all the while still working full-time. By the time I submitted my seventh novel, I was able to quit my day job.

And what did people say then? *You're so disciplined.* Not talented, not amazing. They didn't even call me driven or ambitious, words that carry their own fraught freight; *ambitious* is never really a compliment. Still, I would have preferred it to *disciplined.*

About the time that I broke free of my newspaper job, *Publishers Weekly* included me in a roundup of ten mystery writers to watch. There were only three women (and only one writer of color). And, while the thumbnail descriptions of the male writers centered on their ideas and their talent, I was depicted as a worker bee, head down, nose to the grindstone. Orderly. Organized. *Disciplined.*

I have never seen myself that way. After all, there have been many things I have wanted in life. To be one of those women who always looks very pulled-together, clothes and hair and makeup just so. Nope, never got that down. To maintain a perfect household, not a Martha Stewart one, but a homey, welcoming one, where beds are aired, then made, and the pantry is always in order. To keep meticulous income tax files. To be skinnier. (Shallow, but true.) But I have achieved none of these goals. Wouldn't a disciplined person be able to do these things?

But being a full-time writer was different. I was willing to do whatever it took to achieve that goal, and that quest didn't feel like discipline. It felt like desire to me. Passionate and selfish, something I pursued by myself, for myself. The fact is, I hadn't chosen that first husband; he had chosen me and I had shrugged, thinking, "Why not?" I'd felt lucky to be loved. I had lost sight of the fact that I was allowed, perhaps even entitled, to choose what I wanted. Anne Lamott once wrote that she thought if people knew how she felt when she was writing, they would set her on fire. That seemed about right to me. I knew no more powerful feeling, that was for sure.

The books mounted, as did awards. Critics increasingly cited me as someone at the top of my genre. But no one ever suggested that I was talented, much less a genius. Good, yes. Hardworking, surely. Intelligent; committed. But never a *natural*. There was a scrap of a sports story I couldn't get out of my head, about the Boston Celtic Larry Bird, who allegedly knew, from unending practice, every place the ball might take an errant bounce in his home arena. This anecdote had been flagged as racist; its subtext was that Bird worked harder than African American players with more "natural talent." But in writing, where men and women compete, it seemed to me that "natural" was considered better than obsessive perfectionism.

Women, even the best women, are seldom called geniuses. If they are geniuses, then they are emotionally unstable. Whereas men can sit at their desks under banners of the famous Flaubert quote—"Be regular and orderly in your life, so that you may be violent and original in your work"—then wander into the house and stare plaintively into the refrigerator, asking where the butter is. We demand that women be practical, then we use their pragmatism against them, arguing that it proves they are not geniuses.

The first person of my acquaintance I heard described as a genius was a *Baltimore Sun* colleague who wrote an absolutely obscene and graphic message about me. This was post–Anita Hill but two decades before #MeToo, so all the, um, gentleman received was a stern talking-to. The editor in chief then told me that the guy just couldn't help himself. My colleague was neurotic, a *genius*. "He goes to a therapist every day but can't remember to brush his teeth!"

Me, inside my head: *So is it his lack of oral hygiene that makes him a genius or his desire to titty-fuck me? Both?*

How do women become known as geniuses? If we are slovenly or unpredictable, we are much more likely to be called "difficult." If we follow the Flaubertian dictate, we are apt to be seen as meek little rule-followers, absent the spark of true genius. What if discipline is our genius?

At any rate, I keep to my schedule and get more work done than almost anyone I know. I get up, I write daily, I honor my deadlines. As a crime novelist, I often meet literary snobs who believe genre writing is easier, lesser, because it allegedly has rules. Well, as I understand it, physics has rules, but Einstein, our go-to for the definition of genius, interpreted those rules differently than Newton did. Yes, my genre has rules, of a sort. But the best writers break them and subvert them, even while honoring them.

Why is *that* not genius, I wondered. What makes one a genius? I was, at the very least, *ingenious*. Shouldn't that count for something?

More than a decade ago, my husband and I decided to have a child. I needed a little coaxing. I knew that I would do a disproportionate amount of the work involved because my husband's job in television required twelve- to fourteen-hour days. And there was a period of time after our daughter was born when I was bitter and resentful, when I felt the hours I "lost" to parenting meant that I couldn't possibly do my best work.

Then I began to think about the old Astaire-Rogers axiom, about how she did everything he did but in high heels and going backward. Wasn't my ability to write a novel a year *more* impressive if we factored in planning menus, keeping track of the family calendar, making cookies for the school bake sale? And, okay, I took the cookies to school on the wrong day, but does that make me more of a genius or less of a genius?

Now, it happens that my second husband is an official genius, anointed by the MacArthur Foundation, which gives out those annual genius awards that everyone is told not to call genius awards. But even before that phone call came in 2010, I had often heard my husband described as a genius—for example, when a TV honcho turned to me after a screening and said, "That man is a genius."

I said, "That genius literally cannot change a lightbulb." This was not true. He could, but he wouldn't. I had waited six months for him to change a lightbulb that was out of my reach while he was in production.

Honcho: "It would be a privilege to change that man's lightbulbs."

It wasn't. But I wanted light, so I got a stepladder. Problem solved. Doesn't that make *me* the genius? Come to think of it, why isn't my husband, who routinely puts in fourteen-hour days and often juggles up to five projects at a time, considered disciplined? He also keeps perfect tax records and is very good at filing paperwork. We both lose our keys frequently, but only one of us goes to DEFCON 1 and immediately changes the locks.

Anyway, I'm okay with my husband being described as a genius because, after all, he chose to marry *me*.

A few years ago, a man on a train, desperate for my attention, looked over my shoulder at the book I was writing and said in a sneering tone, "Oh, is that the great American novel?"

"It may very well may be," I said.

The final rule of *genius* is that no one may claim the mantle for one's self; it must be bestowed. But I am tired of waiting. It's a rigged game, this genius business. I am going to seize the dice from the board and throw them so hard that they will never be seen again. So you'll just have to trust me when I say I've won.

YELLOW-BONE
LIHLE Z. MTSHALI

Mama has clear, satin-smooth mahogany skin. When we go for facials, she comes out of the session beaming, proud to let us know that yet another expert did not believe that she is over seventy. The contrast of her always-coiffured, nearly all-white hair gives her round face a glow you could easily mistake for expensive makeup. But the glow is natural. When my sister and I were young, Mama's beauty routine consisted solely of a dresser lined with jars and bottles of Oil of Olay and Nivea. We would watch, fascinated, as she applied them to her face and body. She would explain that the products were not for changing her skin tone but to keep it healthy and supple. We couldn't wait to grow up so we could do the same.

She did not always have reason to be proud of her dark skin. Mama was born in 1946, two years before apartheid was made law in South Africa. *Apartheid* means "apartness" in Afrikaans. The 1950 Population Registration Act separated racial groups into a hierarchy: white at the top, followed by Asians and Indians, then coloreds and, way at the bottom, blacks. (Coloreds were their own mixed-race group; the government was pedantic.) That same year, the Group Areas Act assigned each racial group its own residential and business sections in cities. Then they created ten Bantustans, homelands. There lived the majority of black people. The rest were confined to semiurban townships.

Mama grew up in the 1950s in one of those Bantustans, KwaZulu, "Place of the Zulu." Though KwaZulu was beautiful—*Zulu* literally means "heaven"—it was rural and underdeveloped. Life there wasn't as beautiful as its rolling hills.

Mama was the darkest of five girls. Her sisters had inherited their mother's light complexion, as had two of her six brothers. Mama looked like the remaining four brothers—dark-skinned like their father. Her family was privileged, her father a successful businessman, so she did not want for material things. But people with her dark complexion, no matter how wealthy, were not considered as attractive as those who were light-skinned. To get approval, she had to excel at everything she did, from her schoolwork down to how neatly she kept her appearance.

When Mama was as young as five, when family and friends commented how much she looked like her paternal grandmother, Khulu, the old woman would bitterly reply, "Why is it that every bad thing is always likened to me?" If Mama so much as refused a plate of food, Khulu would be livid and call her names like *mnyamana*—a derogatory term for a dark person.

As a young girl, Khulu would have grown up getting praise for her own dark skin. She would have been called *indoni yamanzi*, a dark berry that grows alongside rivers and becomes sweeter as it ripens. It is a term that Southern African Nguni people use to describe the beauty of their young women. It is the same berry Tupac rapped about in his 1993 hit, "Keep Ya Head Up," with the lyric, "Some say the blacker the berry, the sweeter the juice."

But once apartheid came along, Khulu's generation, who had grown up loving their dark skin, became tainted by self-hatred. Apartheid's hierarchy was alive within the black community as well, and nowhere was this clearer than in the pencil test. If a light-skinned individual wanted to be reclassified as white, they would put a pencil in their hair and shake their heads. If the pencil fell to the ground, congratulations! You were white. If it stuck to your hair? Sorry, no white privilege for you, because no white person could possibly have hair that thick and kinky and coiled.

Because coloreds also enjoyed just a little more privilege during apartheid, black people took the same pencil test to be reclassified as colored. The procedure was the same. If the pencil fell out, you passed. You were colored. You were no longer black. Some black women hated their dark skin so much they took artificial measures to change it. Since they couldn't be white, and their Afro hair would not let them be reclassified as colored, the next best thing was to be light-skinned.

———

I thought of that hierarchy when I started seeing on my social media timelines *yellow-bone*.

Yellow-bone is a loathsome term that we borrowed from American blacks. Though it refers to all light-skinned black people, in South Africa, it is mostly used to refer to light-skinned black women. Yes: people are woke, black pride is a thing, and #melaninpoppin is a popular hashtag. But black men post pictures of light-skinned black women, writing that the "yellow-bones" will give them beautiful kids. I have seen friends on Facebook calling themselves and each other, albeit in jest, yellow-bones. Rappers wax lyrical about yellow-bones in Zulu, my native tongue. There is such a skin-lightening craze that the government banned bleaching creams, which can contain a cancer-causing compound called hydroquinone. There is a company in Johannesburg that calls itself the Yellowbone Factory and promises its products are safe for us to use.

Colorism has stuck in South Africa, even as apartheid has fallen. These days, *indoni yamanzi* feels less like a compliment to dark-skinned women and more like a comparison. It reminds you that you are not the coveted yellow-bone.

Colorism was still prevalent in 1983, when my older sister and I were sent to a Catholic boarding school 110 miles away from home. She was eight and a half and I was four months shy of my sixth birthday. Our boarding school was no Hogwarts. We lived on canned food. There was no electricity or running water. During the day we used outdoor pit latrines. My sister and I had to learn to do our own laundry by hand, using freezing cold water in the winter months. Once you hung up your laundry to dry on the clotheslines, you had to limit your playing to that area so you could watch over your clothes, which tended to grow legs if the owner was not watching carefully enough.

The dormitory was a huge open hall with rickety bunk beds that slept over forty girls. There was no indoor toilet. At night, we relieved ourselves in buckets that sat in the corner by the door. The buckets would be filled to the brim by morning, and the older girls would bully us young ones into taking the buckets out. They were too heavy for our little arms, and we would sometimes spill pee all over our legs. But if you were light-skinned, the mean girls would spare you the demeaning chores and adopt you as their play child.

Needless to say, this was a blacks-only boarding school. Other races had better facilities. If you could pass for colored, your parents would change your name to an English one and you could go to a colored school, where you could learn in English. The rest of us wouldn't be able to go to multiracial public schools until 1991, the year after Nelson Mandela was released from prison.

But although boarding school was brutal, the schools were safer than our homes. We were tucked away from tribal violence in the townships and homelands, violence between black political parties, and harsh realities for black people in our country. After all, 1983 was not long after the 1976 Soweto uprising, when twenty thousand schoolchildren took to the streets to protest against the introduction of Afrikaans into teaching, spurred on by Stephen Biko's Black Consciousness Movement. In that uprising, the apartheid police wounded nearly a thousand children and killed hundreds. Radicalized students disappeared, some presumed dead in police custody, others exiled. There were always police everywhere, not to protect but to take somebody away.

Until boarding school, my sister and I had lived a life of blissful ignorance, unaware there was another race enjoying a more perfect life. Our parents made sure we knew that we were loved and cared for and that we were beautiful. All we knew about white people were the stories we overheard. Baba, our father, worked at a Toyota plant as an engineering inspector. If he received praise, he would come home skipping like a little boy. But the next day he would be angry, talking about how he had trained that white rubbish Johannes, and now he was the boss.

At school, we would only catch glimpses of white people once a month when we were allowed to go to town. They always looked carefree, the children in their pretty clothes, holding their parents' hands, while we only got to see our parents every four to six months. Our school's priest, Father Michael, was the first white person we had ever known. But if you had asked us and any of our school friends what we wanted to be when we grew up, most of us would have confidently replied that we wanted to be *umlungu*—a white person.

They were our standard of beauty. We didn't have dolls that looked like us, only blonde-haired, blue-eyed ones. We would brush their silky straight hair and wish ours, which was kinky and would break a comb if you tried to run it through the hair without dampening it first, was just as soft. Magazines were full of white faces. We would leaf through the pages, yelling, "This is me." Those magazines and newspapers showed us pictures of the winners of the Miss South Africa pageant. It never dawned on us that there was something strange about the fact that the pageant was lily white and the contestants all looked like the dolls we played with, blonde and blue-eyed—in Africa. There were separate pageants for black women, Miss Black South Africa and Miss Africa South. They were rarely publicized, so we never got to see that black women could be beautiful enough to be in beauty pageants too. It was no wonder that if you wanted to pay someone the highest compliment, you would say they were as beautiful as *umlungu*.

After boarding school, we befriended kids who had remained behind at home and became politically aware. They taught us about Mandela and Biko, and we started moving away from the notion that white people were better than us. When my sister and

I were the first black kids to attend a public school that had previously been for whites only, some white kids teased us and said the monkeys swinging on trees in the school's outside lunch area were our relatives. But we remained unmoved. We knew that we had every right to be there, that we were just as smart as they were.

But outside of our schools, the idea that only light-skinned blacks were beautiful persisted. Skin-lightening creams were abundant. They burned your skin and made your cheeks an unnatural scarlet red, a telltale sign that you were bleaching your skin—that and the knuckles that remained dark even if you used the creams on your hands. But women used them anyway. They even used light-brown shoe polish as foundation. Some B-complex vitamins and injections promised to give black women light skin. Anything to be lighter.

One of Mama's cousins, born dark-skinned but now a lighter complexion from the neck up, would offer my sister, who has Mama's complexion, her miracle creams. My sister was very pretty, she would say—it was just a shame that she was dark. We paid her no mind. She looked ridiculous. Her cheeks were abnormally rosy, and while her face was now lighter, her hands were still dark. When she touched her face it looked as if somebody else were touching her.

Black consciousness, Biko wrote in a 1971 paper, "seeks to demonstrate the lie that black is an aberration from the 'normal,' which is white. It is a manifestation of a new realization that by seeking to run away from themselves and to emulate the white man, blacks are insulting the intelligence of whoever created them black."

Biko's words, long after his death, had instilled in us, along with millions of black South Africans, a sense of black pride. The release from prison of Nelson Mandela and his comrades, the unbanning of Mandela's African National Congress and other black political parties, and the country's first democratic election, which led to our first black president in 1994, further instilled that black pride.

And yet, here we are, nearly fifty years after Biko's death, and one of the most popular words to describe black women's beauty was born of American slavery. Despite the fact that black people are the majority in South Africa—a fact made glaringly obvious every time I step out of a plane in Johannesburg from the United States—despite the fact that everywhere you turn, you see black people. You would expect us to be more accepting of ourselves. But we are still steeped in internalized colonialism and self-hate.

Walking through any South African city or town, you are still assaulted by remnants of colonialism, not only in the architecture but also in the fact that at least almost three-quarters of the land is still owned by white people. The Group Areas Act is long gone, but living in the suburbs is still seen by black people as living in "white areas," and townships, where the black people were moved to, are still black-only. Black people are still protesting for the removal of statues of late nineteenth-century white leaders and the change of street names that celebrate apartheid leaders. We have held political power since 1994, but many are still poor. Some still feel it is better to be white than black. And colorism is here again.

It is disheartening to think that if Mama were young today, her relatives and the larger world would not see her as attractive and would call her *i-darkie*, a dark person. We have not transcended seeing people beyond their shades. In South Africa you don't have to look hard to see black people everywhere—they are on TV, they are major celebrities, they are CEOs and professionals. Young women and men growing up today have no want of examples of beautiful dark faces.

But white people still hold economic power; they still own the land; they are our bosses. When they own everything, they also own our standards of beauty. Shortly after the 2004 elections, ten years after the first democratic elections, which Mandela won, I overheard one of my white editors saying to a group of white colleagues, "They may have political power, but we are still in their heads." I can see her in my head, smug, as if saying that it didn't matter, white people remained in charge. We might have had a black president, but they still controlled everything. Including us.

ZAFTIG
LIZZIE SKURNICK

The first time I was ever called "zaftig" was by my grandma Dora. My family was on vacation, and I had just completed one of my punishing hour-long runs, runs I took every day in a vigilant regime to remain un-fat. Running was a bad sport for me—I couldn't do it without gasping and immediately wanting to lie down and take a nap. But once I could breathe, I enjoyed it despite myself, because my body found a strength and power in the rigor, the sweating, the solitude.

Anyway. Grandma Dora looked at me, said, "Zaftig!" and nodded approvingly.

I think I actually wailed in response. "Zaftig means fat!" I said.

My grandmother looked outraged. "Doesn't mean fat," she said. "Means strong!"

A brief interruption for the naysayers. Yiddish was my grandmother's first and primary language. On her meandering path from Ukraine to the Bronx, she also picked up Ukrainian, Russian, a bit of Polish, and, during a two-year stint in Buenos Aires, Spanish. She spoke perfect English too. She was a corner-store translator. She did the taxes of half of the people in her building. She was a particular fan of Danielle Steel. If she said *zaftig* meant "strong," it meant "strong."

But ask the Jews of your Facebook feed, and they will disagree—with her, and with each other. (I'm sure some of you have objected already.) Some say *zaftig* means "pillowy" or "soft"; others, "plump." Some insist a certain height is called for; some say Nigella Lawson still qualifies. A goy who was sure it meant Mama Cass was shot down. My father, as he often does, brought up Mariah Carey. I enjoyed a definition I'd never heard: "Big in all the right places."

But I knew my grandmother meant none of these. She said I was zaftig with approval, and my grandmother *hated* fat people. She was a fiercely smart, lovely woman, a bookish housewife who pressed a loaf of rye with a side of farmer cheese on all visitors. But let a chubby person stride into view, and she would mutter, "Uch, she's so fat!" with the type of vigorous disapproval usually reserved for a drunk peeing in the subway.

Let me also be clear: I actually *wasn't* zaftig, by any definition. I wasn't even "normal," whatever that means. I was thin— very thin, exactly the kind of thin I despaired I wasn't. All I was lacking was knee definition. But from the commentary I provoked, I never would have known it. From my aunt: "You've still got that baby fat." From my best friend's mother: "When we were your age, *we* were bony." From a frenemy: "I know your hips are as big as mine!" My mother would look at other girls and nod approvingly: "She's *really* thin."

Only my grandmother, in my entire adolescence, looked at my young, strong body, heaving with effort, and gave it her unvarnished approval, even respect. But she called it the one word I hated to hear.

The first time most non-Jews likely heard the word *zaftig*—at least on a regular basis—was during the Monica Lewinsky scandal. Then, it was practically a byword for the girl herself. Ah, the American public said. *This* is how you describe the subtle heft of that girl in her black beret, bobbing along in the crowd to meet the president, her eyes both acquisitive and alight. Her one-time date Jake Tapper illustrated how to apply the qualification. "She was cute," he said, "*if* a little zaftig."

Then, when people said *zaftig*—Jews and gentiles alike—they meant a regrettable, if tolerable, weight. It was the fifteen pounds you could put a positive spin on, like "pleasantly plump," "voluptuous," or "curvy." Unlike *goy* and *shiksa*, Yiddish terms of derision that became jokes everyone was in on, *zaftig* was now an insult that everyone knew. It wasn't as bad as "Such a pretty face!" But you could see it from there.

Now, in America, *zaftig* has come to mean almost anything—that is, anything that's not skeletal. Google the word and you will find a New York skyline of bodies. Size XXXLs have reclaimed it, much like *curvy*, in the name of body positivity. Large-sized models—which is to say, average-sized women—stride down runways, looking strangely unlike coat hangers. Hippie chicks show off cleavage and generous hips. It is all unabashedly sexual: the women preen and vamp like pinups, sporting skimpy bordello wear, lots of bare flesh, and spikes.

All this confusion is strange, because *zaftig*—which, incidentally, is pronounced more like "zaftik"—*does* have a precise meaning. It just means "juicy." It's not about being fat, curvy, busty, or even well molded. It's not about boobs, or breasts, or size, or heft. It's not something you can weigh, something you diet away. *Zaft* means "juice" or "sap," and *zaftig* means "full to bursting, delectable." It's explicitly sexual, and it's approving. It's not, as Jake Tapper suggested, something that detracts from hotness. It embodies it.

When I think of the journey *zaftig* made from praise in Yiddish to insult in Americanese, I think also of my grandmother's journey from Ukraine to America. Dora—then Dvoire—grew up in Kamenetz-Podolsk, a city that once had a thriving Jewish community. But in 1941, as part of the Final Solution, it suffered the first large-scale Jewish mass murder. Eighteen thousand Jews were marched over from Hungary, and they, along with the five thousand local Jews, were massacred.

But my grandmother had left long before then, in 1921. The city was rent by pogroms before Jews were massacred. In her hometown, she had seen Czar Nicholas on his imperial train, but she had also seen heads rolling in the street after a visit from the Cossacks. She, her brother, Carl, and her mother, Miriam, took a ship to Ellis Island. It was turned away and went to Argentina. She lived there for two years. In 1923, they came to America.

When she first came to the United States, Grandma Dora told me, she was too scared to leave the house for a year. Then, like many of the Jewish *shmatterati*, she found work in the garment industry. Like *The House of Mirth*'s Lily Bart, she trained as a milliner. In Kamenetz, she had been a prize-winning student. Now she sat at a table adorning hats for rich ladies.

In my twenties, I lived on Seventy-Second and West End, and I took long walks up Riverside Park, twenty or thirty blocks up and back. When I told this to my grandmother, she told me she had taken those same walks in the same park when she first came to New York, down from Jewish Harlem, as she had taken them in Buenos Aires, up and down the beach for hours, every day. When I walked, I was also fearful, alienated, afraid of my future—with far less cause.

And here, our paths diverge. At eighteen, I did not flee my country but instead went to Yale, then off to further and bigger degrees, further and better jobs, writing and publishing books and essays. I traveled for pleasure, not terror. I lectured and taught; I stood before crowds; I judged and dispensed awards. I had a baby alone, and the world welcomed him.

Set beside mine, my grandmother's story looks like that of the typical immigrant woman: marries young; unfulfilled potential; a life collecting schmaltz rather than degrees. But, as I learned later, that wasn't exactly the story. Grandma Dora, too, had a chance to go to the Ivy League.

In the 1920s, the International Ladies' Garment Workers' Union, of which she was a member, offered scholarships to Barnard. They told her to apply for one. We don't know if she did and was accepted, simply stood at Barnard's gate and peered in, or just brought the paperwork home. What we do know, however, is that her two sisters shut the whole project down. They, who had come to America earlier, told her everyone would call her a greenhorn and a Jew. They told her people would see her red hair and laugh. They told her not to go.

And she didn't.

It's still difficult for me to not be enraged on her behalf. If my grandmother had gone to Barnard, I, of course, would not be here. But where would she have gone? Would she have been one of the first professors of literature? She definitely liked to read. Would she have decided to become a chemist? Her chopped liver was phenomenal. Would she have traveled on different ships, to other countries, at her own pleasure?

Recently I made another strange discovery. I knew the black side of my family—my mother's side—were academics and taught at historically black colleges and universities. But I did not know that one great-grandfather, starting in 1919, while my grandmother was terrorized by Cossacks, went to Harvard for summer school. And in 1926, while my grandmother was adorning hats, he, a black thirty-five-year-old, was accepted to the Harvard School of Education.

But there, his story is also cut off. Because in December, someone came into his boarding house and beat him into a coma. One month later, he died.

That both immigrant Jews and poor black folks three generations back in my life were a hair's breadth from degrees in the Ivy League is astonishing to me. (Take that, WASP legacies!) That they did so as refugees—one from pogroms, one from lynchings—makes it even more astonishing. And that they were not allowed to finish—one because he was murdered, and one who escaped murder but not her bitchy sisters—is, to me, agonizing.

In all ways, I have the life they were shooting for, at far less cost to myself. Yet what do I do with it? While I read, I look at my thighs under the book. (There they are under me now, waxing and waning!) When I bike, instead of enjoying the breeze, I think about the time, at sixteen, a man yelled, "Look at the ass on that!" as I sped by. It shamed me for a decade, then it occurred to me it could have been a compliment. Does it matter now? Did it ever?

I do not know what my grandmother was thinking in the decade she walked up and down Riverside Park, up and down the beaches of Buenos Aires. But I know that I was partly walking in a grim march to keep myself trim, to make sure any black-and-white cookies and Gray's Papaya hot dogs kept to their appointed journey. It was also, of course, making me strong. That I could only see the former then irritates me.

Because what if we reclaimed *zaftig*—and, like my grandmother, left the proportion of lipid to lean out of it entirely? What if we took out the sexy part too? What if we made it, like my grandmother did, about being *strong*?

When my grandmother, who walked the shores of New York and Buenos Aires and was shamed out of the Ivy League, looked at me coming back from a run—ruddy, chest heaving, and powerful—and nodded in approval, I like to think she was opening the door to this possibility. That to be zaftig was not about whether you were sexy to Jake Tapper, or sexy, whatever your weight. That it was about presence, substance, how strong I had become, how strong I could be.

I live in Jersey City, a stone's throw from the Statue of Liberty and Ellis Island. When I think of the word *zaftig* now, that's who

I see—her strong planes and flat sandaled feet, how she holds that torch up day after day, her wide shoulders and powerful stance. I think—and I am entirely sure of this—how terrible she would look in Ann Taylor.

Then I bike along her path. I run. I walk. I try not to think about my ass. I try instead to be strong. Full of sap. Fully alive—to bursting.

CRAZY

MARY POLS

He has set the course for a far-off island, and we are sitting companionably in the cockpit of his sailboat when he asks, "Did I tell you about the crazy one?"

It's an iffy June day and we are in layers. He likes to wear orange, I've noticed. A bright fleece, a rusty-orange parka with the down beaten and funneled into sleek rivulets. He eats bread only on weekends; it makes sense he wants his down slenderized too. He is a man whose attractiveness is not a gift of features but rather something acquired through self-care, restricted calories, and maybe attendance to grooming articles, in *Esquire* perhaps, which he might say he is only reading for the Charles Pierce columns.

Even though at that point I was in my late forties, I was still too dense or plain hopeful to be properly alarmed. Or to say anything. This was in the halcyon days of Obama's second term, and I was generally less angry.

Everything feels different now. In late 2018, the actress Natalie Portman spoke at *Variety*'s Power of Women event, making recommendations about ways to achieve gender parity in the workplace—including, but not limited to, Hollywood. Her whole intense, furious, hyperarticulate speech was received with cheers and clapping, but she got the biggest reaction when she brought up how the code words *crazy* and *difficult* are used to discredit women. Portman suggested a new response. "If a man says to you that a woman is crazy or difficult," the Oscar-winning actress said, "ask him, 'What bad thing did you do to her?'"

On the sailboat in the Gulf of Maine, I do not say, "What bad thing did you do to her?"

The terrible truth is, as he introduces this topic, in one half of my brain, a line of trumpets tilt merrily into the air, announcing that I must be better. Special, really. He's already told me about many failed relationships, including his marriage. What I don't get, even though I should, is that his telling me about the other ones is not an endorsement of me. It does not indicate I have been distinguished from a herd of troubled women. It's a quest for validation for him; these are the things wrong with her. And her, and her. Also, so many men have told me about "crazy" women who came before me that this conversation feels like part of the romancing process. Like that first thoughtful gesture, like his stocking up on Twinings because he had only coffee in his place and you drink tea.

I say evenly that he has not told me about the crazy one. But I'm sure my expression, some shift in my posture, is saying that I would very much like to hear about her. He's going to tell me about a woman who crossed some line and ventured into dangerous territory and got stuck in this category as a result. I am very interested in the lines he draws. I don't want to cross them, because I like him so very much.

This story about the "crazy one" is a lesson he's about to give me. Because I am nearly positive he's not going to tell me about someone with a psychiatric diagnosis. You don't say that with a half smile on a sailboat. I have been a good student of the lines men draw, generally, but in middle age I'm wearying of this school.

In our culture, the c-word is a warning. The sailor is signaling acceptable parameters for behavior from female companions. I both know this and want to not know this. I toss away that truth when I find it inconvenient. I move it aside because it is spoiling my view. The sailor is also signaling a distinct lack of gentlemanly qualities, which is at least a small indication there may be a contradiction in all the nice things he's done and said. This, too, I disregard in the moment. I sit and listen as the boat continues on its course. We're going to an island I've never been to. I'm very excited.

My first brush with "crazy" as an insult specific to women was Iris McCarten, deemed so crazy my entire family hid when she showed up in town. Iris had been part of a couple my parents were friendly with—although we all knew, all five of my brothers and sisters, that no one liked Iris. Everyone liked the man, who was charming and funny, a performative sort, always the life of the party.

When they split up, Iris was no longer tolerated. If my mother got wind that Iris was in town, she would rush home to close the curtains and order us to pull down the garage door. We sheltered in place while Iris knocked imperiously and fruitlessly on the front door, then the back door. Eventually, Iris would go away down the street holding her handbag tight—tall, stooped, a woman discarded by her husband and his friends.

My mother's attitude toward Iris set a point on a chart for me. Here is crazy. Avoid it. When crazy showed up in the books and stories I plowed through as a teenager, I followed along, which is to say, I joined in on the societal shunning. In *Jane Eyre*, Bertha Antoinetta Mason, Edward Rochester's first wife, the one in the attic, was insane and dangerous and literally burned the house down. She was practically an animal. (Poor Ophelia; I dismissed her as a drama queen back then too.)

Meanwhile Jane Eyre, so competent, so neat, so tidy—"small and plain as you are," in Rochester's words—was, despite being the heroine in a Gothic romance, one of the more notable feminist icons of my young reading life. She did not take shit and she regularly saved her hero. Moreover, she toyed with settling for security in a loveless marriage and then didn't, saving herself. She was rational and competent. I was romantic, but I liked rational romantics. I didn't love Jane the way I loved Jo March, but I admired her.

But Bertha was crazy in a hopeless-case kind of way. Jean Rhys's 1966 feminist classic *Wide Sargasso Sea* tells Bertha's backstory through her own point of view, but even in the early 1990s, when it seemed every sidewalk sale in San Francisco included a paperback copy, when women and then more women urged me to read it, I couldn't be bothered. I was ruthless in my dismissal: *Listen, if Bertha ended up crazy, there must have been something seriously wrong in the first place.*

By that time, I'd had one major personal experience with crazy: feeling it when I discovered that my longtime boyfriend from college had been two-timing me for the better part of a year. We'd been living in different states, and while there had been a lot of clues that his friend Nancy was more than just his friend, he'd countered all my suspicions by telling me I was crazy for doubting him. If I saw her, he added, I would understand that they were just friends. (Always throw in an ego stroke when gaslighting.)

The whole thing blew up in his face, and mine, when my college roommate became friends with one of Nancy's friends. I was standing in a kitchen in Washington, DC, clutching the cord of a landline when she told me. The detail I could not shake was that when Nancy found his crumpled-up boarding pass from visiting me—for Valentine's Day—he told her he had to rush to my side because after he'd (allegedly) broken up with me, I had become suicidal.

I saw red. These are the times Shakespeare no longer seems theoretical. I had eaten on the insane root that takes the reason prisoner. Macbeth and me, for at least a little while, unhinged. The wave of grief and rage and impotence was like nothing I'd ever felt before. *Crazy*, by the way, has its origins in an old word for "cracked," meaning "broken, full of flaws." I felt cracked that day. Cracked Mary.

What does it mean when a man calls a woman crazy? That boyfriend had used it as a way to make me accept his lies as truth. He was assuring me that our relationship was intact and that to think of it otherwise would be crazy. Meanwhile, he was telling another woman that I was so crazed with grief he'd had to rush to my side, when in fact, we had not broken up and were just enjoying a fun Valentine's weekend together. I was furious about him lying to me, but also maybe just as outraged at the betrayal of him lying *about* me, tossing me into the same category as the feral, attic-dwelling Bertha Antoinetta Mason. Years later he visited San Francisco, where I was living. He was married; I was in love with someone else. We went out to dinner. It was pleasant, although I remember distinctly that I was armored in some way, as if I had put on a coat woven from thistles. I drove him back to his hotel and we sat in the car listening to the Grateful Dead and talking of the past, and his side of my black Jetta was redolent with nostalgia. I felt a door might open if I wanted it to. I wanted no such thing.

There is a psychological term to describe someone who is accused of being crazy but ultimately is proven not to be, "the Martha Mitchell effect." This term doesn't get a lot of play, probably because the person it is named for has been mostly forgotten. Martha Mitchell was married to John Mitchell, who was Nixon's campaign manager in 1968 and 1972 and served as attorney general in between presidential campaigns. For a while there, she was more famous even than her husband, appearing on the covers of both *Time* and *Life*.

Both names were features from my Watergate-era childhood, but until I learned about the Martha Mitchell effect, I remembered Martha mostly as a punch line on *Laugh-In*, the jokes Lily Tomlin was delivering slightly over my head, but my father's roars of laughter signaling they were good. I could see she was ditzy, I assumed in the manner of Gracie Allen, who played dumb to her husband, George Burns, for laughs. Maybe that was true, but Martha was also outspoken and bold. She was friendly with reporters and called them regularly to gossip, earning the nickname "the Mouth from the South." She'd call the legendary wire reporter Helen Thomas, then with United Press International, late at night. Her opinions were not the kind a nice conservative wife would share (as Vietnam dragged on, she told Thomas, "It stinks!"), but Americans loved her because she was funny and audacious. (She compared peace protesters to Russian revolutionaries.) She listened in on her husband's meetings and phone calls, and shared what she learned. After the Watergate burglary that led to Nixon's downfall, she accused the White House of framing her husband, John, and of spreading rumors she was an alcoholic and crazy, particularly because she'd said she was kidnapped to suppress the Watergate story.

Mitchell's claim was that she'd been held against her will in a hotel in Newport Beach in June 1972 as the story of the burglary was breaking. She'd been in California with her husband, but he flew back to DC early to deal with the crisis, leaving orders with a bodyguard that she be kept away from papers and television. He, having helped plan the burglary, knew that his wife would likely make the connection between one of the accused burglars, James McCord—whom she knew through her husband—and Nixon. The person John Mitchell left guarding Martha, Steve King, ripped the phone from the wall right as she began telling Thomas she was being held against her will. She fought back, was wounded, and was then tranquilized by a doctor while being held down by five men.

The story was dramatic, when she got a chance to start telling it. Her husband laughed it off. "The press dutifully reported the claim and did virtually nothing to check it out," Nora Ephron wrote in an essay called "Crazy Ladies: II" in her 1975 collection

Crazy Salad: Some Things About Women. That was the year Mc-Cord, convicted in the Watergate burglary, confirmed that what Martha had said was true. She had been intentionally discredited and her husband had helped. Fun fact: the bodyguard, Steve King, went on to lead the Republican Party in Wisconsin and in 2017 was named ambassador to the Czech Republic by Donald Trump. And, yes, was confirmed.

Even after her early death from cancer in 1976, Nixon continued to work to make Martha Mitchell seem crazy. He told David Frost in 1977 that if it hadn't been for Martha, there would have been no Watergate. "God rest her soul," Nixon said. "Because she, in her heart, was a good person. She just had a mental and emotional problem that nobody knew about." John Mitchell, he said, should have been watching "that store."

Tricky, dick. Martha Mitchell told the truth. And while it was crazy, she wasn't.

On the boat, his story about the crazy one is good. Long windup, great delivery. The sailor and the crazy girlfriend lived near each other as children, both the spawn of liberal, do-gooder Mainers with too many children and too few dollars. As his peripatetic family was moving away, his mother gave her father a dime and said, *When those girls grow up, if they are looking for a good man, have them call one of my boys.* (I love that detail; it seems right out of Steinbeck.)

When they met as adults at a party in Maine, both divorced, both with nearly grown children, this caused him to think it was fated on some level. She recognized him, blushed, and said something flirty about having had an embarrassing dream about him when they were children. No, she would not tell him what it was. Yes, he could have her number.

She was great-looking, he says. Face, smile, beautiful hair (he gestures to mimic first its waves, then more curves below her neck). But she got needy quickly, he tells me, texting a lot, wanting to know when she could see him again. Sometimes, he says, he has a habit of getting involved too fast, and he's noticed this and he's trying to not do that. And then one night, she showed up at his house uninvited and he came home and there she was in the kitchen and things got weird and he actually felt scared, because there was a knife on the counter, lying right near her hand, and what if?

The sailor and I both came of age in the era of *Fatal Attraction*, a 1987 film in which a woman (Glenn Close) who has an intensely sexual weekend with a married man (Michael Douglas) becomes obsessive after he ends the fling. There's a knife involved. And a pet bunny who gets boiled. The movie was a cultural touchstone for many years afterward. Someone might say of a troublesome woman, *Are you worried she might boil your bunny? Was she that crazy?* The sailor was triggered by the knife on the counter. Then when he asked her to leave, he says, she got angry. And then—here he pauses in the telling, adjusts some ropes, moves about the boat for a minute while I admire his ease with the mechanics of sailing—she told him her dream from when they were kids. In the dream, she said, they were on a rowboat. She looked up his shorts, and she could see his penis. Then it fell off. After his penis rolled around the bottom of the boat, she picked it up and put in in her pocket.

On the boat, listening, I'm impressed by how out-there this is. The symbolism, the boat, the knife on the counter.

I remark that I hope he changed the number on his combination door lock. But it's the last four digits of his phone number, and I know this because that's how I have been letting myself in during the last few months of what has been a dreamy romance. So maybe he wasn't all that scared? My brain tucks that away, to digest later.

I ask when they dated and he says, "Winter." It is June, nearly warm enough to swim in Maine. Winter seems a long way back.

As he's driving me home the next day, we talk about it again. The sky is yellow with a strange sunset rain, and both of us have been quiet in the eerie light. I compliment him on his delivery and tell him it would make a great radio story on one of those public radio shows. "Like the *Moth Radio Hour*," I say.

He smiles and faux shivers and says, "What if she heard it?" He doesn't want to get her mad. Because remember, she's *crazy*.

The next month I instigate the end of the relationship with the sailor. Something about all the others I have heard about, including the "crazy one," makes me think he's in the whole business of hunting and gathering women for something other than love. I put it to him more subtly than this, but I've cracked the narrative of our mutual attraction.

He puts a fresh profile up on an online dating site while we're still discussing terms. I wanted to be proven wrong, so I'm sad. Then he ghosts me. I miss my funny, smart, charming friend who seemed so intently interested in every aspect of me. Naively, I had hoped he might do some self-reflection and we could try again. Honestly, I feel a little crazy. I mean, was it me, or was it him?

When I reach out to the "crazy one," who is easy to find on social media, I am conscious that the sailor would think me crazy, too, for crossing this social barrier to investigate how crazy she may be. I call anyway.

It's only been a few months since they were together, she says. She expected to hear from him after that terrible night, and when she didn't, she told her friends he must have met someone new. Must have replaced her.

Together we are a forensic team reconstructing a narrative of an emotional criminal with a true modus operandi: meet at a party, send texts before he's left the party to establish contact, social media friend requests across all platforms. Full-court press. First date ends with him carrying woman to a guest room in his house for consummation—we puzzle over this choice of room—then lots of talk about the boat and sailing and where he wants to take her. And me. Us.

The night of the knife? That was less than twenty-four hours before I met him. They had been to the city's art walk, made out on the street, posed for photos in a black-and-white photo booth, and then headed back separately to his house for dinner. He'd told her to wait for him while he got groceries. He was considerate that way. The knife was on the counter because they were cooking together. Salmon. Strawberries. Asparagus. I am nodding, remembering eating this same meal.

What went wrong with them? She is still puzzling over that. He told her that he thought they should decide where this was going—were they going to be together forever, or just be friends?—and she said she was just following his lead. A muscle in his cheek began to pulse. He was mad. Maybe he wanted her to be the one who would say, "Let's be together forever"? Anyway, he wanted her to leave.

She suggested that this was sudden and odd, although she did not say, "That's crazy." She pointed to the photos on the counter, of them kissing, from that night. The man running the photo booth had told the sailor, when he bought the prints right then and there, that he might like to use the photos of the sailor and his beautiful girlfriend on his website, because they looked so in love.

But now, two hours later, they were not in love. He would call the police if she did not leave right then. He offered her some of the photos; she told him to put them on his trophy wall. As she left, she turned and told him the dream, with the rowboat and his rolling penis. And that was where their stories came together as one.

"Was the dream real?" I ask.

"It was," she says. She'd never understood it, but there it was. The dream was crazy, but then again, dreams often are.

In my own small romantic life, I had unmasked the Martha Mitchell effect at play.

When I called the woman maligned by the sailor, I did not tell her he referred to her only as "the crazy one." I spared her the direct quote because I know how volatile and cruel the word is, and that it carries for women the special shame that we have somehow overextended the emotional capabilities of womanhood. By talking back. Questioning. By becoming too attached. Think of Monica Lewinsky, whom Maureen Dowd once compared to Glenn Close's character in *Fatal Attraction* and of whom some of us, many of us, thought, *That girl is crazy.* She could have stayed shamed for life, the young woman who the world saw as more foolish than the man risking his presidency to have sexual relations with her. Lewinsky did not. And in her public appearances, including a much-watched TED Talk, what is most riveting about her is how extraordinarily level-headed she seems.

There are signs that the word *crazy* itself is being reclaimed. My favorite remains the way Natalie Portman wants us to translate it as we hear it, then toss it back at its sayer. Would Nora Ephron, if she were still alive, blithely name a collection of essays about women *Crazy Salad* today? Probably not. But while that title and its subtitle, *Some Things About Women*, could be taken to imply women are like a crazy salad—a mishmash of elements, maybe even kind of a mess—that wasn't the point. Ephron was referencing a William Butler Yeats poem, "A Prayer for My Daughter." It's about his hopes for his child, including that she not be too beautiful, lest she succumb to narcissism or attract the wrong kind of men. Shallow ones. Unworthy ones. As Yeats saw it, these men were something fine women often endured, perhaps because they did not understand their better worth.

It's certain that fine women eat
A crazy salad with their meat.

I marveled over this origin story for a while. It is undeniably strange that a Yeats poem published in 1921 described bad men as "crazy salad" and that Nora Ephron in 1975 repurposed the phrase as a book title, at a time when feminism was in full swing, along with the contradiction of women starving themselves on salad-centric diets to stay thin and presumably attractive to men. Now here I am in the twenty-first century, telling you that if a man says to you that another woman is or was "crazy," you should do as Natalie Portman suggested, then walk away. Me? I gave up eating crazy salad for good, bought myself a kayak, and finally learned to set my own course.

SMALL
BETH BICH MINH NGUYEN

One day in eighth grade, Aaron Lewis picked me up by my legs and swung me around and around.

I had been sitting in the hallway with my friend Tricia, waiting for an after-school activity to begin. When Aaron picked me up by my legs, it was so sudden and surprising that I couldn't get away. I was terrified—of falling, of hitting my head against a wall. But mostly I was terrified by the understanding that there was nothing I could do to make him stop. I was powerless. And it went on and on. Tricia, sitting there, covered her mouth and laughed.

At some point Aaron stopped. I lay on the hallway floor. Tricia was still giggling. When I sat up my tears were unstoppable, and he and Tricia both looked stricken. Tricia asked if I was okay. Aaron said he was sorry.

And then he said, "You're so small, I just wanted to pick you up."

I can feel it now, all these years later; I see his face as he gathered strength to keep spinning me. *You're so small, I just wanted to pick you up.* Aaron wasn't a bully or a threatening figure in the middle school hallways. He was an average kid with plenty of friends. We'd had a few classes together. I thought he was kind of funny.

I don't recall what I replied. Most likely I told him it was all right, everything was fine. I was well practiced in letting situations go. No good would come to me by raising a fuss, by letting anyone else know what had happened. Already I was telling myself it was dumb, no big deal. Aaron was just having fun. I wasn't physically hurt; the whole thing could have been much worse.

In eighth grade, I didn't want to think about how people saw me. I still had all of high school to get through with the same group of kids. So I didn't speak about this again, not even with Tricia, who had been my friend all that year, who was good at math, who had cloudy blue eyes and a melodic, throaty voice that reminded me of Stevie Nicks singing "Gypsy." Soon we would drift apart, and she would never know why.

It would be years before I would begin to understand the shame I felt at how Aaron had grabbed me as if I weren't a person at all but just a thing on the floor. A small object that he wanted to pick up and grab, because he could. I never asked what he was thinking, why he did it. I didn't have the courage to ask, because now I feared him.

I was raised among the tall, blond people of West Michigan, because that's where my refugee family was resettled after fleeing

Vietnam at the end of the war. I grew up hearing comments like *You're so small.* I heard it even more than *What are you?* and *Where are you from?* I was the shortest one in class, and people never tired of pointing that out. And by "people" I mean the non-Vietnamese, non-Asian, almost entirely white group of people who dominated and determined my life every time I left my family's house.

I understood that when they called me small, they didn't mean it as a compliment. They meant: *You're so weirdly Asian.* They meant the strangeness I embodied, that all Vietnamese embodied, because we were foreigners to them, enemies, forgotten allies, uncomfortable reminders, unwelcome. When someone referred to me as *small*, I heard it as *small Vietnamese girl.* Someone to overlook.

Being small was another way of being silent, and that's what white people were always expecting of me too. I kept that silence going. At home, I never said anything about Aaron because that's how things were. My siblings, uncles, parents, grandmother, and I all lived in a ranch house where we were used to sharing food, sharing clothes, sharing every bit of space. Like me (though not like every Vietnamese person), the people in my family were smaller in size than the white Americans who surrounded us. We were used to not taking up too much space.

I often wondered what it would be like to be tall, to be big enough that no one would ever think about picking me up, big enough that a person walking toward me on the same sidewalk wouldn't expect me to step out of the way. Years later, I wondered if maybe we had trained ourselves to take the diminishment, to diminish ourselves. To keep out of view as a way to stay safe.

Almost everyone I knew outside of my family and our slowly growing community was white, a descendant of Dutch immigrants who had arrived in Michigan in the 1800s. The dominant narrative of immigration to the United States allows white Europeans to become fully American within a generation. But immigrants and refugees from Asia are always seen as foreign, never truly American. I knew this even before I learned this, because white people made sure I knew.

Sure, they did the usual racist things—laughed at our names, called us chinks and gooks. But they also pretended not to see us in class, didn't invite us to birthday parties, told us our food was gross, told us Buddhism was wrong, told us we were going to hell. Our bodies, sneaky and slitty and small, proved that we didn't belong, that we could never be like them, could never achieve the so-called dream goal of assimilation.

I learned to love the inside, the indoors, the quiet spaces, because that's where I wasn't anything but myself, to myself. Alone, I didn't think about my race or gender; I didn't think about being short or small. I felt fine; I was fine. It was only when I left the house that I understood how other people saw me—how they expected me to be.

Small is a complicated word in America. It can be insult or praise, shame or aspiration. It can be privilege. When people talk about feeling small they mean they feel insignificant, ignored, belittled, almost erased. When we say something is "small potatoes," we mean it is unimportant. But when we size each other up we spout contradictions: "Go big or go home," yet "Good things come in small packages." "You're in the big leagues now," but "It's a small world after all."

Small has always been used to control and limit women: the old, Darwin-backed belief, for example, that women must be inferior and less intelligent because they're usually physically smaller than men. We are *still* working against this idea. It also reinforces a related, heteronormative belief: that smallness in size is desirable in women. The specifications might shift with trends—which of our body parts are supposed to be big or small—but women are still expected to be smaller than their male partners. This notion is so entrenched, we feel it even if we don't agree with it—as if women are supposed to crave being diminished, as if smaller must mean less powerful.

It is a perversity that the smallness that I grew up associating with insignificance was also a measure of protection, because it adhered to a beauty standard for women. I didn't realize this until high school and college, when I saw how often girls lamented, and were told to lament, their body sizes. Sometimes these girls, who were always taller than me because everyone was taller than me, would tell me that they didn't like being next to me because I was so small that I made them feel huge. I took no pleasure or power in this; it made me uncomfortable, worried. I'd been used to thinking *small* was a negative word. But it wasn't negative at all here: it was something to strive for.

I've never reconciled or figured out these contradictions, except to pull away from the idea that my body should be something else for someone else. I don't want to participate in that kind of conversation about desire. Sometimes I think about how my grandmother, who taught me about Buddhism through her daily example, meditated in order to be released from both her body and her mind. In that space she was most herself, and to me that was beauty beyond beauty.

———

One afternoon when I was about six years old and playing in the yard, a strong gust of wind literally picked me up and tossed me back several feet. I remember the feeling in the same way I remember Aaron in eighth grade: the shock was my awareness of how little power I had to secure my body to the ground.

It is no surprise that I became a cautious person with many fears. I fear ocean tides. I fear storms. I fear standing on subway platforms. I fear crowds. I fear men.

Because of where and when I grew up, I had to unlearn *small* in the same way I had to unlearn the way people identified me as Vietnamese, which is to say through a lens of war and imperialism and otherness and righteousness. I had to reconfigure, for myself, definitions of *small* and *Vietnamese* that are sometimes twined but often not, that are essential to my origin, family, history—without shame. To get there (here), I had to refuse the gazes of the people I grew up with.

I had to learn to respect what my body can do, how it can maneuver. I learned that my size lets me climb fences more easily. In a crowd, I can squeeze myself through to the front or to safety. I have learned when to be louder. Learned to stop feeling small while at the same time accepting its strengths and complications.

If you were to ask me now, I would tell you that I don't *feel* small—not in the way that signifies being hidden or demeaned. I would tell you that I feel like myself, alone at work in a room where no one else is looking at me.

Recently I was on an airplane sitting next to a guy who felt free to extend his left leg into my space, beyond that invisible line that divides the seats. Finally, I pointed to his leg.

"Do you mind?" I said.

"Oh," he answered. "Sorry. But you are a lot smaller than I am, so . . ."

"That doesn't mean you get to take up more space," I said.

He held up his hands as if to say "Fine, fine." I turned to look out the window. I like window seats. I thought about how this man was once my size, as he was growing up, and I wondered if he could remember when that was, what it felt like. The plane glided above the clouds, above so much land, and I thought about how the interaction with him could have gone wrong. He could have gotten defensive, as men often do; he could have started an argument, could have become hostile, could have rolled his eyes and called me a bitch, could have called me a stupid chink. All things I have experienced. For a moment, in the silence, I felt lucky.

I settled in to where I was sitting, facing the window. There was no reflection, just a long view outward and outward.

FUNNY
MEG WOLITZER

One of my earliest attempts at hilarity involved a baked potato. To be precise, it involved a rock from the backyard posing as a baked potato. I had noticed the rock while playing outside and thought I might fool my father with it when he came home from work. I waited for his blue Rambler to pull into the driveway, and by the time he sat down at the dinner table, the mock potato was there on his plate, between the steak and the mound of Birds Eye french cut green beans.

He said, pointedly, "This baked potato looks delicious," then lifted his fork and knife in a flourish of anticipation. Across the table, I was fibrillating and nearly squeaking with excitement, which reached its crescendo as he attempted to cut into the unyielding surface. There was a loud clang of cutlery against geology. "Why, this isn't a baked potato!" my father cried.

"I know!" I confessed. "It's a ROCK, Dad, a ROCK. I fooled you. It was a joke. I was being *funny*."

The pleasure I felt at being funny, and then immediately being appreciated for it, was extreme. I could barely keep it in the container of my body. I would have liked to do handsprings across the kitchen linoleum, if I had been the kind of girl who could do handsprings. But I was not. I was something else: a girl with an instinct for making faces and doing voices. Still, I was shy, though when I pushed myself out of that state and into the province of funny, I felt its rewards.

The funny women I studiously watched and loved on TV when I was very young were sometimes funny in the service of situations to which I did not exactly relate. Lucille Ball, brilliant and physical and daring, played someone frequently afraid of getting in trouble with her husband. Phyllis Diller told stories about *her* husband, "Fang." (Why would I want to grow up and marry a man named "Fang"?) And the droll humor mined by Audrey Meadows as Alice Kramden on *The Honeymooners* depressed me, as I imagined living in a black-and-white apartment with a loudmouthed husband. Mary Tyler Moore as Laura Petrie on *The Dick Van Dyke Show,* with all her allure and her strong presence, was quivery voiced and superdomestic. Carol Burnett, whose sketch show I adored, seemed so maternal to me that I related more to the idea of being her child than to being her.

In my own experience back then, humor was connected to a feeling of overexcitement. I fell off the sofa repeatedly while watching *Rowan and Martin's Laugh-In* on Monday nights. And I recall the time my next-door neighbor, a much older, cool, and arty teenaged girl, fell in love. She and her boyfriend lolled in the yard while I observed them through a thin scrim of bushes. Finally I broke through those bushes and marched over to the lounge chair where they lay entwined. My way to get them to notice me was to sing for them a parody song I had written, which at the time I believed was deeply witty. Sung to the tune of "I Want to Hold Your Hand," it went like this:

> *Oh yeah, I told you something*
> *I think you understood*
> *When I told you something*
> *I want to suck your blood*
> *I want to suck your blood*
> *Please let me suck your blood*

And then I spread my arms wide and pounced like a vampire, leaving them shrieking in laughter. In some way I did want to suck their blood, by which I mean I did want what they had. Much later, reading the Carson McCullers novel *The Member of the Wedding*, I saw that particular kind of desire intricately described. Frankie Addams, McCullers's protagonist, is a twelve-year-old girl who longs to belong; she craves what she calls "the we of me." Humor was a way toward my version of "the we of me," whether that meant connecting with sophisticated teenagers or with my father.

When my family went to the mall (ours was called the Walt Whitman Mall, an oxymoron that didn't strike me as funny at the time but certainly does now), my father and I would often peel off and go to a store called Foods of All Nations, where together we would sample then exotica such as tahini or goat cheese. And then we would go a few stores down to the novelty shop. I loved buying joke buzzers and dribble glasses, already planning the mechanics of my next prank. I was fascinated by those boxes labeled "Honeymoon Kit" or "Hangover Cure," which contained candy in the shape of pills or joke sexual props that I didn't understand. Once, from the back of an *Archie* comic, I ordered a rubber cast that I could put on my arm so I could pretend to have broken it. Oh, the hilarity of it all!

For a long time I unselfconsciously embraced my own brand of being funny, despite the fact that at school, the openly and extrovertedly funny people tended to be boys. One was a talented impressionist, and even though he sometimes struggled academically, I remember his excellent Ed Sullivan. Another boy was slightly out of control and often got reprimanded, but he found his groove on the school bus during class trips, where he would turn around in his seat and "conduct" the entire bus in renditions of a few different sexually suggestive songs. Everyone sang and whooped and, of course, laughed.

My own humor tended to be more modest, and my performances, such as they were, were ad-libbed. Being funny, or at least trying to be, felt like a real part of me, and I never questioned it—until suddenly I did. The change began one day in the cafeteria, when I was telling a joke or performing a manic little skit, and I noticed two boys observing me with a kind of disapproval. They were not the "funny" boys, and I wasn't friends with them. But one of them whispered to the other, and he nodded and smirked, and then they turned and walked off. I still recall how startled I was, and how suddenly self-conscious. The impressionist would keep doing his impressions for years, and the boy on the bus would take his act as far as he could before being stopped by the threat of detention. I wish I could say that I ignored the boys in the cafeteria, whose manner seemed to suggest that what I was doing was too loud and somehow unseemly for a girl. I wish I had thought, *Fuck them*, or even, *I'll show them*, and that the next week I went on to create a funny variety show called *Girlzapoppin'*. But that's not what happened; my early 1970s girl self wasn't able to do that. From that moment on, I checked the audience before doing my shtick. I didn't feel as free anymore.

The delineation of the genders had become more defined in my social world, and I had a vested interest in conforming. I didn't yet comprehend that being oneself, fully oneself, is a key to pleasures of all kinds. Soon I performed less at school, though when I was in an all-girl environment, I felt as free as I'd ever felt. In my bunk at camp that summer I recall being part of several variety shows that the girls put on for one another's entertainment. Everybody had to have a special toilet-paper ticket to get into our bunk, where we sang and danced and clowned around before an appreciative audience.

Back home in the fall and alone at night in bed, I became the occasional host of a talk show called *Meg's Treasure Box*. The name is ripe with Freudian implications, but I took the show seriously, serving as host, sidekick, bandleader, singer, audience, and various guests, which included stand-up comedians. I loved lying in my dim room, controlling the fantasy of being funny and expressive and extroverted.

Later on, when I was sixteen, *Saturday Night Live* came on the air, bringing with it Jane Curtin, Laraine Newman, and Gilda Radner. All of these women were thrilling to watch, but it is Gilda I think about now. To me, Gilda Radner achieved maximum poignancy in the portrayal of her character Judy Miller, a little girl who starred in her own TV show in her bedroom when no one was around. I watched as she put on her version of *Meg's Treasure Box*, called *The Judy Miller Show*, and I realized that those secret one-girl TV shows were probably a common phe-nomenon in bedrooms throughout the land. In the character of Judy Miller I saw myself, and with a start I knew that the antic, goofball ways in which I sometimes processed the world were legitimate, and that it was just fine to bring them out, for anyone to see.

SWEET
MONIQUE TRUONG

"Sweet, cute and with a good attitude."

"I found her to be a very competent individual. I liked her as a person. I thought she was a person of integrity."

Attributed to different interviewees, both statements purport to describe Dr. Christine Blasey Ford, or more specifically, Christine Blasey, the young woman these two individuals knew while she was at Pepperdine University, first as a graduate student working toward a master's degree in clinical psychology, which she earned in 1991, and then as a visiting faculty member from 1995 to 1998.

On that 830-acre campus in Malibu, California, with a sweeping view of the Pacific Ocean, graduate student Christine Blasey met and began an eight-year relationship with a young man named Brian Merrick, who decades later would describe her to the *Wall Street Journal* in terms that suggested that they went to the prom together in the 1950s. This *WSJ* profile of Dr. Ford was published on September 19, 2018, a week prior to her testimony before the Senate Judiciary Committee, in which she publicly accused Supreme Court nominee Brett Kavanaugh of sexually assaulting her when they were in high school.

On the same day as the *WSJ* profile, the second quotation appeared in the *Graphic*, the Pepperdine University newspaper, and was attributed to Distinguished Professor of Psychology Cindy Miller-Perrin, who knew Christine Blasey as a visiting faculty member. Professor Miller-Perrin's recollection suggests that Christine Blasey had more to her personhood and her personality than a pithy inscription scrawled in a high school yearbook.

Considering the reason Brian Merrick was being interviewed by the *WSJ*, he should have given more thought to the monosyllabic descriptors that came from his mouth. Borrow a few from Professor Miller-Perrin's statement, for instance. Because Merrick did not or could not think through the implications of his words, I will do it for him. I will begin and end with "sweet" because Merrick undermined the credibility of both Christine Blasey, the younger, and Dr. Christine Blasey Ford, the elder—with that one word.

It's a compliment! Jeez.

I'm sure that someone—perhaps even you, dear reader?—has uttered that retort in an attempt to neuter *sweet*, put a rhinestone collar around its neck, and call it pet.

These too are compliments: *sugar, honey, candy, sweetmeat, honey bun, honey pie, sugar pie, sweetheart, sweetie, sweet cheeks, sweet lips*, *sugar tits*, and *sweet piece of ass*. The slippery slope from compliment to insult begins with *sweet*.

As cultural anthropologist Sidney Mintz noted in *Sweetness and Power: The Place of Sugar in Modern History* (1985), there's a distinction between the basic taste that we understand as sweet and the "ingestibles" that can trigger it. His treatise focused on refined sugar, derived from sugarcane, and how it overtook fruits and honey as the most commonly available and cheapest source of sweet in the United Kingdom and elsewhere in the Western world. Mintz's short answers were colonialism, slavery, the Industrial Revolution, and capitalism. Here's his timeline:

In 1650 sugar was considered a rare medicine, and if it was found in the kitchens of the United Kingdom, then it was only in those of royal households. By 1750 sugar's culinary use had increased, but it was treated as an expensive spice and was very far from what it has become today, a kitchen staple to be measured out by the cupfuls. By 1850, when the subjects of the United Kingdom and its unruly former colony, the United States of America, said "sweet," they meant "sugar."

This road from rarity to ubiquity was paved by the labor of enslaved people and indentured workers on the "Sugar Islands" of the British West Indies, beginning with the empire's "settlement" of Barbados in 1627. The increasing availability and accessibility of refined sugar—white sugar being the most coveted among the varieties—and its by-products was made possible by the subjugation and violence inflicted upon black and brown bodies. The sensorial pleasures afforded by the taste of sweet and the inhumane cruelties of slavery were inextricably twined.

This incontrovertible fact casts a grotesque light, a too-revealing X-ray, as it were, on the "little girls" in this classic nursery rhyme:

What are little girls made of?
What are little girls made of?
Sugar and spice
And everything nice
That's what little girls are made of.

Attributed in part to the British poet Robert Southey (1774–1843), the rhyme shows the transition in sugar's culinary role taking place: a century before, "sugar *and* spice" would have been oddly redundant, but by Southey's lifetime sugar was already separating from spice, with its powders and judicious pinches, and offering itself up as a distinct ingredient to be purchased by the pound.

The rhyme also neatly captures sugar's gendered role in the British imagination. The verse begins not with little girls but with little boys:

What are little boys made of?
What are little boys made of?
Snips and snails
And puppy dogs' tails
That's what little boys are made of.

Southey was echoing here a divide that assigned sugar and the taste of sweet to the "fairer sex." A connection between females and the excessive consumption of sugar was often commented upon by male "observers" of Southey's time and onward and, according to Mintz, was put forward without research or investigation.

While the science was missing, Mintz found that there was a socioeconomic underpinning to this supposed sugar predilection. In the United Kingdom of the Industrial Revolution, sugar was, in fact, the only thing nice that poor and working-class women and their young children had in their meager, monotonous daily diet. The limited animal protein at their tables—the meats, cheeses, and fresh dairy—was reserved for the man of the house as he was the wage earner. Women and young children were habitually malnourished in order to keep these men better fed.

Without animal protein, cheap sugar stepped in to provide the bulk of feminine and infantile calories: sugar in their many cups of tea (also courtesy of colonialism); sugar in the sweetened condensed milk—an inexpensive stand-in for fresh milk and cream, which had the added benefit of being preserved and slower to spoil—in those same teacups; "golden syrup," which was lightened treacle, a.k.a. molasses, a by-product of sugar processing, poured over their morning porridge; and sugar in the store-bought, mass-produced breads and jams that together stood in for their midday meals.

As Dr. Ford and countless examples before and after her make clear, men often blame women for being victimized and point to their bodies as the very reason for their downfall. So, yes, male observers, the fairer sex did adore and was weak for sweet, because without sugar, its cheapest delivery device, generations of mothers and their little girls and boys would have collapsed in an energy-less heap in London's East End.

It's a compliment! Jeez. (Part 2)

Before sugar, there was honey. When sugar pushed honey into a cobwebbed corner of the UK cupboard, sugar also pushed itself into the culture's linguistic and literary imagery. *Honeyed* was set aside for *sugared*. *Syrupy-toned* found itself in a losing competition with *sweet-talking*. Here, for instance, is the 1784 version of another enduring British nursery rhyme:

> *The rose is red,*
> *The violet's blue,*
> *The honey's sweet,*
> *And so are you.*
> *Thou are my love and I am thine;*
> *I drew thee to my Valentine.*

Here's the modern-day version of the same rhyme:

> *Roses are red*
> *Violets are blue*
> *Sugar is sweet*
> *And so are you.*

What didn't change, according to Mintz, was the underlying sentiments and feelings associated with the taste of sweet: "happiness, well-being, with elevation of mood, and often with sexuality."

In the realm of "sexuality" is exactly where we find Dr. Christine Blasey Ford, the elder; Christine Blasey, the younger; those sugared and spiced little girls; and the grade-school Valentine's Day cards, where you probably last read "Sugar is sweet / And so are you" and thought of it as high compliment.

Perhaps Brian Merrick meant to say to the *WSJ* that when he met Christine Blasey on the campus of Pepperdine, as the Malibu sun shone and the Pacific reached toward the horizon, he felt "happiness," a sense of "well-being," and an "elevation of mood," and that he continued to feel this way during the course of their eight-year relationship, and that decades later, when he was asked to think of Christine Blasey, he thought of her still in these terms. Merrick instead reached for the juvenile shorthand "sweet." He sugared and spiced her. He little-girled her. He sent her a Valentine's Day card with a cartoon bear on it. With "sweet" he set the princess-pink stage for the "cute" and "good attitude" that followed. All were intended by Merrick as compliments.

Stop, You're Giving Me Diabetes!

During the period from 1850 to 1950, sugar, according to Mintz, crossed another line, from being an ingredient to being a food group in its own right: "By 1900, it was supplying nearly one-fifth of the calories in the English diet." More accurately, sugar became a pervasive food substitute, offering the poor and working class their much-needed calories and fulfilling their desire for the taste of sweet as well as for qualities such as softness, tenderness, moistness, and a longer shelf life in their comestibles. Sugar as food could do it all and do it for less, if you didn't take into account the utter lack of nutrition, rampant dental decay, and type 2 diabetes.

In 1961 Roland Barthes published the essay "Toward a Psychosociology of Contemporary Food Consumption" and declared that food is "a system of communication, a body of images, a protocol of usages, situations, and behavior." Barthes was stating the obvious, but it often takes a white man's stating the obvious to include it on university syllabi and to impart it to young impressionable minds, encouraged thereafter to think that a French academic named Roland Barthes was the first human to stumble upon this nugget of truth that any cook could have told you from the time she gathered berries or snapped the neck of a small animal and fed it to her little girls and boys.

At the open of his essay, Barthes cited the fact that Americans consumed twice the amount of sugar as the French, 43 kilograms versus 25 kilograms per person per year. (According to the US Department of Agriculture, as of 2011 sugar consumption in the US has risen to 156 pounds or 70 kilograms per person. FAOSTAT, a database of the Food and Agriculture Organization of the United Nations, reported that France's consumption in 2013 was 32 kilograms, a decrease of 1.56 percent from the previous year.) Barthes followed his citation of a fact meant to be comparative in nature but that smacks more of shaming by asking facetiously what Americans do with all that sugar. He answers with another obvious fact: we "saturate" our foods with it, from pastries, ice creams, jellies, and syrups to foods that the French would not think to sweeten, such as meats, fish, and salads. Barthes concluded that for Americans sugar is not just "foodstuff" but an "attitude" and an "institution" that "imply a set of images, dreams, tastes, choices, and values."

Another French author, Jean Anthelme Brillat-Savarin, had already written the same thing in a more memorable, succinct way in his book *The Physiology of Taste* (1825): "Tell me what you eat, and I shall tell you what you are." His mother probably said it to him first. Thanks, Madame Brillat-Savarin, because that observation remains devastatingly true.

Our tastes, choices, and values are literally killing us. There's a straight-line connection between excessive sugar consumption and obesity, and obesity is one of the primary triggers of type 2 diabetes. According to the American Diabetes Association, in 2015 diabetes was the seventh leading cause of death in the

United States, and 30.1 million Americans, or 9.4 percent of the population, had diabetes.

We are a country of sugar eaters. We are sweet. Actually, we are the sweetest. No country in the world consumes as much sugar as the United States, with 126.4 grams of sugar per person daily.

So, of course, *sweet* is a compliment. We prefer our girlfriends the way that we prefer our everything. This was why Brian Merrick didn't have to think twice. The Christine Blasey he had known was "sweet, cute, and had a good attitude." Dr. Christine Blasey Ford, the woman she had become, the woman who would have to ask for a bottle of Coke with its sixty-five grams of sugar in the form of high-fructose corn syrup in its twenty ounces in order to keep her energy level up—nutrition be damned; Dr. Ford had work to do and no one was going to give her a plate of animal protein—as she withstood the four hours of questioning in front of the Senate Judiciary Committee, that woman would have been better served by a steak, medium-rare, and better complimented by "competent" and "integrity" or, most accurately, "person."

NURTURING

RAQUEL D'APICE

My innate response to most people telling me that women are more nurturing than men is to say to those people, "Hey, feel free to eat a bag of dicks."

And before I do anything else, let me please, please say that *I am in no way* a person who casually yells things like "Eat a bag of dicks" at people. I am a person who quietly says "Shit" when she stubs her toe on the corner of her oversize bed in her too-small room (every four seconds), or who mutters "Fuck fuck fuck fuck fuck" when her computer freezes before she remembered to save changes to a document. I am a frustrated curser, not an aggressive curser. Not only am I not an in-your-face user of expletives, but I am the type of person who, when someone bumps into me on the sidewalk, says "Sorry" and then spends twenty minutes being quietly frustrated that the person did not say "I'm sorry" back.[*]

---

[*] I.e., a woman. Sorry for generalizing, and since I'm already here, sorry for apologizing about generalizing.

And to clarify, I'm not angry at anyone who's ever said that women can be nurturing. I have occasionally met perfectly lovely people who've said this as something they've observed, like, "Children are extremely needy!" or "Netflix has too much original content!" My frustration lies with the people who say "Women are more nurturing" but mean "Women are nurturing and emotional rather than practical and logical," which bleeds into "In a family, someone should stay home with the kids, and I think the people who should be doing that are women."

Those are the ones who say it with self-satisfaction, as if they were paying all of womankind a compliment. They announce that their mother was nurturing and was one of the finest women they've ever known, even though if you ask them about her passion in life, they'll say it was making sandwiches when their friends came over.

I'm not a mean or aggressive person. But I will occasionally say things like "Eat a bag of dicks" or "Go shit a bucket of needles" or "Hey, I hope your genitals get stuck in an escalator" because when people who don't know me insist that I must be more nurturing because of my gender, my gut reaction is to say something outlandish that (a) won't be perceived as nurturing and (b) has some chance, however small, of getting their attention. The type of people who insist that women are inherently nurturing are often the type of people who tune women out. Too often the phrase "Women are more nurturing" feels less like an observation that women are nurturing (many certainly are) and more like an expectation that women will nurture because men are somehow incapable of doing so.[*]

---

[*] And anyone implying that can light their asshole on fire while they fuck a dead bird.

Pregnancy, the world says, will transform you into a Mother Earth–type being—someone perfectly at home in a meadow, doted on by fawns and songbirds—so inherently nurturing that flowers will grow where your tears fall. There is supposed to be something very "natural" about giving birth, which is why so many maternity photo shoots are done in wooded areas as opposed to open-plan offices or basketball courts.

Which was why it was surprising that after I gave birth, I did not immediately become someone with leaves in her hair and a babe at her chest, suckling an infant betwixt the tangled roots of an oak tree. I couldn't tell my own baby's cries from those of other babies, though I had read a BabyCenter article that assured me I'd be able to, and breastfeeding came about as naturally as juggling knives while riding a unicycle, that is, even after extensive reading and repeated meetings with a juggling/unicycling consultant, I struggled to make any progress.

Rather, I felt, throughout my first son's infancy, like Tom Selleck in the movie *Three Men and a Baby*—a person who was reluctantly learning to be nurturing because a baby had been left on her doorstep. Or like Steve Guttenberg in *Three Men and a Baby*. Or possibly like the baby itself, had it been forced to care for a second, even more helpless baby. Which is to say: Comically inept. Overwhelmed. Frustrated.

But a baby's cry is a powerful motivator. My infant son would cry and I would say, "Okay, I will obviously do whatever is necessary to get him to stop making this awful sound." And I did many things and some of them worked and others didn't, the same way, as a child, I pressed all the buttons on my controller while playing *Street Fighter II* and some things worked and some things caused me to be kicked or electrocuted to death. And with time I learned which moves were more likely to achieve my goals, and I mastered those moves. For *Street Fighter*, a spinning bird kick or a drill headbutt; for a baby, holding him close to my chest and making a hushing sound directly into his ear while rocking back and forth on the balls of my feet.[*]

I learned to be attentive to a child the way I had previously learned to attend to frustrating things that were not children. My son would cry and I would rock him and feed him so that he would stop crying, the same way that, if my hypersensitive smoke alarm went off in the middle of the night, I would check to make sure there wasn't a fire and then either hold the button down for five seconds to make it stop beeping or (in my fantasies) chuck it out an open window into the pitch-black night so that it would never again go off when I was trying to boil an egg.

And that is where love enters the equation. I obviously do not love my smoke detector. I love my son. Love is what makes you hold a sobbing baby close to your chest instead of hurling him out an open window into the pitch-black night.[**]

It's because I love him that I would pace my living room in the wee hours of the morning, singing "The Safety Dance" by Men Without Hats, which may not be the lullaby that you hear mothers cooing in idyllic diaper commercials but which is, it turns out, a song babies like, while also being a song I know the words to. I would hold my son's tiny body to my chest with the other hand cradling his head, which was roughly the size of a

---

[*] Obviously, mixing these two pieces of advice is disastrous.

[**] Although postpartum depression is very real and I can't imagine a parent who didn't, at the very least, wish babies had a button you could hold down for five seconds to stop their crying.

Magic 8 ball. I would whisper, "You can dance if you want to, you can leave your friends behind," and with all the strength in his tiny lollipop-stick of a neck, he would crane his head upward to look at me—his dark, barely focused eyes asking, "And if my friends don't dance?" To which I would whisper, "If your friends don't dance, and if they don't dance, then they're no friends of mine."

Having a baby was, for me, the essence of becoming what one might call nurturing. Not "having a baby" as in "having a baby come out of your body," because I have done that twice and, heads up, it ranks somewhere between having a thirty-six-hour root canal and an anus full of bees. But "having a baby" the way you can possess or have something transformative, like chronic pain or a Dyson vacuum. And there *was* a transformation, but rather than becoming a primal nurturer, I found myself transformed from a person who did not have a newborn baby into a person who did.

I learned to nurture because I gave birth to (and slowly grew to love) someone who needed help, and I can't imagine loving anyone and seeing that they need help and not trying to help them. And to be clear, I am not saying "and not helping them," but "*trying* to help them." From my experience, a lot of nurturing is just failing with the best of intentions.

The best part of *Three Men and a Baby* isn't watching three men fret over the correct way to feed a baby every two hours or fasten a disposable diaper. The best part isn't even watching the men immediately try to trick their girlfriends and mothers into taking care of the baby full-time only to have the women *immediately* shut them down by refusing to do it, although yes, okay, that part is also terrific. But the best part is watching the men angrily struggle with their failures and inexperience and emerge as three-dimensional characters.* All three men became nurturing *as a result* of caring for a baby, which is certainly a more believable part of the movie than the idea that three extremely well-off bachelors in their thirties would be for some reason sharing an apartment.** There is no universe in which Tom Selleck discovers the baby on his doormat and leaves her there, stepping over the bassinet every day the way I see but ignore the pile of unopened mail on my counter. The only way Ted Danson could discover she's his child and then cease to care for her would be if his character were plucked from the movie and written into the script of *Trainspotting*. Not that everyone finding a baby would decide to raise her to adulthood, but the vast majority would care for her until they could make the calls and find someone else to do it.

And finding someone else to do it is okay. I'm not pretending raising a child is not hard. Maybe the hardest part of being nurturing is emotionally investing in something that is weak and can be easily hurt. Loving a child is like loving an extremely delicate ceramic vase on a low shelf. It isn't a question of whether it will get broken; it's a question of how often and how badly. But to casually assume women should be the ones to nurture children is to place something fragile and valuable into a woman's hands,

---

* I want to insist that I was fully three-dimensional before having kids, but if you ask me what my twenties or teenage years were like, it's a struggle to present them as anything but a lighthearted montage set to "I Wanna Dance with Somebody" that ends with my husband and me in matching flannel shirts, anxiously looking at a pregnancy test.

** Although "becoming more nurturing" is in no way synonymous with "being a perfect parent," as evidenced by the pretty in-depth extortion-and-narcotics subplot.

strap her into a pair of roller skates, and push her into a tornado while whispering, "I heard women are just inherently better at doing this."

Women are not nurturing and emotional as opposed to practical and logical. To effectively nurture, you have to be, at times, some degree of all of these things. You need to multitask and think outside the box. The other night when my toddler ran face-first into a door, I held him and then spent five minutes chastising the door as if it were a thoughtless person. (I want you to apologize for hitting him in the face, door. If you hurt him like that again, I'm going to take you right off your hinges and buy a newer, better door at Home Depot. You think I'm kidding? Do you want me to get the screwdriver? I AM GETTING THE SCREWDRIVER, DOOR. DON'T TEST ME.) Which kids love—probably since, like adults, they want someone to be held accountable when they are hurt.

Nurturing involves knowing when to be kind and when to be strict. Yes, I will hold you because you seem sad; no, I will not let you watch that Netflix show featuring an anthropomorphic frog army on a weeknight. Every year I add new areas of expertise to my parenting résumé, not because I am inherently nurturing, but because I am learning as I work at this job, the same way after two years in an administrative position I learned to use the Mail Merge with Envelopes function in Microsoft Word.

Are people missing out by not having to learn to nurture? Yes. Although I worry that some people—often the same type of people who feel that women should do the nurturing because "they're so much better at it"—will interpret that to mean that everyone should have children. And *no*, that is not what I mean. If you do not want kids, do not have kids.[*] There are other children or animals you can nurture, and also it is okay to miss out on some things. I have been told that I am missing out by being too scared to attempt skydiving, but I will continue to miss out on the transformative experience of skydiving from the beautiful, safe ground. Literally the only thing that might get me to skydive would be having a bunch of young kids in the plane with me constantly asking me to refill their water bottles, because I can only process the idea of leaping out of a plane if it means having ten minutes to myself.

Learning to nurture my kids, while I fought it tooth and nail, has been a transformative experience. And part of the reason I think more men should learn to nurture is obviously because I'm very selfish and tired of having this transformative experience all the time. I want to be very up-front about that. I am more than ready to have the nontransformative experience of lying around the house, reading books, and watching food documentaries while scrolling through Twitter. But part of the reason I want more men to nurture is that I know how much they'll grow from it. Because I know how going through it will transform them. Because I know that they will emerge from it as more hardworking and more understanding people.

I want people to grow. Because while I may not be a Mother Earth–type figure, I have always, in some respects, been nurturing. Which doesn't mean I've been overemotional or coddling. Which doesn't mean I love smelling babies' heads or singing "The Itsy Bitsy Spider" while sitting cross-legged on a rug. It means I

---

[*] Honestly, even if you do want kids, I'd go into it with a sense of trepidation.

want people to be better people, even if that means they have to do hard things.

And I would like to be better as well. The list of the best people I know is synonymous with the list of the most nurturing. I would love for both men and women to be nurturing, and by nurturing, I mean people who actively care about the growth and well-being *of other people*. I'd rather not adhere to the world's sometimes misguided definition of the term, because that definition can eat a giant bag of dicks.

PRETTY

STEPHANIE BURT

To me *pretty* means "almost." Almost beautiful, almost desirable, almost a woman. Almost respectable. Almost there.

I'll take it. Frankly, I'd love to feel pretty; I wish I felt pretty more often. I am delighted when I hear from people I trust that a butterfly-print scarf or a new pair of silver flats or my *Jem and the Holograms* earrings (a lovely gift whose batteries died almost immediately, so they stopped flashing) or the earrings I made out of D&D dice (let me know if you want some) or the bell-sleeve, burgundy, floral-print, V-collared blouse that I got from Stitch Fix (part of my clothes-I-can-teach-in project) look pretty.

I want my poems to be pretty sometimes too. I think pretty is underrated, in the same way and for the same reasons that a lot of what we now call Girl Culture or Kid Culture is underrated. Nobody's going to mistake *Frozen* for an Éric Rohmer film, but you know what? *Frozen*'s great. I cried a lot. I even cried at the five-minute sequel to *Frozen* that showed before *Coco*, the one where Elsa has a box that should have held all the Girl Culture things she played with as a child, but she doesn't have any, because she didn't get to play with other girls. (I also cried at *Coco*, but everyone cried at *Coco*.) She retreats to the sublime and flexes her superpowers, building a scary (that is, scary to kids) ice monster, and a spectacular ice palace, and yet because she's who she is, the results are still pretty.

Given a choice of attributes, would you want to feel pretty, as in the Sondheim and Bernstein number "I Feel Pretty"? Wouldn't you rather—if you had to choose—feel "witty and bright"? (Why do I often misremember the words to that song as "pretty and witty and gay"? Is it because the movie version of the song substitutes "gay" for "bright" in order to rhyme with "today," or is it because I'm definitely gay?)

Pretty—like *witty*—is a belittling word: not just femme, or feminine, but girly, or girlish. It's something we are (or are not) rather than something we do.

It's also about being or feeling inadequate: to be pretty is to be not quite beautiful, not quite finished, not quite serious, not quite enough, almost in the way that a girl is by definition not quite finished, not quite adult, not quite ready, not quite independent, not quite a woman. Nobody ever got a gold medal for running a pretty good race or launched a career by doing a pretty good job; it's a word that shies from competition, that wants praise—or possibly cuddles, or pats on the head—but does not want to stand up, stand out, reach for the top.

Stevie Smith seems to have hated it. That wonderful, underrated, understated, acerbic, and very femme British poet and novelist wrote a whole poem to undermine and attack the term *pretty*, or maybe to attack hypocrisy. Smith's thirty-six-line poem applies the word to owls, to pike ("the pike is a fish who always has his prey"), to "Nature," "always careless and indifferent . . . and this is pretty," to a nameless wanderer in the woods who stops to lick icicles, and to oblivion: to "be delivered entirely from humanity / This is prettiest of all, it is very pretty."

Crinolines are pretty, and cupcakes with beads on the icing, and birthday candles in all the pastel colors, and T-shirts with capped sleeves in the misses section at Target, and covers for calendars Great-Grandma had, and none of those things look like they could last five minutes in the company of Smith's pike, or Smith's owl, or Smith's hypothermia-inducing winter, or Smith's despair.

Or yours, or mine. To be pretty is to be appreciated and girly but small and impractical and, also, perhaps, defenseless. The girliest (prettiest) outfits we give children are outfits that make it hard to run around; Natalie Wood's character in *West Side Story*, the one who sings "I Feel Pretty," might get fought over but won't get into a knife fight. Nor will she run for public office. If we don't want to be pretty, or to feel pretty, one reason might be that *pretty* means "girly," and some of us would like to be seen as adults. But another reason might be that we would like to feel strong, to feel able to defend ourselves. *Beautiful*, *sexy*, *attractive* can go with *powerful*. *Pretty*? Not so much.

So why do *I* want to feel pretty? Why does the word mean for me not a pitfall but a real goal? For one thing (and nothing here says that trans women aren't women; of course we are), I feel less like a woman than I do like a very lucky girl. Like many trans people who start their social or medical transition in adulthood, I've felt like a teen or a preteen for a very long time, felt as if everybody around me was growing up, meeting social milestones, developing, while I wasn't. "Last girl in her class to develop"—socially or physically—is a cliché of middle-grade fiction, and of some teen lives: I've been that last girl for a while, and I'm developing—coming into my own and also physically developing, in the way my brain tells me I should—right now, in 2018 and 2019, nineteen years after my PhD and thirteen years after I became (as I now put it) a mom.

No wonder, then (or so I tell myself), that I want to feel pretty: to be affirmed as the girl I took myself to be.

But what does it mean to be a girl today? Why would I want to be a girl when I can take steps to skip the intermediary states and be seen as a woman? Why would I *want* to feel pretty when I could try to feel, instead, attractive, or cool, or beautiful? I've been asking myself that question since before I transitioned: Why do I want this? Why does this term, with all its baggage, fit me? And I've been asking it in another key as a mom. Our older kid seems to be a cis boy and has to confront these questions in the lives of his friends but not in his own; our very confident younger kid, however, who sometimes wears a lot of pink—for that kid, these questions are more personal.

Should I be saving what's pretty, the feeling of being pretty, for . . . girls? Shouldn't I try harder to (as the kids say now) adult?

Maybe I should. But I can't. I care to be pretty, at least for now: it means something I want. Why? I think I've come up with three answers.

1. *Pretty* means something attainable. I can do it. Even bad designers can do it. Floral prints can do it. Cartoon unicorns can do it. (If you are not already reading the newspaper comic strip *Phoebe and Her Unicorn*, go read it! It's online for free!) You can pretty something up, or go with another shade of the same thing

and make it pretty; the other femme adjectives seem harder to attain.

When I was first learning basic makeup (and we're talking one layer of Revlon foundation plus muted pink lipstick, or maybe lip gloss or lip stain, not High Degree of Difficulty Eyeliner), I told my partner, and anyone else who was trying to help me learn, and anyone else who would listen, that I didn't need to get an A in makeup or in femininity; I wanted to work hard enough to earn a B+. The attitude I had carried up to that point—where if I knew I couldn't get an A in something I wouldn't attempt it—had been bad for me: I wouldn't apply myself to learning languages in which I might have to converse (because I would never sound fluent), and I wouldn't transition—I put off coming out as a trans woman, and social and medical transition—not least because I was afraid that I would never be able to do it right; that I would have to get an A; that the bar for being seen by the world as the woman I wanted to be was just too high to clear. I can't make myself look perfect or beautiful. I probably can't even pass (be taken for a cisgender woman by strangers), although one never knows. But I can be pretty okay at being pretty. The word *pretty* means, to me, a bar I can clear.

2. Pretty isn't just or always for girls, as much as it's associated with girlhood; it's also for cats, and for tableware, and for the old lady I someday want to be. It's decoration. It's lace.

It is, in other words, for versions of the feminine that are not (or shouldn't be) directly sexual. It's not sex appeal. And maybe I don't want much sex appeal (or not in how I look to strangers). I am already partnered, after all. I'm also a teacher—I spend a lot of time in the classroom and onstage—and if I can find a way to read as pleasantly feminine without even trying for hot or available or please-look-at-my-body . . . maybe I'm in favor of that.

(I have a recent history of taking that goal too far; some of the tops and dresses I have ordered or purchased and worn and then discarded on advice from People I Trust Most are bad Laura Ashley–esque prints that bring to mind Prairie Dawn from *Sesame Street* and/or floral tablecloths. I don't want to look like a tablecloth.)

3. *Pretty* means girly, not womanly: more cute than beautiful; more light pink than hot pink; more floral print than two-inch heels (girls aren't permitted to wear awful heels). I sometimes describe my style as "low femme," in contradistinction to the spike-heel, serious-mascara, décolletage-conscious high maintenance of high femme. *Pretty* means—for me—low femme.

But it does not have to mean powerless. Sparkly unicorns can be the most powerful magic entities in the universe, if you draw them that way (the lead unicorn's name in *Phoebe and Her Unicorn* is Marigold Heavenly Nostrils, and yes, she's pretty, and loves rainbows, and can probably kill you with a glance, although she won't). Pretty dresses (tops, hats, gloves, scarves), for kids or adults, will never be workout gear, but they don't have to immobilize; they might not be great in a fistfight, but who says power means fistfights? Not even superhero comics (not the good ones anyway), and certainly not real life.

The association of girly, low-femme, pink cursive hearts-on-*i*'s handwriting, floral-print looks with disempowerment is not a necessary fact about femme style in the modern world; it's an artifact of the same prejudice that says girls who like being girls are less than boys and also less than boyish girls and also less than girls who act like adults, a prejudice not against women and girls but against femininity, the same cisheteronormative, femme-phobic nonsense that tells us that boys who look girly are suspect, while girls who look and act "like boys" are laudable or tolerable tomboys (although of course they'll grow out of it: they'd better). The enemy here isn't just sexism in general but the particular brand of toxic nonsense that the cultural critic Julia Serano has labeled anti-feminine sentiment or femmephobia, a prejudice not against kinds of bodies so much as against their free and vivid expression. It's nonsense that runs deep in our culture and language, nonsense that has helped make the word *pretty*—which I embrace and pursue—a word I do not often apply to others, a word I know many other people don't want.

And popular culture is—at last, at least—turning around and doing something about that nonsense, something to counter femmephobia; today's girls and young women can get, if they want, messages not just about female empowerment but about femme empowerment, about various characters in various worlds who can do whatever they want, or who save the day with their heroic efforts, or who don't need strangers' approval, and a lot of these characters are . . . pink, or surrounded by glitter, or at home in tulle, or aggressively uninterested in what older popular culture thinks that symbols of power should be.

That's *Frozen*, the first Disney movie about a trans girl. It's *Phoebe and Her Unicorn*. It's also *Jem and the Holograms*, the recent comic book (you can skip the movie). It's the *She-Ra* reboot, now with more princesses (retitled *She-Ra and the Princesses of Power*).

And it's contemporary poets from Angie Estes to Dorothea Lasky who have less than one-ten-thousandth the audience of *Frozen* but share the hit movie's commitment to the costume department at the Met and to the elaborate articulation of snow-flakes. Preferably pink snowflakes. (That said, it's surprising how hard it is to find a serious contemporary poem that uses the word *pretty*; the most recent famous one is probably Elizabeth Bishop's "Crusoe in England," where the repeated word functions as homoerotic code: "Pretty to watch; he had a pretty body.")

I used to turn nearly red with suppressed frustration when parents at our kids' preschool (mostly dads, but some moms) told me they were sad about their young children who wanted to wear lots of pink: as if pink, and tulle, and lace, and other accoutrements of pretty were inherently disempowering. They are not. They don't have to be. And that's a lesson that does not apply only to literal girls; it applies to me. Sometimes I feel pretty. Sometimes I wonder what took me so long.

INTIMIDATING
TANZILA AHMED

I pull into the parking lot late and frantically wrap the loose end of my sparkly turquoise sari around my waist as I race up to the front door of the wedding venue. The room is full of women in elegant saris and men in crisp suits, and the smell of goat biryani is wafting out of the kitchen. The couple getting married are Bangladeshi American, distant family friends whom I know only tangentially, through my parents.

Though their wedding is fully underway, I blend in easily as just one attendee among the four hundred guests at this Desi affair.

I quietly sneak my way to my parents' table. I need to have Mom retie the sari because, by the time I find my seat, the folds have completely fallen. Mom looks at me with a tight-lipped smile and informs me that I'm late.

"I know," I respond, looking down.

Then Mom looks at me with that look that only moms can give, assessing my level of presentability to her peers. "Why didn't you take that thing out of your chin?" she says. "What will people think?"

On my chin, I have a little silver ball. I got the labret piercing when I turned twenty-three years old. I like it—it makes me feel punk and rebellious and pretty. And Mom didn't get too upset by it, unless we were at events where all the Bangladeshi aunties and uncles might see it.

"I like it," I say, defensive. "And I can't take it out without my hole closing up."

"Hide it with your hand, then," she says. "Don't bring attention to yourself. That thing is intimidating."

"I'm pretty sure I'll bring more attention to it by having my hand covering my chin all night."

I don't tell her that I like that it is intimidating. That I like feeling powerful and like I can't be reined in. That I am tired of being seen as quiet and obedient—the expected good girl. I am a good girl, but maybe I like looking a little intimidating too. With the piercing, I am signaling that there is a side of me that cannot be tamed.

He is playing with my toy—that redheaded four-year-old with the freckles and chubby arms. I'm only three years old, and Ammu says I have to be nice to him. But it looks like in his hand is the plastic yellow van that converts into a helicopter that I fly around my living room and drive over the crushed-green-velvet sofa. I know he has his own plastic yellow van-copter—a nicer and newer one that his mother bought him when I refused to share my toy—but this time I am sure he is playing with mine. If I could only just get closer, I'd be able to see whether the black sticker is ripped on the side—the way mine is—and if it has a black mark on the bottom, the way that mine does.

Every morning, Brandon's mother drops him off at our house for my ammu to babysit. When she opens the door, she becomes strangely polite. Her voice rises an octave and changes to a fluttery, whitewashed English. She never sounds like that with the Bangladeshi aunties and uncles—only when she is talking to white people.

I know that Abbu goes to work in an office every day, and for Ammu, babysitting is her job, and jobs are important for grown-ups. But how is she able to change her voice like that? I can always tell, even when she's talking on the phone, what kind of person she's talking to on the other end of the line. Her voice changes like a switch.

But I don't understand why I have to let Brandon in my space when I myself have daily important jobs of my own to work on. I have Lego homes to build and paper-doll clothes to make. I especially don't like this kid playing with my toys, because as an only child, I don't believe in sharing my toys.

I inch closer to see if I have reason to be full of rage. I debate if I should scream for Ammu, who is in the kitchen making Brandon's lunch. She has told me before that I need to play with Brandon and be nice to him because she's his babysitter. But I don't want to be nice, especially if he is playing with my toy.

"That's mine!" I say quietly while pointing at the toy, when I finally find my voice.

"No, it's mine," he responds confidently, grasping the toy tighter. "Go play with your dolls. Cars are for boys to play with."

I feel the rage inside bubble to the surface, but I can't say anything. Instead of using my words, I use the only thing I can think of using through a red curtain of rage—my teeth. I grab his chubby short white arm and bite him. Hard. Not to the point that he is bleeding. I have just barely grown my baby teeth. But hard enough to leave a ribbed oval indentation in the skin of his arm.

Of course, he starts crying, and Ammu runs right in. I know I am in trouble and I start crying. But I also feel the powerful rush behind using my bite to express myself instead of saying anything.

She looks at the toy in his hand as she comforts him and wipes away his tears. "You are fighting over this?" she says. "Isn't that your yellow van over there? Why do you need to play with his toy?" She points to the corner of the living room. Sure enough, there is my yellow van. I guiltily realize my mistake.

I bite him a few more times over the next few weeks. Each time I bite him I get into more and more trouble with Ammu— she always yells at me after Brandon is picked up. Sometimes I don't even need to bite him; I can just give him a look that says I will most likely bite him, and it has him cowering in a corner. Soon, his mother finds him another babysitter. She tells my ammu that my behavior is intimidating, that her son is scared of me because of my bites. My mother says she understands, though she pleads and pleads, saying she will try better to control it.

But I have already felt the rush of intimidation. It will be my new life theme.

By the time I am a teenager, I am far from intimidating. I wear big glasses, am awkwardly skinny under baggy clothes, and usually have my nose buried in a novel. In school I am often overlooked because I am so quiet, and I play the role of sidekick to a series of much more popular girls. At home, my parents keep me sheltered. They want to keep my American life separate from my home life, and they want me to set a good example for my younger sisters.

Within these margins I find freedom, in a way. When you don't even have the option of being the cheerleader or the class president, and boys don't find you attractive because you are a brown girl, and even if they did, it's not like you're allowed to date, anyway—you have to figure yourself out in different ways. I find myself drawn to the energy of rebellious punk shows; I find passion in fighting for the environment and purpose in participating in student government. I shop at thrift stores for a unique sense of style (and because it's all that I can afford) and fold into my quirky personality.

Suddenly I learn that people find me intimidating—the undateable punk rocker with quirks, the unique political environmental activist, was a formidable peer. I am no longer the bland and meek Brown, the Other. I can intimidate by simply having no other option but to find my voice.

Back at the wedding hall, I stand against the wall as I watch the bride and groom onstage looking into a hand mirror, sharing their first official look at each other as marrieds under the intimate covering of one dupatta over both their heads. They are young, at least a decade younger than I am. I am always surprised to see two Bangladeshi Americans find each other in the dating minefield of this world that we live in. I wonder how they met, how they knew. I find out later that they were "introduced"—the contemporary version of an arranged marriage.

An auntie smiles at me, then gives me a hug. She asks me when it's going to be my turn. She tells me I'm in my thirties now, and time doesn't stay still.

I am frustrated by her comment and the implied agency it gives me. It's not like I haven't been trying—I have been on numerous dating sites since I was twenty-two years old, have been on countless first dates with all kinds of men, and of all the men I've been in relationships with, three of whom I thought were on the path to marriage, well, they didn't see a future with me.

But of course aunties don't want to hear about the sordid details and frustrations behind the reality of marriage hunting. Instead of responding as I usually do—with a tight-lipped "Yes, Auntie, very soon, *inshallah*"—I decide to flip the script and put the agency back on her.

"But no one wants to marry me, Auntie."

"What do you mean no one wants to marry you?" she says, pinching my chin. "Look at how gorgeous you are. Why wouldn't anyone want to marry you?"

"I keep trying and trying. And it's so hard out there, Auntie. Do *you* have anyone for me, then?"

"Me? I don't have anyone. Just go on the web. What are you looking for?"

"Well . . . someone who has a job and isn't a Republican."

"*Hai Allah* . . . you have to keep an open mind for these things. You can't be so limiting."

"I mean, I work in progressive politics, so it just won't work otherwise. . . ." I mumble.

"*Array*, I can't ask if these men are Republican or not," she responds, scandalized. "That's asking for too much. You should have gotten married before getting your master's degree. That must be why you are not getting proposals. You are too successful and too educated for these men now. You are too intimidating."

I look at her, stunned. Is she really saying that I shouldn't be smart or, at least, appear smart?

"Now, listen," the auntie says quietly. "When you talk to these men, don't tell them you have a master's degree or work in politics. Just let them speak. Make yourself seem smaller."

"You want me play stupid?"

"No! You are smart—you keep being smart. I'm just saying at first, when you meet them, don't show them how smart you are. These men, they are weak, with their egos. A woman like you is intimidating to them. So be less so. Temporarily."

***

"Remember, you must always learn how to be an independent. I want you to be able to take care of yourself when you grow up. You should never depend on a man."

Ammu always said it forlornly, looking off into the distance. It was her favorite life lesson, and it was always when she was feeling particularly morose about her own life—usually, after getting into a fight with Abbu—that she reminded me of it. I heard it the first time when I was little, maybe even when I was a toddler, before I knew words, really. And I heard it over and over again every few months for the rest of my life.

"You don't want me to get married?" I'd always respond.

"*Chee*. Of course I want you to get married. That's not what I'm saying. I just want you to have options. To be able to take care of yourself if anything should happen. Just look at what happened to me and your abbu . . ." She'd trail off.

My mother had married my father sight unseen, because to her, it didn't really matter whether she saw him before the wedding day. She was going to see him the rest of her life. My father had established himself in Los Angeles and had gone back to Bangladesh to find a wife over his summer break. His family had sent over several proposals to my mother's family. At first her family refused because his family was from the country and they wanted to make sure my mother was marrying up. Eventually my mom relented. In her deliberations, she weighed that she'd be able to pursue a graduate degree in America. She had always wanted to get an advanced degree in economics. She wanted to give her children the opportunity to be raised in America. Love would come after marriage, she thought.

Just months into her marriage, she got pregnant with me. By the time she emigrated to America with the stranger of a husband and me in her belly, she realized her life would be very different from what she had expected. As my abbu jumped from job to job as a struggling electrical engineer where his language and culture were big barriers, my mother realized that in this immigrant life scenario, her pursuit of an advanced degree was a pipe dream. They had no fallback for the gaps when he was between jobs. She had to hustle. She babysat, taught preschoolers, worked in an airport parking lot.

She would never admit that she was disappointed in her life. But she made sure her three daughters knew the importance of learning how to take care of yourself first, and not a man.

I thought this was what most Bangladeshi mothers told their daughters. I thought this because I imagined that most women who had arranged marriages would want different futures for their daughters. It wasn't until I became a teenager that I realized that this wasn't the case. There existed a whole cadre of aunties who were all about making sure their daughters married "well."

They wanted their Desi daughters to be able to depend on a man. If the girls got an education, it was only to make their biodata profile stand out. And god forbid they get too educated, because a woman should never have a degree higher than her partner's.

I studied hard, maybe subconsciously because I knew that it was something that my mother had always wanted for herself but never achieved because she got pregnant with me. I often credit my mother with the reason I pursued social justice—because women who survive and hustle deserve to have their rights protected. I think about this often—how getting an arranged marriage was the ticket to freedom for her and for her daughters. I was eternally grateful that Ammu would defend my marriageless status to all the aunties and uncles, proudly stating that I was pursuing a degree or getting an award instead.

She died suddenly and prematurely at fifty-five years old. And the struggle to survive as a family without her was an uphill battle. But to her credit, seven years later, all three of her daughters are living independently and self-sufficiently without depending on a man for survival. And we learned how to tie our own saris. So I guess there's that.

Over the phone, the psychics had me say my name. Three times. That was it.

It was a year after my mother's death, and I was seeking her in my dreams. I was feeling lost in my life without her and ungrounded by a recent heartbreak. I was in my midthirties and down on myself for still not having found a man to start a family with. I had found the psychics through a psychic friend of mine who had suggested I try them out when he saw how I was struggling. So at the determined time I had to call the psychic hotline. I was skeptical, but in my grieving state of mind, I was open to believing anything.

"I haven't been able to sleep lately," I told the psychics. "What does it mean?"

There were four of them on the phone, all keying into my auras, my chakras. They said that I was in a period of regrowth, that I was still searching for a higher path, though the truth remained strong within me. That using divine light to heal was a gift I had. That religion and the structure of religious practice were strong parts of my identity. That seeking an understanding in truth gave me a deep sense of purpose and centered me at my core. And that in my dreams I was very busy, constantly going to other universes, learning things, and storing that knowledge.

They told me that my body was recalibrating. That I was passing through the other side of grief. I was going from one phase into another and clearing old karma.

"I have to ask, being the single woman that I am. Will I ever find love?"

"You are attractive to men of all types. They find you intriguing, but almost frightening. Even though you project a deep level of internal beauty, men are afraid to talk to you. Slow down your energy level to match theirs. Allow them to come to you," the male psychic responded over the crackling phone line.

Hold up. Did the psychic just "auntie" me? Did he just call my aura intimidating? Did he say men find my cosmic energy too strong and that I need to slow my psychic roll?

I didn't need a psychic to tell me that.

"It's someone you have met, but you just don't know it yet," he continued. "It will feel like family. And when you know, you'll recognize it and just know. . . . So don't be too concerned with it. It will take no effort. And it will happen; you just need to let it."

Even the psychics thought my aura was intimidating. And I found it very concerning.

I reflect back to the night of that wedding and how, as I was walking out of the wedding hall with Ammu, she turned to me suddenly. She could see, in her motherly way, how frustrated I was by the auntie's comment. It had made her upset as well. I had told her not to confront the auntie but was regretting it. For as long as my mother was alive, I never told her about any of the guys I dated. I kept all my relationships secret because none of them were relationships worthy of my mother's knowledge. But I think she knew that I was dating, and brokenhearted.

She reached out her hand and grabbed my arm. Her arms jangled with the sound of her bangles clinking and I could feel the brush of her silk sari on my skin.

"I believe that Allah created someone for everyone out there," she said while rubbing my arm. "Don't lose hope; your time will come." Given everything she had been through with her arranged marriage and her mantra of raising her three daughters to be independent beings, I found this statement incredibly optimistic. But she still believed that I was destined for an eternal love pairing, when even I couldn't believe it.

It's been seven years since she's died. I am turning forty this summer, and I have spent almost the entire past decade single and searching for love. I have heard the phrase "I don't know how a woman like you is still single" on a first date more times than I can count. I see now that my mom's fierce need to have independent daughters who didn't have to depend on a man came about because she didn't have that choice. But I wonder what she would say now if she could.

Society has all these expectations of how women are to show up in this world. Be yourself, they say. Be less of yourself. Be independent, but not too intimidating. Take care of yourself, but make a man feel like he can take care of you. Be everything, but not too much.

Sure, I'd love to find love someday. But not by sacrificing myself. It's taken me too long to get here, and my ammu taught me better than that.

I'd rather be the woman with a bite.

GOOD
TOVA MIRVIS

I escaped being named Gertrude in memory of my great-grandmother, who died a few months before I was born. Not wishing to saddle me with this name, my parents turned instead to Gertrude's Yiddish name, Gittel. But since this was hardly better, they made use of "Gittel"'s Yiddish meaning, "good." They arrived at "Tova"—which means "good" in Hebrew.

I was grateful for the save. Yet this swapping left me with a name as cumbersome as "Gertrude" might have been. *Good* hangs over me. As a child, when I told adults what my name meant, they would respond, "Well, are you good?" I took the question seriously. Was I? Did my name command me to be good, or was my name, by definition, who I was?

I may have lain awake puzzling out this conundrum, but I knew from a young age exactly what it meant to be good. There were divine commandments to be followed for every aspect of life. Every action was decisively allowed or prohibited, good or bad. In the small Orthodox Jewish community in Memphis where I grew up, to be good was to do as you were told. To be good was to sit quietly, to speak gently. To be good was to be pleasing to those around you, to fit the shape others imagined for you. Good was not slippery or wily or crafty; good was not loud or demanding, not insistent, not angry, not strong. Most of all, to be religious was to be good—they were presumed, in fact, to be synonymous.

Whether you were in fact good wasn't determined by your own internal reckoning but rather by the eyes of others. A communal surround of eyes and ears was watching, judging, deciding. Any private wrestling to understand what goodness actually meant might have existed in the background, but what mattered most was whether others deemed you to be good.

In high school, good became linked inextricably to our bodies. Good girls adhered to a dress code prohibiting the exposure of knees and collarbones. Good girls—surely this went without saying—did not touch boys. When my skirts skimmed the knee, I had to pull them down. Good girls also did not doubt the all-encompassing authority of God or the rabbis when it came to enforcement. But it wasn't just a wayward knee I was covering. It was not just body parts that were problematic but some core aspect of who you were. Some part of ourselves was in need of cloaking.

In class, we studied the book of Genesis, in which God made day and night, the beasts and the fowl, man and woman. At the end of His creations, God surveyed His work and declared it good. All this goodness was marred by Eve, who tempted Adam to eat from the tree of life, the tree of knowledge of good and bad. We learned that now they knew they were naked; they entered into the world of knowledge, and also of shame. They who had once been good had become bad, and for this, they were exiled, cursed to toil and suffer.

The word *good* appeared, too, in the prayers we said each morning, the ones recited in synagogue when the cantor blessed the new month. As my name was sung aloud, the prayers felt personal, an admonition and a message. A life of peace, a life of sustenance, a life of blessings, a life of good. It was clear what this life was supposed to look like: marriage to someone like me, children, a home in the same kind of religious community in which I was being raised. The word *good* was ubiquitous at the start of the Jewish new year, when the greeting "*Shana tova*" was exchanged and exclaimed. We wished that we might have a good year—a year in which we were kept safe, a year in which nothing bad befell us, a year in which we were blessed with goodness by being good ourselves.

The word *good* might have been repeated over and over, but it was the prospect of its opposite that had the real power. Hiding underneath the word *good* was something far more dangerous. To be bad was an ever-present possibility—if you were not good, then automatically you were bad. To be bad was to be difficult, desirous, provocative. To be bad was to insist, to dare, to challenge. To be bad was to go against the path laid out for you. If to be good was to say yes to the world of rules, to be bad was to utter a willful, intransigent no.

Am I bad? I asked myself, as often as I wondered if I was good. In a world of rules, there were infinite ways to be bad. My infractions at the time were minor—the short skirts, a few kisses from a camp boyfriend—but when even the smallest of deeds mattered, these counted as genuine trespasses. Each bad act filled me with guilt and fear. But to be bad didn't even require an action. Bad was a state of being, some inner malignant spot that would grow and grow. If I was indeed bad, I was at risk of displeasing everyone around me. If I was bad, I would be without love.

After I graduated from high school, I spent a year studying Jewish texts in Israel, as was the custom for Orthodox girls like myself. As I immersed myself in religious life, the fear of badness receded. For this year, I sat in front of my books. I emulated teachers who showed me the right way to be. To be good I simply had to do what was expected of me. There was an ease to following wholeheartedly; the self didn't have to be so embattled.

I started college intent on holding on to this goodness lest it become corrupted—not just by others, but by my inner rebellious parts. I was now regarded as a good girl, not quite as good as some more-religious peers—who seemed to be almost ethereal, rosy and pink with the flush, it appeared, of God himself—but good enough to make an appropriate wife for the kind of guy I wanted to marry. While we were good girls, they were great guys; it was universally acknowledged that they were in search of girls who dressed according to the religious strictures, who would make good wives, who would create good Jewish homes. Good girls grew up to be good wives and good mothers.

I began dating someone who seemed good in the way I had been trained to be: Orthodox like me, unopinionated, unassuming, obedient. He did not have any hint of the dark streak that I worried was inside me. Or if he did, it was buried deep, far from where I would have access. I had again started to fear that I didn't match the world inside of which I was trying to remain. I wanted to be a writer; I wanted to turn over every truth handed to me and examine it for flaws. I wanted to be good, yet I felt a curiosity and a stirring hunger to explore—a Russian nesting doll of alternate selves.

We got engaged in the middle of my senior year of college, after twelve weeks of dating. This rashness wasn't an act of rebellion. To get married was to permanently seal that good girl in place. With marriage, there were other kinds of good to be. I covered my hair with hats and a wig, as was now required of me according to religious dictates. I had children. We moved from New York City to the Boston suburbs where my husband was from— he wanted this, and I wanted to do this for him. I so badly wanted to be happy, to be safe, to remain good.

Years passed, and I began to feel discontent. I felt like I couldn't say what I really thought. My religious doubts were rising to the surface, but to voice them would be to risk an unraveling—there were no words that could bridge the gap, no conversation that didn't end before it began. So long as I remained contained, we were fine. If I said everything was okay, then it was. I didn't think there was any other way it could be.

More years passed, and I continued to feel that I was upholding religious strictures that had come to feel like a prison. Most of all I felt the problem was with me—that core of badness I had long feared had been lying in wait, and now there was no hiding it. I was bad because I could not make myself believe, bad because I could not overlook the loneliness and the urge for something else, something more. If only I could not feel this way. If only I could be different than I was. Make it through, I told myself. Don't think. And always, try, try, try, try harder, try again.

But those whispers of doubt grew more insistent. I lay awake wondering what would happen if I stopped trying so hard to hold everything in place. I started with a few minor trespasses of religious law: a forbidden food, a cell phone used on the Sabbath. I stopped trying to act like everything was fine in my marriage. There was no single moment when everything changed, just a slow erosion of the ability to not know what I really knew. Just a recognition that what had felt like a stone fortress was actually capable of crashing down.

What scared me most was that I didn't feel bad about my trespasses. They felt like an inevitability. Despite all those attempts to the contrary, it was as if I'd long known that the day would come when I would stop trying to be that good girl.

Over the course of the year leading up to my fortieth birthday, I left my marriage. I ceased to follow the religious rules. I fell in love with a man who was not religious. Every new action, every change, felt like I was repeating the word *no*. No, my mind and my body screamed. *No.*

My divorce was a battle of good versus bad. You are bad, my soon-to-be ex-husband repeated until it was hard to distinguish in my head which was his voice and which was my own. Bad, bad, bad, I heard from those who had been part of my religious community, some friends, some merely acquaintances who were so sure of their own goodness and so ready to cast judgments and affix labels—self-appointed guardians of good, there to defend its borders, to uphold its name. We had lived in a world of black and white, and we would divorce on those terms. I, who had once been good, had publicly revealed myself to be bad. In order to leave, being good was one of the things I would have to surrender at the gates.

Bad was a label that ripped me apart. I roiled with self-doubt, unmoored, unrecognizable to myself. And yet, in that rending, some other world was being torn open. It was time to stop running from bad. To be bad meant that I wouldn't have to subject myself to the opinions of others. To be bad meant that I wouldn't have to hide from what I believed, cloak what I thought. More than anything, to be bad was to be free.

Leaving behind the actual religious rules wasn't the hardest part. Instead, it was easing the imprint these rules had made in my mind, that insistent voice asking if I was good or bad. But slowly, slowly, the press of these words began to ease. A new set of possibilities began to assemble that felt neither good nor bad, just present. You are allowed to change. You are allowed to decide what you believe. You are allowed to think what you think, feel what you feel. It turned out that there were other ways to be. To really leave was to let go of not just the answer to the question of "Am I bad or good?"; it was to let go of this kind of question altogether.

These days, I mostly cringe at *good*. It's a word I use sparingly, especially with my own daughter, aware of its shadowy opposite. Instead, I try to remind myself of words like *kind* and *compassionate*, like *open* and *thoughtful* and *generous*. As though I could take this word *good* and smash it to the ground, so that it shatters into so many small stones that are varied and rough, dappled and craggy.

And yet, there is still the matter of my name. At the start of each Jewish year, when the greeting "*Shanah tova*" is handed out, I am reminded of all the associations that come with my name. I remember how fervently I once prayed to be good while standing inside a synagogue wishing to be anywhere else. Most of all, I feel the pain of exile from the world that I grew up in, even if I chose to leave it myself.

On this new year, when the word *good* rings the loudest, I have also taken to celebrating what I have gained by choosing not to be good.

Each year, I spend this holiday away, as far as I can be, inside a wilderness of other possibilities, other definitions. While on the other side of the world my name is sung in sanctuaries, I can be climbing up red-brown rocks, kayaking along lush rushing rivers, hiking in green verdant forests, surrounded by a different kind of new year and different way of being.

This past year, I spent the Jewish new year in Iceland, in a landscape so stark it felt primordial. Hiking out onto a glacier, surrounded by icy white and blue, any notion of good or bad felt remote; in this seemingly unformed world, those words ceased to have meaning. Out here, inside this raw, rough beauty, no one owned goodness, not even those who tried to capture it and store it in a small, tight box.

On one of these hiking ventures, an Icelandic woman asked me my name.

"Tova?" she said as I waited for her to ask what it meant. But she wasn't looking for my definition. "We also have that word," she said.

She searched her vocabulary for the right translation.

"In Icelandic, *tova* means 'fox.'"

TOMBOY
WINTER MILLER

täm̦ boi. *noun. a girl who acts like a boy*

It's 1978 and a half, August 15. I am standing by the porch in my Dorothy Hamill haircut, which, if you didn't live through the seventies or aren't a figure skating fanatic, is a bowl cut that fades into a wedge, with feathering. Picture a hairstyle for a senior citizen, but on a child. I am leaning against the yellow bicycle I'm about to learn how to ride, wearing a short yellow gingham dress.

In the photograph snapped on my fifth birthday, I pull the dress up to my shoulders, flashing underwear like bloomers and my short white socks and patent leather shoes. This is because someone else dressed me for my birthday.

Usually I'm in sneakers, overalls, and a shirt with patterns: fruits, frogs, maybe fire trucks. Not only have I never met a pattern I didn't like, but I've never met two opposing patterns I didn't want to wear together. When my mom's friend comes to get me at day care, he asks if I'm trying to blind the other kids.

I've been the boss of my clothes since I was two. Stripes with plaids: excellent. The look of a red long-sleeve shirt, red corduroy overalls, red shoes, and red barrettes: wicked. No one in my family says, *This is what girls wear; this is what boys wear.* What I like, I wear, my picks chosen for comfort and readiness. Who's to say a kickball game won't materialize out of thin air? A race? TV tag? Trees that need climbing? Preparation is crucial. Dresses are impractical.

I can run naked at a lake or play shirtless in a sandbox. No one cares how I perform gender, and neither do I. On a hot summer day, you can lift your dress over your head as long as you're a little girl.

Pie chart one:
clothes I liked to wear as a girl + now

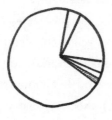

62% jeans
25% boots + sneakers
5% pants
5% shorts
2% overalls
1% skirt or dress

☐ clothing viewed as more masculine
▨ clothing viewed as more feminine

The popular girls in fifth grade are talking ballet again: who's *en pointe*, whose teacher is best. I sit quietly, following along.

"Can I take ballet?"

"Ballet?" My mom lowers car-radio Springsteen to a murmur. "You said you weren't interested."

"Everybody talks about it."

"I would find ballet tedious."

"Is tedious hard or boring?"

"Tedious is *unbelievably boring.* And ballet isn't cheap."

Ballet doesn't sound all that appealing.

After school, neighborhood boys and I ride bikes. We have nowhere to go; we circle the blocks. Boys' bikes have boys' bars, the steel bar running from handlebar to seat. Boys' bikes have thick, nubby tires for quick stops and spraying dirt. Girls' bikes have puffy seats, plastic flowery baskets, and bells. A boy at school says we can come see him race his BMX. The track has boys in helmets bobbing up and over packed dirt mounds.

"Can I get a BMX?" I ask my dad.

"What's wrong with yours?"

"Mine's heavy. Brooks's bike is so light he lifts it one-handed."

"Someone should tell Brooks bikes are for riding, not carrying."

"Dad. Can I ride the BMX track?

"You can ride around the block and I'll time you."

"It's not a track!"

"We're not paying for you to break your neck."

"I can't do *anything* fun."

"It's dangerous. These kids' parents are out to lunch."

That's fine, because in May 1984, the movie *Breakin'* comes out. I have a linoleum square atop my bedroom rug at my dad's and a can of lemon Pledge to make it shine. I wear a slick navy-and-red nylon tracksuit for maximum spin. My parachute pants have a zipper from ankle to knee; my jacket folds into its own pocket and zips closed into a little pillow. It came from the boys' section, and to my eleven-year-old mind, this is the ultimate utilitarian sartorial majesty: after you've pop-and-locked till you drop, you just unzip the legs to air out your knees and lay your head on your tiny pillow. The back spin is my signature move, and I seal it with flair: an abrupt shift into casual freeze. Casual freeze is when you're stretched out horizontally, one hand behind your head, one elbow out, legs crossed, your face like a model's surveying the distance. It looks very suave, trust me.

At my mom's house I rough it, dragging a flat refrigerator box down to the street corner. My grandma's hand-me-down boombox eats D batteries while older boys and I plant ourselves on cardboard with back spins, worms, windmills, and dolphin dives. Nobody does head spins; some kid over in Connecticut broke his neck. The only time I ever see another girl breakin' is at the teen center. We challenge each other, a circle forming around us. It lasts all of a minute and ends in a draw. I never see her again.

Based on what I like to do, wear, and think about, on the cusp of becoming a teenager, I start to hear it: *tomboy*.

No, I think. *I'm a girl, I'm me, and this is what I like.*

I'm twelve, thirteen, and the messages from the outside world get louder.

My friend's mom looks me over in her kitchen.

"You like playing outdoors; you're such a little tomboy."

I'll be punished for sassing back, so I go neutral.

"I like sports."

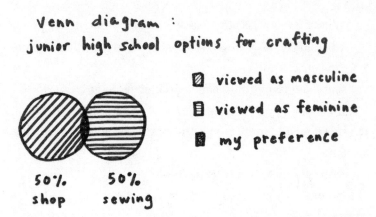

Venn diagram:
junior high school options for crafting

▨ viewed as masculine
▤ viewed as feminine
▨ my preference

50% shop   50% sewing

"Be a kid as long as you can." She looks relieved her daughter isn't me.

The term *tomboy* appears in the mid-sixteenth century: a rude and boisterous boy. By the turn of that century, *tomboy* shifts: boisterous girls who act like boys. By the mid-nineteenth century, *tomboy* is a blunt instrument of patriarchy and white supremacy: young women are urged to go outdoors and be healthy in order to birth strong babies to counter the influx of immigrants who will take over America.

Tomboy is for white girls; mainstream society has never protected or encouraged black girls—the implication: *Why bother, black girls aren't ladies.* By the mid-twentieth century, *tomboy* reverts to describing independent (white) girls who like "boy stuff," with a caveat: *Mama, don't let your tomboys grow up to be lesbians.*

Tomboy is someone else's ideas about my gender. *Tomboy* assumes I want to be a boy, implies boys are better—like Jo in *Little Women* or Scout in *To Kill a Mockingbird*.

What little boy is called "sissy" as a compliment?

Once she leaves girlhood, she leaves the *tomboy* label behind.

Tomboy is finite.

Once you grow out of *tomboy*, there's no *tomteen*.

If I don't buy into the either/or of things, don't stick to the feminine script, sooner or later someone's going to call me a lesbian.

Same girl, now in a woman's body.

No one, save my high school boyfriends, is surprised when I come out.

Come out as what? I am presented with only two options: bisexual or lesbian. Bisexual sounds confusing to me; if you're in a monogamous relationship, how do you maintain a fluid identity? Lesbian. That's just ridiculous. A lesbian is someone from Lesbos; no ancestor of mine came through Greece. A Ukrainian or a Lithuanian would make more sense.

My first girlfriend picks me out of a lineup at my college pre-orientation. S— is a junior, a self-described out, proud butch dyke, and she plants a flag in me. I like the attention.

I am *slightly* dating an ex-boyfriend until S— presents an ultimatum: lose him, keep her. I ditch him, which is easy because on a date during the Hill-Thomas hearings, only one of us believes Anita Hill.

S—'s dorm walls are a paean to all things lesbian. She nudges me to come out—to my new college friends, my family, my oldest friends, the registrar, the librarian. "I only date out dykes," she says. It's been three weeks since we met.

S—'s parents visit and the lesbian propaganda disappears.

"It upsets them," she says, retaping her ACT UP postcard of two women kissing.

"You hide, but you demand that I be an out lesbian?"

"I am out. You don't understand them."

"That sounds really hard." My tenderness surprises me.

"It bites." She looks genuinely sad.

I may be falling in love.

Once sepia, sex is a radiant ROYGBIV. I overlook the hypocrisy.

I call my mom for advice. "Should I get her four roses, one for each week? Or a single rose for our month anniversary? Or is that cheap and I should do a half dozen?"

"Do the four? That seems nice." My mom offers to send money.

"Can I call you tomorrow? S— is on the other line."

S— has called to break up with me. I sit sobbing on my single bed. I call my mom.

"How can a woman be so cruel? I thought sisterhood was powerful!" I'm bawling into the phone.

———

"Like, what are you?"

First question in college is, Which dorm? Second is, What's your major? Third is, How do you define your sexuality? Lamont. Double major in women's studies and theater. Not straight.

But it's backward to self-identify with that which I am not. I wouldn't say I'm not black, not Catholic, not male, as true as those things are.

I kind of like *dyke*. It's one syllable and has the satisfying, plosive *k* sound—the reason why, among curse words, *fuck* is a fan favorite. *Dyke* is also what men lean out of car windows to yell at my girlfriend and me holding hands. *Carpet muncher* doesn't sound appealing to anyone who isn't a vacuum cleaner, and it just refers to sex.

Homosexual seems too midcentury, self-loathing, like *The Children's Hour*: forbidden love, tragic ends, which doesn't fit how I feel at all.

Homo sounds great: it's quick, rhymes, and reclaims *homosexual* without being antiquated. But using it in a sentence— "No, that's not my boyfriend, I'm a homo"—doesn't roll off my tongue.

Gay is a good word, simple and happy. A drawback is its erasure of women, the way "hey guys" is a male term that envelops female presence. I sometimes use *gay*.

Queer liberates. A queer person exists fluidly on a spectrum of sexuality and identity not just outside of straight but without parameters. But . . . *queer* is insular; queers use it, but the people I need to tell won't understand. They'll ask me what I mean. *Why that word?* People who haven't been slurred against often don't grasp the power of reclaiming a word.

Tomboy is a most innocuous slur. Girls don't notice the patriarchal assumption that to take on male traits bestows power; girls think, *Cool, I'll take more power.* The word is so sneakily subcutaneous that reclaiming *tomboy* is apt to be mistaken for embracing it.

I do like coming out. We make queer look cool. Some women try it on to be in the glow of cool; some hope it sticks, others pray it won't. It's the ones who pray they aren't who are. The curious women trade on it, an eventual footnote of a person of mystery.

At Thanksgiving, I consider my options: *Please pass the queer some turkey?* Or more subdued? Yes. I ask my dad and stepmom if we can talk.

They hover on the edge of their bed, alarmed. I face them from the burgundy velour-cushioned rocking chair. It tilts back and forth, putting me literally on edge.

"Okay. I'm dating a woman." My sentences meander awkwardly and aimlessly.

To my surprise my dad is visibly relieved. "I thought you were going to tell us you have AIDS."

Accidentally, a decent strategy: first, terrify them.

"Freud says everyone's bisexual," he says, and they both nod.

"Are you bisexual?" *Have I underestimated them?*

"No."

"No."

My dad's eyes look full. Is he going to say he loves me no matter what?

"Keep an open mind. You don't have to label yourself yet."

"Can I tell my sisters and one grandma?"

"There's no reason to talk about your sex life with them." *My lefty parents are the vanguard of "Don't Ask, Don't Tell."*

I can't identify even one person who was out or perhaps concealed queerness on *any* side of my family. But I know my grandma will be in my corner. When I tell her in the spring, she leaves the world's greatest unconditional love message on my voice mail. I share it with my friends wanting to tell their families, too, that sometimes there's a rainbow.

Needless to say, my dad's reaction is a gut punch. I tell him, "You could say, 'I love you; I support you.'"

"I do," he says, "I'm sad your life will be difficult. It's a harder road."

"So get out there and help make the road smoother."

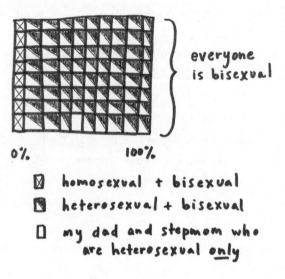

I'm out long before queerness is a trend, a rite of passage, or a party trick that means nothing but turns on voyeurs. But I'm not on the front line of any fight. I'm admired for being out—at a women's college, what did I stand to lose? Turbulence in my family would subside. No one kicked me out. No one beat me. No one picked me up at a bar and tied me to a post until the life ran out of me. I didn't have a god to abandon me. It was all going to be okay.

In my dorm's dining room, a coterie lingers after dinner regularly to discuss the meaning of life. We cover the four essential topics: relationships, women we long to date, periods, and orgasms. We are young, so the personal is the personal; the political will come soon enough.

"You're a soft butch." A dyke is describing me to me. "Not femme, but not a stone-cold butch dyke."

"I don't like *butch*. Compared to what? Soft is weak."

Nobody in college calls me a tomboy; the girl playing outside with boys is gone. The woman, now a sexual being, is butch.

"It's your look, the way you walk."

"This is how I *walk*. This is how I *am*. It's not anything."

After a moment she asks, "How about *androgynous*?"

"Is that me?"

To be seen as neither or as both male and female is androgynous. I don't like it; is it a step up from *butch* and *tomboy* or more of the same?

Androgyny, among a community of women, a dozen years before the trans movement goes (relatively) mainstream, is a dating commodity. When it settles in that it's not "tom-man," just a less identifiable performance of gender, the label feels less freighted and I don't fight it.

—————

I am twenty-five. My hair is short. I'm wearing black pants, a white shirt, a luminescent baby-blue jacket, lug-soled boots, and a tampon. I feel fly in my corporate casual attire. I'm an associate producer in the news department of the two-year-old Fox News Channel. Queer, female, and a Democrat, I am the outlier's pet outlier. There are three other out lesbians—and one closeted future lesbian. I fall in love with the future lesbian. It's very "Don't Ask, Don't Tell" at Fox.

I'm working on an hour-long TV special on JFK and the Bay of Pigs invasion. We've booked Kennedy biographer Arthur Schlesinger. He's a trim, white-haired white man with a floppy bow tie. In the interview, my producer asks him questions while I scribble notes. She asks if I want to ask him a question. I do, and, mercifully, I hold my own.

We are waiting for his car, which is nowhere to be seen. I am standing by a wall of windows, making small talk with Mr. History, making a go of it, but clearly out of my depth.

He's talking and I'm nodding, hoping the car will arrive, which it doesn't.

"Must be a lot of traffic," I say helpfully.

"Yes," he agrees, and to fill the silence he commences another stage of small talk. "Where did you go to college?"

"Smith College." At the very least, he'll know I'm not a dum-dum.

"Is Smith College coed now?"

Arthur Schlesinger thinks I'm a man, ergo Smith must be coed. Maybe through cataracts, I could pass for a fourteen-year-old boy. In Arthur Schlesinger's eyes, perhaps I am a wunderknabe, *producing an hour of television on the Bay of Pigs.*

Arthur Schlesinger thinks I'm a man! Perhaps I am his first encounter with a woman with short hair and trousers. An irony: while waiting for his car to show up, I'm counting the minutes until I can go change my tampon.

"No." I choose my words. "Smith is not coed."

He's old guard. He didn't get the memo about androgyny.

pie chart two :
things that scared me when I was a girl + today

60 % Nazis
25 % white men
6 % white women
5 % unanticipated mice
4 % centipedes

☐ things viewed as masculine :
Nazis, white men, centipedes,
over half of all unanticipated mice

▨ things viewed as feminine :
white women, less than half of all unanticipated mice

In my late twenties, my straight friends engage in a marrying frenzy, even as the nation's resting bitch face is the Defense of Marriage Act. I'm often one of one or at most one of five out queers at these weddings. We recognize each other, the subtle or obvious semiotics of footwear, hairstyle, swagger, or flounce.

At one wedding I go to, the tables are named for geographic locations where the couple has vacationed or aspires to go, like Panama, Buenos Aires, Maldives. Our table is affectionately called the Gay Table. We are a destination. We laugh loudest, and the other guests stop by to tell us they envy our gay fun.

Is it a surprise I'm never asked to be a bridesmaid? Maybe I'm not close enough to my friends. Or we can't imagine me standing in a row of matching dresses, my idea of the sartorial ninth circle of hell—*treachery*.

The word *bridesmaid* is itself a disappointment, beginning with *bride* and ending with *maid*. I'd rather be called *groomswoman* or even *tomboy* than *maid* (or *handmaid, maiden, mermaid*) if linguistic push comes to definitive shove.

Maybe my friends think I'll stage a coup if paired with a groomsman. Or they'll sense my inherent dislike of marital traditions, like the patriarchy sandwich: Dad "gives her" to her husband. Maybe I'm not asked to be a bridesmaid because I ask questions that seem like I'm judging their choices. I mostly am.

"Are you going to keep your birth name?" I ask them all, even when I know the answer.

"I'll still use mine for work, but we want our family to share a last name."

"If he took your name, you'd all match. . . ."

"Yeeeaaaahhh, I know . . . This is just easier. I'll still use my maiden name for my career."

Maiden is mind-control reverse *tomboy* for heterosexuals. The fine print is carefully coded: marriage bestows womanhood. *Maiden* becomes *matron* and is disappeared into her husband's identity. How often do you see a museum donor referred to as a matron of the arts? I guess only men have money to burn.

I appreciate that when my parents wed, my mom kept her birth name and my dad kept his maiden name, and they took it a step further. A headline in the local newspaper read, "Couple Bucks Law by Giving Daughter Mother's Last Name." It was against the law. When they tried to give me my mom's last name, Miller (spoiler alert), my birth certificate remained blank for months as their petition traveled all the way up to the Massachusetts attorney general to eventually establish precedent. Afterward, children born to married parents with different last names could be given either last name.

Along with never being asked to be a bridesmaid, I've never been asked to be a godparent, though I've diapered a small army of babies. It could be because I'm an atheist, or my friends think I hate all labels. Or it may be just that I seem noncommittal. I mostly am.

Androgyny these days is evident everywhere, perhaps even over-shadowed by the ever-broadening definitions of gender and the popularization of *nonbinary*. My androgyny feels less pro-nounced these days. Maybe we're finally ready to trade in *tomboy* for *a-gender.*

A love of piano is a-gender.

A love of horses is a-gender.

A love of running is a-gender.

A love of cooking is a-gender.

A love of puzzles is a-gender.

A love of gardens is a-gender.

A love of walking is a-gender.

A love of jaywalking is a-gender.

A love of broccoli is a-gender.

A love of love is a-gender.

A love of "the end" is a-gender.

ALOOF
ELIZABETH SPIERS

My freshman year of college I went to a lot of parties and didn't talk very much. Some of this was garden-variety shyness; I didn't know anyone at Duke going in and didn't even visit the campus until after I got admitted. It was the only school I applied to, and I didn't have a good sense of what it would be like. So I arrived from a small town in rural Alabama to what I quickly discovered was essentially a New England boarding school exported to North Carolina, full of people with ungodly amounts of money and networks of people they already knew on campus. I came with freshly signed student loan agreements and a southern accent, the latter of which was unexpectedly out of place for a school south of the Mason-Dixon Line. (Turns out, 99 percent of my classmates were from New York—or it seemed that way, at any rate.)

So I spent a lot of time that year trying to figure out where I fit, and with whom. My primary mode of doing that was observing and listening—and that was easy to do. I'm short, quiet, and I don't stand out in a crowd, and I often prefer it that way. So I had conversations with friends one-on-one, but in group settings, I was the "quiet one." Which people tended to assume meant I was either scary or scared of everyone else.

But I tended to be a lot more vocal in class. I had opinions and was engaged in what I was learning, and I liked provocative discussions. (And of course, I wanted to get something out of the education that was costing me the GDP of a small country in debt.) Toward the end of one seminar, a professor had us pair up to give each other feedback about how we were contributing to the class, and I was paired with an acquaintance who later became a close friend. He was one of the New Yorkers who came to Duke with a network of friends from high school and bafflingly referred to his hometown of Manhattan as "the City," as if there were no other densely populated metropolitan areas anywhere in the country.

His feedback to me was less about the class than his impression of me generally. "You have to stop being intimidated by everyone," he said. "You can compete with anyone here." It went uncomfortably into Stuart Smalley territory—"You're smart enough, you're good enough"—and I was relieved that he didn't suggest that we wrap up the session with a self-esteem-building affirmation. I knew he was well intentioned and meant it to be some kind of pep talk, but I didn't really need it. I wasn't intimidated by people; I was just quiet.

I realized later that he assumed I was timid and intimidated because he viewed me as someone who didn't really have power or standing at a place like Duke. I came from a working-class background, without the money or connections my classmates started with. I had the smarts, sure, but what about all of these other things? If I was quiet, it must be a function of meekness or fear.

It's possible that my friend would have had the same impression if I had been a man instead of a woman, but I doubt it. I think he would have viewed a quiet man as intentional in his reserve.

I left college, got a job—in the City—and spent a long time building a career in media and doing things that, at least externally, appeared to be the opposite of what someone who was fearful or meek would do. I had brash, snarky opinions that I made public. I took risks. I did some smart things and a lot of dumb things—decisively and without hesitation in both cases. I recovered from most of the dumb things and tried to learn from them. And by the time I was in my thirties, I had some professional standing and a reputation as someone who was not easily intimidated, even when I should have been. I was still reserved in social settings, but now no one assumed that I was timid.

The people who knew me weren't bothered by the fact that I was quiet. But the people who didn't were. Suddenly, my reserve meant something else. I obviously wasn't shy or afraid of people, so I had to be *aloof.*

I've been called variations on *strong* that are flattering and variations on *silent* that are neutral or negative, but I've never been referred to as "the strong, silent type." Somehow, a five-foot biracial forty-two-year-old woman fails to embody the archetype the way, say, Gary Cooper does. But I don't think it's my height or my age or race that makes the difference, or even my utter failure to produce a career as a legendary Hollywood film star, a development that surprised no one. It's the fact that Gary Cooper and strong and silent people like Gary Cooper have one thing in common. They're men.

Strong, silent women exist. Yet women who exhibit emotional control (women are always emotional!) and are taciturn in social situations (and they never shut up!) don't get the benefit of being "strong, silent types." In women, that alchemy of reserve and resolve makes a lot of people uncomfortable. They are people at once feminine and at odds with traditional ideas of what femininity connotes.

If you've ever stood in a group of people and managed not to deploy your vocal cords in service of telegraphing an idea to the humans around you, you may think, *Well, that's just silly. I was just being polite! I was listening, which is ostensibly a nice thing to do, and something that people often appreciate!*

I understand your logic, but I have to ask: Are you a woman? Because if you are, there are a variety of aspects of this behavior that may be offensive to people, especially if those people happen to be men. I know this isn't fair, but here's an impression you might unwittingly create:

You are not saying anything because you're sitting there quietly judging everyone else.

The most remarkable thing is that you can earn this critique by doing absolutely nothing. I know you may have reasons for being quiet. Especially if you're not naturally a talker and are not laboring under the impression that if noise stops coming out of the front part of your head, you'll die on the spot because it affects your breathing. Maybe you're shy! Maybe you don't have anything of particular import to say at the moment! Maybe you have laryngitis!

But evidence of an actual superiority complex isn't a prereq-
uisite. All you have to do is put yourself in a social situation, be a
woman, and keep your mouth shut while everyone else is talking.

People who are not quiet often assume that quiet women use
most of their brainpower to formulate negative opinions about
everyone else and not to, say, wonder whether that mole on their
right arm might be cancerous, feel sudden anxiety about three-
month-old emails they forgot to reply to, or consider Wiles's
proof of Fermat's Last Theorem. It does not occur to them that
these quiet women may even be listening to what others are
saying and thinking about those things, which, Occam's razor,
takes far less brainpower than nihilistically picking someone
apart for sport. The silent lady is just assumed to be a judgmental asshole.

I'm convinced that this sort of thing never happened to Gary
Cooper. When Gary Cooper went to a cocktail party and pro-
jected steely resolve while producing zero decibels of sound and
sipping a Gibson in a way that was strong and, by extension, very
manly, I doubt anyone thought, or said, "Did you see the way
Gary just stood in his corner, quietly judging everyone else? Sure,
he's famous and I like his work, but he's just so . . . aloof."

Men have natural standing when they're inherently quiet. As
women, we have to explain ourselves. I'm reserved, very even-
keeled temperamentally, and given a choice between observing
and talking, I tend to observe. When I was a kid, I used to spy
on my parents when they had friends over because I wanted to
understand adults and hear what they were saying. I like sitting at
bars alone with a novel, in part to read the novel and have a glass
of wine, but also because I enjoy picking up ambient conversation and thinking about what other people's lives are like. My

personal spirit animal is a fly on the wall. But being an observer is a modality directly at odds with being a speaker.

And observation is a kind of distancing. It creates an implied remove: space between the observer and the observed. Is it accurate to say that aloofness, applied accurately, is indicative of some kind of distancing? Sure. But that doesn't mean detachment is inherently indicative of aloofness, which itself implies a form of lightweight malice—an intentional remove driven by the observer's feelings of superiority. So the act of observing, by itself, isn't the problem. It's who's doing the observing, and why.

You might think that being an observer would be easier for women, given how frequently we're told to shut up by misogynists. But even misogynists want women to speak in contexts where they're expected to serve as validators. Express insufficient appreciation or support for a dominant point of view and it's considered a sin of omission. And it's not enough to be polite; you must be enthusiastic. You must smile. If you're incapable of effervescence, you could at least try to muster a few bubbles. Your participation is required when it benefits someone else, and your delivery matters. Any woman who's ever failed to endorse the idea of a male colleague and been told she's not a team player as a result can attest to this.

I once met a technology reporter whose byline I knew at a book party and exchanged a few pleasantries, only to have him drunkenly scream at me hours later because in his words, I didn't "seem very impressed" with him when we were introduced. (I was neither impressed nor unimpressed; he was one of probably twenty people I met that night and we only spoke for a minute or two.) He was furious at me, and at none of the men he'd met at the same party who responded to him in exactly the same way.

In his view, I was not a human with my own agency and history and personality; I was just a potential reflecting pool for him to evaluate his own self-worth, and as a woman, I was expected to be fawning, effervescent, possibly flirtatious, and definitely subordinate. Even though, professionally speaking, we were peers, I should have been impressed with him and expressed it in a way that was loquacious, warm, and made him feel better about himself. The word he used to describe me later? *Aloof.*

I try to imagine what it would be like to move about in the world with this kind of mentality, where every time I meet someone of the opposite sex, I expect him to say or do something that validates me personally and/or professionally. In this scenario, I introduce myself, and my would-be validator's eyes always widen. "Oh, wow," he says, every time. "I love your work." Then he coquettishly bats his eyelashes at me, and . . . dear God, I can't.

I can't even imagine it in a way that's credible, because it's inherently ridiculous. And I don't even think having that sense of entitlement would be empowering. It must be exhausting to need members of the opposite sex to assure you that you're professionally competent, sexually appealing, and irresistibly charismatic all the time. How do men live like this?

And why is it so offensive to them when we have the temerity to behave the way they often do, like normal human beings who are not 24-7 paragons of vivaciousness and reserve the right to exist while not speaking? My armchair theory is that in a man, reserve—being taciturn, selectively or wholly—is viewed as a form of control. If a man isn't yammering incessantly every five minutes, it's indicative of intelligence and restraint. He's not saying anything because he's waiting to say the perfect thing at the perfect time. He is not shy, or dumb, or introverted, or just zoning out while others spew endless boring words out of their perpetually open faceholes. He's just thinking brilliant appropriate thoughts, and there's nothing antisocial about it. It's a given that he's acting in good faith and should be given the benefit of the doubt.

The motives and actions of women, on the other hand, are to be viewed with skepticism. This has been true possibly since the beginning of time but definitely since centuries ago, when some guy (obviously a guy) scribbled down a now-canonical story about a man and a woman, the latter of whom consumed a bad apple on the dubious advice of a talking snake, and that, the story goes, is why we have pain and evil in the world. (The man ate the apple, too, but essentially did nothing wrong because, really, it was his wife's fault, and even centuries ago, men routinely blamed their own dumb mistakes on women.)

And what was Eve's sin here? I'm no theologian, but I grew up Southern Baptist and was subjected to this story repeatedly in my impressionable youth: Eve disobeyed God. But secondarily, Eve arrogantly decided to use her own brain and make a judgment call instead of taking orders from men. Eve exhibited agency and control. And, well, look what happened.

Nothing is scarier to men than women exhibiting control of our own lives. Women in the workforce are scary because we're financially independent and can now live without economic subsidization by our (always male) partners, and we can operate in positions of power over men. Women with access to contraception and abortion are scary because we have sexual agency and can have sex for no other reason than that we enjoy unadulterated pleasure. Women with access to education are scary because we're empowered to use our intellect to navigate the world with skills and critical thinking that are conducive to success and upward mobility. And women who can vote and run for office facilitate our own ability to assert and utilize control in all of these realms.

Silence is a form of control, and it's easy to recognize that in men and in male narratives. In women's narratives silence is usually viewed as a product of oppression or censorship. We're silent because we're conditioned to be, or because someone isn't allowing us to speak. These narratives are not false: self-silencing is something we learn to do in childhood because we're told stories about what women can and can't do and which actions are safely in the realm of the acceptable.

In that sense, silence is often rewarded for women when it's interpreted as compliance.

The twist for those of us who are viewed as aloof is that our silence is viewed as noncompliant because we already have some other kind of standing. This is where the "strong" in "strong, silent type" comes in. Strong women—and I use the word broadly to mean women who exert any kind of power or influence—are doubly expected to be validators because on some level we have to apologize for allowing ourselves control and agency. If we're in positions of power, we are expected to go to great lengths to make others, and men in particular, feel comfortable with it.

In my case, I've been in positions of leadership and had fancy job titles. I also write opinion pieces in large outlets, and they're, well, *opinionated*. I am not meek.

But I am a bit shy, which is not the same thing. I struggle with anxiety, and this is exacerbated by the fact that I'm incorrigibly drawn to anxiety-inducing situations: working on risky

projects, publicly criticizing powerful people who could probably destroy me, pursuing professional trajectories that offer no financial stability, living in New York generally. I also enjoy being
around other humans despite the fact that I have social anxiety,
and I have to steel myself sometimes before I go to a party. If
I were better designed physiologically and psychologically, my
risk aversity would correlate to my anxiety, but it doesn't. I run
toward the explosion, every time. And I sometimes have panic
attacks en route. I know why this is confusing to people. It's confusing to me, and probably doesn't speak well of my capacity for
self-preservation.

The upshot of this is that on more than one occasion, I meet
people who've read something I've written and they expect me to
shove an opinion down their throat, loudly, and act like a boss
(loud, authoritarian, or commanding the room in an explosion
of charisma and charm) because I'm, professionally speaking, the
boss of something. When I deviate from that expectation, they
take it personally. They think my silence is about them. They
can't read me as someone who is both strong (in the sense described above, with agency in certain areas) and quiet because
it's not a combination that's valued or recognized in women the
way it is in men. It's aberrant behavior. There are no women Gary
Coopers. There are only aloof bitches who are busy judging everyone else, as evidenced by their silence and refusal to apologize
for their standing.

My husband and I met at work, and I was his boss. So needless to
say, it didn't bother him that I had professional standing or strong
opinions. (That would have come up.) He understood instantly

that if I wasn't saying anything in a group conversation it wasn't because I was being self-absorbed or judgmental—aloof—it was because I was listening and analyzing, and we'd talk about it later.

Our son, who is now three and a half, is, as far as we can tell, more extroverted than all of the extroverts we know put together. If you ever meet him, he will climb in your lap and talk your ear off about everything he saw, touched, tasted, heard, and smelled today, and it will not matter that he has never laid eyes on you before. I sometimes worry that should the clichéd kidnapper in a van ever present himself proffering candy, Ford will be the first kid into the van, enthusiastic and ready to tell the nice man all about the spiderweb he found on his science outing.

He's also fiercely independent and observant. He notices everything. I imagine that at some point, that will also result in his developing the sense of skepticism his father and I share, and I won't have to worry about the kidnapper vans so much.

And of course, I can't determine how he thinks about and remembers his mother as he gets older and becomes an adult himself and I eventually cease to exist in any formal sense, except maybe as a Wikipedia footnote alongside full entries about Gary Cooper and Presidents Who've Been Impeached. But I wouldn't hate it if, in addition to being a loving mother who did her best to make candy-laden van drivers as unappealing as possible, he remembered me as the strong, silent type.

EXOTIC
EMILY SANDERS HOPKINS

On the "race" line of my marriage certificate it says "mulatto." That's what the ladies at the courthouse insisted on putting there, before asking me how to spell it. While the younger woman clacked on her noisy typewriter from the 1970s, the older woman stood over her shoulder checking the work, maybe curious to see the exotic word in print. My husband-to-be and I stood awkwardly, shifting from foot to foot in the cramped basement office. They didn't ask him his race; they just typed "white." (Maybe race is just what you look like to white people.)

As you probably know, *mulatto* comes from the word *mule*, that animal resulting from the mating of donkey and horse, two distinct species. To my mind, many words used to describe non-white people have that same *mulatto* feel—*octoroon*, *quadroon*, *Negro*, *colored*, *mixed*: they are flavors, rare hybrids, embarrassing and fancy at the same time.

Half of me is glad it says "mulatto" on our wedding certificate, because it's true and it's funny and it's a tangible memento from an era so outrageous, it almost sounds made up. But I have more than one half, maybe more than two, even. The white southern girl part of me thinks, *Oh, lighten up. Those poor women in the basement never thought it was an insult.* But then there's the part of me that wonders, *Why does my wedding certificate have to be marred this way? Why did I have to have our wedding day colored by that reminder that I'm a second-class citizen to somebody, even if it's just somebody in the past?*

This was in the little town of Princeton, West Virginia, in 2007. It's the town my white mother grew up in, although it has grown so much uglier since then. Why are all the Wendy's and KFCs and ostentatious bank branches set at weird angles to the roads? From that central snarl of retail and fast-food trash architecture, there are modest streets lined with little houses, one of which my grandfather grew up in, shooting off into the wooded hills, along with unregulated roads with names like Cornbread Ridge, Possum Hollow, and Old Pepsi Plant Road. Trailers, trucks, cinder-block houses, leafy glades where retired coal miners live out the remainder of their days. My grandparents' grand brick house, a gorgeous Georgian thing built in the 1950s but modeled after the house my grandmother grew up in Emporia, Virginia, used to have the whole mountain to itself, on more than a hundred acres, but over the years, my grandparents had to sell off the land to cover business losses, and now the house is encroached upon on three sides by McMansions.

If you told Granddaddy your last name, he could tell you all about your clan and would never forget you were a Blankenship or a Lilly, the way an astrologer will never forget that you're a

Scorpio. Granddaddy would also latch on to his first perspicacious verdict about a person—they would never work hard, they were brilliant with horses, they were decent country folk—and worry it like a bone over the next years and decades. He told me many times, "There are good blacks and there are bad blacks, and your father was not the good kind." There was a stretch of several years in his eighties when Granddaddy had a bee in his bonnet about Muhammad Ali changing his name from Cassius Clay. He would corner me at family gatherings and tell me yet again about what a great man the original Cassius Clay, a Kentucky politician and abolitionist in the nineteenth century, had been and what a friend to black people. "Now why would that boxer want to change his name from that?" he asked me, truly hurt and perplexed. And Grandmama once said to me, as if she'd wrestled with it and arrived at a magnanimous solution to an old conundrum: "Do you know, nobody is *all black.* Everyone has a little bit of white in them."

The next town over, Bluefield, used to be home to more millionaires than any other town in America, legend has it. Coal mine owners. One of my first jobs, in the 1980s, was in Bluefield at a fancy clothing boutique, where the owner told me stories about the coal-rich past when coal barons' wives would shop with stacks of hundred-dollar bills in their purses. My mother told me stories of the men whose faces were always black with coal dust impervious to soap and water. To me, coal barons *and* coal miners were exotic.

My nearly all-white boarding school, founded in 1844, was originally called the Virginia Female Institute, which sounds a little like a place where Confederate men study your vagina. During the Civil War it was in fact requisitioned as a Confederate military hospital. When the war was over and it returned to being a school, it was given a better name: Stuart Hall, after headmistress Flora Stuart, wife of General J. E. B. "Jeb" Stuart, who had commanded a cavalry unit in the Confederate army.

Stuart Hall didn't enroll black girls until 1973, twelve years before I arrived. They did so only at the insistence of one righteous alumna—Lucy Venable, class of 1944, who endowed the scholarship that helped me attend the school.

We had an inferiority complex at our school. We knew we weren't as fancy or as rich as the girls at our nearby sister schools—Foxcroft, Chatham Hall, St. Katherine's, Madeira, even the slightly raggedy St. Margaret's. Ours was not a hard school to gain admission to—many of us were dropouts from other schools, myself included, or had been sent away from home by parents who didn't have the time to parent. The tuition and board were something like $14,000 per year. Our nickname for our school was "Stuart Hell." I'd been expelled from a ritzy coed Quaker school for almost never attending class or turning in homework. The daily recitation of the Lord's Prayer in the auditorium at Stuart Hall, the "burrito nights," the dimly lit little swimming pool in the basement, and the creaky halls and ghost stories all struck me as shabby but lovable.

We had an annual fund-raising tradition: Slave Day. Seniors bought juniors to be their slaves for one day. Juniors were lined up on the stage in the auditorium. The seniors sat in the front row, close enough to inspect us and make their bids. The rest of the school filled the other seats as spectators. Your name was called. You stood, turned left and right. There was laughter and talking. The seniors lifted auction paddles or hands, just like in a real auction.

There were eighteen of us in the junior class. Most of my best friends were in my class. Reynolds, the granddaughter of a very wealthy longtime Florida state senator, had Ralph Lauren model looks and a beautiful set of collarbones and shoulders—wide but sleek. Reynolds was our swim team champ. Before coming to Stuart Hall, she had competed to make the Junior Olympics in the butterfly stroke, but, despite all her sacrifices, effort, and willpower, she had missed qualifying by a fraction of a second. On the heels of that disappointment, she arrived at Stuart Hall with the idea that she would dedicate herself now to something else entirely: school.

Emma Dare, from South Carolina, was a petite mother hen to the younger girls, with whom she spent most of her time. She had the best southern accent of us all. (I have a theory about southerners putting on their accents to some extent, consciously and to signal status as southerners. I don't think northerners put on their accents or push them to the max on purpose the way southerners do, partly because southerners are alive to their own glamour and Yankees aren't. The northern equivalent of *Garden & Gun* magazine would have to be called *Fleece & Complaining* or *Traffic & Cheese*.) Emma Dare had been in residence at Stuart Hall since eighth grade, and her dorm room was like the apartment of a twenty-five-year-old, I thought—fully stocked with neat stacks of extra sheets and rarely used items like ice skates and a sleeping bag. She drank water from a white plastic cup decorated with her name and balloons and flowers in colored marker.

There were two kinds of people in the world, I realized at Stuart Hall: the kind that had personalized drinking cups and the kind that didn't. I was in the latter category because I could never do the planning—purchasing the cup and the indelible markers, sitting down to execute the design, keeping track of the cup, remembering to drink water. Emma Dare also exercised nightly, doing vigorous twists with her hands balled into fists—like a woman in a 1940s movie about girls in the secretarial pool trying to land rich husbands—in order to slim her waist, she said. I shook my head in wonder. What dedication! What faith in a remedy so seemingly incremental! And anyway, she was already very slim—who knew how? I preferred to sculpt my own figure through more dramatic and satisfying methods, like deprivation and laxatives and vomiting up dinner.

Brannon, also a junior, was another of my best friends. She looked just like her handsome father, who visited on Parents' Weekend, with his same fat beak of a nose, lantern jaw, and shocking light-blue eyes. Brannon loved rock music and drinking and boys. I can picture her now in her tie-dyed tee, at her leisure in the TV room. When I said, "Who wants to see who can go the longest without eating any food?" Brannon said, "Sure, why not?" I won, at nine days (over which I lost fourteen pounds!), living on just water and gumballs, but Brannon came in a close second, giving up after something like three days, after which I just kept fasting for the thrill of it.

Another of my best friends was Jenny, from Louisiana, who was about six feet tall and the spitting image of Mariel Hemingway—blonde hair and heavy dark eyebrows, long limbs and the bad posture of the very tall. She held a patent already on something to do with an orthopedic implant—at least, that was the word on the street. She lettered in every sport you could letter in and was effortlessly good at things on and off the field, but she worried about being thin enough. She worried a lot in general, I think. I remember walking into her room and finding her lying on her back, her shirt lifted up. With her hands she was carefully feeling the sharp valley where her ribs ended and her concave belly began. I joined her on the floor and checked my own valley, which wasn't steep enough either, in my book. We must improve, we concluded. No more food!

Occasionally, Jenny would say something I considered racist in my hearing, for instance about how terrible the black people in Louisiana were, and I would bristle and even, in one instance, confront her. "But Emily," she retorted, "you just don't know what you're talking about. I'm speaking from experience." And it was true, I didn't know what she was talking about.

Floppy-haired Heath and I were, I think, the only Democrats in our class. Once our US history teacher gave our class a quiz to determine where we fell on the ideological spectrum. The questions were mostly about how much workers should be able to organize, how much they should be able to demand, and how much power to restrict or protect those demands the federal government should have. The right answers seemed patently obvious to me. To answer in any other way than I had answered, I felt, would mean you were a greedy jerk. My answers revealed, according to our teacher, that I was a socialist. To my surprise, many of my friends scored conservative.

Robin, in the class below us, was a hilariously funny old soul from Tennessee. Short, with fuzzy dark hair and a face that sometimes reminded you of an Irish washerwoman's and sometimes of a young Russian empress's, as in an old painting—bright eyes, pretty little mouth, round face. This wasn't her first rodeo. And yet, in all her lifetimes, she hadn't picked up punctuality and organization. She did not have a cup decorated with her name. My memory is that Robin, who was adopted, was often rumpled or in a fix, which I loved, because wasn't I always rumpled and in a fix too? Beneath her cherubic, freckled cheeks and cloud of dark hair was a mind that was sharp, discriminating, and certain. She had an air of biding her time. There are people like that in life. When you are with them, you get flashes of some other, more momentous future that they will become involved in later.

Robin and I liked to sit in her room and play a game in which one person says something and then the next person has to say a sentence that has absolutely no connection—neither grammatical nor topical—to the thing the other person just said, and so forth. If I say, "I love to eat bananas," you better not say anything that has to do with any sort of food, fruit, plant, preference, self, or really even any statement of opinion. A good counter might be: "Wait! There are only seven minutes before the play begins!" Or: "General Lee surrendered at Appomattox." And then the next person's sentence better not have anything to do with the Civil War *or* fruit or preference or time or winning or losing or famous people or the theater. A good next entry might be: "The deep blue sea churned." And then the next person better not say anything about any place in nature, any description of movement, color, history, war, fruit, time, theater, sailing, or fame. It was harder than you'd think.

When my name was called on Slave Day, I walked onstage grinning and rolling my eyes. *What if nobody bids?* That fear stopped up my throat and made it hard for me to swallow. Someone bid five dollars. Then silence. Then someone else bid ten. In the end, I was relieved to be purchased for a modest but not pathetic amount of money by Donna, from Tennessee, president of the senior class, whom I idolized because of her adorable upturned nose, dark, Natalie Wood–esque looks, and steady gaze. It was a relief to be purchased by someone so popular. Or, on second thought, was it bad? Did it mean that she felt sorry for me and had just bought me to bump up my price as a favor?

After the auction, she made me come to her room and put on brown platform disco boots and a polyester Pucci-patterned dress and clean her toilet bowl. I had to wear the boots and the dress for the remainder of the day, and I teetered to my classes, laughing. Other juniors were decked out in silly costumes too. At least I didn't have to wear a T-shirt with an embarrassing or hateful statement scrawled across it. I can't remember if it was the posh Iranian senior who made the Jewish girl in the previous year's junior class wear a swastika, or if it was a Jewish senior who made a Muslim junior wear something anti-Muslim, but something disgraceful had happened the year before. I just remember that somehow a mention of Hitler was involved, and that there were raised eyebrows and objections and that the dean of students or headmaster had stepped in, disappointed in the show of bad taste. Slave Day was supposed to be good-natured.

We also had Juanita Club dinners, where we dressed up like "Mexican whores" and came down to the dining hall in miniskirts and lots of makeup. Dr. C, one of my English teachers, pulled me aside at the end of one Juanita Club dinner and told me with a twinkle in his eye that of all the girls, I would "be the most successful." It was meant to be a compliment, and I smirked back at him.

Occasional lewd remarks from teachers and professors, unwanted advances from strangers and friends, date rapes, anorexia and bulimia—all these common experiences shored us up and gave us glittering hard shells we could wear later into subsequent difficult situations: more date rapes, workplace sexual harassment, self-satisfied baby-boomer bosses, sinus infections, and 10Ks—protected by our own intimate understanding of the Real World. Someone later might mistake you for just an ignorant girl who didn't know what was up, but secretly (you could pull out your familiarity like a knife) you had all the knowledge and power of a double agent who had spent time behind enemy lines. I said something to this effect to my younger brother James recently (he's a white millennial), and he accused me of not being very "woke" and of belonging to a generation of women who let people get away with shit, in contrast to his generation's women, who are insisting on and achieving real change and better behavior. I was deeply offended and made him take it back, which he did because he's a good brother. How could he dare judge me, his black sister, as less woke than his pretty, white, thirtysomething girlfriends?

But it's true that we weren't scoring direct hits. We weren't taking people down. Today's young people go into battle with something other than tough calluses: they have a special optical tool, a lens that allows them to see the offense and entitlement and inequity at the bottom of every rule or utterance or grotesque Virginia yearbook photo and to pen screeds and takedowns that are read by thousands in a minute.

I might have been within my rights to complain about Slave Day, if I had thought that it was racist. But I didn't think it was racist. I thought it was racially embarrassing but just an old school tradition, one that definitely predated black students in attendance at the school. So why be churlish? Why tie something so innocent and fun (note: it wasn't that fun or innocent) to ugly history none of my classmates or I had anything to do with?

When I Facebook messaged Katreniah, one of two black girls in the class above mine, to ask what she remembered of Slave Day, she said she hadn't associated Slave Day with actual slavery either. "You just worried about who would buy you," she remembered.

While it makes sense to recoil from being called exotic, you can also trade on it, cash in on the difference between you and the self-centered viewer who is othering you. Who gets more mileage out of my being listed as a "mulatto" on my marriage certificate—the white ladies in the basement or me, writing this juicy account?

The summer after graduation, I lived at my mother and stepfather's house, as I had during all my summers of high school, only now I was eighteen and could do what I wanted. They were both trial lawyers and had seven children between them from previous marriages. We sisters were wild. We returned from our respective boarding schools and commenced sneaking cigarettes in their backyard, borrowing their Saabs and Audis, drinking their vodka and beer, going to house parties, and racking up their snack bar bill at the country club.

That summer I had my first love affair, with a boy named Kirk. In August Kirk confessed to me that he'd always wanted to date a black girl and was happy that now he could say he had. We were sitting on the stone steps outside the side porch at my mother and stepfather's large brick house. The bushes were the darkest green, and when Kirk called me a black girl, I was suddenly aware of myself leaning against the railing and how I might look to someone standing behind me. I couldn't think of anything to say back. What could I say? I was black, and if he'd always wanted to date a black girl, then he'd always wanted to date a black girl.

His comment sucker punched me, though. Here I was thinking that we were two people half in love, kindred spirits, not two representatives of types checking off boxes. Maybe I should have told him that I'd always wanted to date a big dumb blond jock, a C student at Princeton, an outside linebacker, a rosy-cheeked white boy with dark button eyes like an intelligent rodent's—a mouse down for whatever. I wonder if that would have stung, if I'd told him I'd always wanted someone—anyone—like him. But I didn't really consider him all that exotic, beyond that he was a boy. (Being exotic hurts worst when it's not mutual.)

How much of that gleeful acquisitive feeling—as if you're a collector of rare butterflies and they just keep landing in the center of your net—is *seemly* in a lover? Probably not very much at all! But sometimes I like to look down the long gallery of past boyfriends and just begin to stroll slowly, my hands clasped behind my back:

Boris. Boris was the most beautiful man I have ever seen in my life. He was black coffee–brown, six foot four or five, and had a massively muscled yet elegant body and practically perfect features—high cheekbones, shapely black eyebrows, and a straight nose with nostrils that flared like a bronze horse's. The insides of Boris's nostrils were bright red, for some reason. He was an outside linebacker too. One night he arrived at my house with a large silver pistol in his pocket and a handful of loose bullets, which rolled noisily down my slanted bedroom floor when he took his clothes off. We didn't discuss what the gun and bullets were for or why he'd brought them, but I remember feeling mildly flattered. Maybe they had something to do with me?

I dropped out of Williams College before my freshman year was even over and joined the army—thousands of fit seventeen-, eighteen-, and nineteen-year-olds on lockdown, being bossed around by a bunch of twenty-six-year-olds. It was a world of gravel and diesel and sexual tension. For a few weeks, I dated a small soldier who liked to insult me. He had narrow black eyes and brown hair that he slicked down from a side part. "You're the most flat-chested girl I've ever seen. I've never seen such small tits in my life," he said one night when I was squished into a tight black dress that flattened my medium-sized breasts. "You're not very smart, are you?" he said another time, when we lay together making out on the top bunk in his barracks room. His insults thrilled me. Did they mean that no matter how terrible I was, he would love me? This was a strange, new kind of romance! I'd never even considered the allure of abuse, but here it was on offer to me, as if on an outstretched platter, and I nibbled, intrigued. It only took me a few weeks to realize that his insults were always factually inaccurate and that it wasn't exciting to be insulted as much as it was tiresome.

After the army, when I was back in college in my home state of West Virginia, I dated Tim, the youngest of twenty-one children, all from the same parents. A third of his adult siblings still lived together in the house they'd grown up in, on a little hill right off a highway. His mother had been killed in a car accident at that very intersection, where you turned off the highway onto the small road that wound its way onto their mountain. I learned to shoot dice at his childhood house, against the outside cinder-block wall by the front door. And inside the house, I learned dominoes at the kitchen table from his older brother, who was in a wheelchair. Tim and I had almost no cultural touchpoints in common, it seemed at first. He had never read Jane Austen or the Brontë sisters' books or *A Separate Peace*, sci-fi, romance novels, astrology, philosophy. He didn't care about the fine points covered in the *Preppy Handbook*. I didn't know anything about football, business (his major), black food, black music, black culture and humor, or being one of twenty-one kids. But our differences made being together more romantic. He called me his "little white nigger," and I blushed.

My next boyfriend, a Polish math professor, wore suspenders and smoked a pipe and did math all day long. He was the same age as my mother. In the summers, he took me with him to his hometown on the shore of the Baltic Sea, to the tiny Soviet-era apartment his mother lived in. I spent the days walking through the forest and along the beach while he worked bent over a makeshift desk in our bedroom, on his paper for the applied mathematics journal that published him nearly every year. The first summer I went with him there, I read all of his mother's English-language books, except for *The Rise and Fall of the Roman Empire*. I read *The Eye* by Vladimir Nabokov, a book of Emily Dickinson poems, *The Swiss Family Robinson*, two early Faulkner novels (one called *Mosquitoes*, about a party boat of drinking friends that gets moored somewhere and the party grows melancholy and poetic, with an inverse relationship between the amount of activity on the boat and the profundity of the adjectives being used to narrate the nonaction), Proust's *In Search of Lost Time*, and three Ayn Rand novels. I read those Ayn Rand books very fast, gobbled them up, and I was briefly a brutal giant, a frightening, fearless iconoclast, my profile chiseled and my eye disdainful of everyone I could see or imagine, for their pathetic weaknesses. Why have weaknesses? Why make allowances? I should be great, I thought.

In the mornings, while he worked on his math, I would walk in the forest or along the beach. Or by the train tracks. When I was in the apartment, I would hear him shout to himself at his desk sometimes, "Oh Catherine! Catherine! I love you!" It was unpleasant having a boyfriend who shouted out another woman's name. It was like being the mousy protagonist in *Rebecca*, with dark glamour swirling around you, making you feel even mousier in contrast. I thought of killing myself by walking in front of the train. Andrzej was supposed to be asking his mother for her sapphire ring, to give to me as an engagement ring (we were already engaged, but without a ring), but I didn't think he had asked her yet. The Catherine he was always calling to had been a student of his at Rutgers, from a mafia family. He'd written love notes to her on her math exams and gotten in trouble for it and now, every other day or so, back in West Virginia and also here in Poland, we'd get crank calls, just someone breathing on the other end, then they'd hang up. Andrzej was sure it was connected to Catherine's family's mob ties. Who else could find him no matter how many times he moved or changed his phone number or went to Poland for three months?

When I look back at pictures of myself from those years, when I was in my teens and twenties, I am surprised at how ordinary I look. My white family members and classmates and even some of my boyfriends were constantly going on about how beautiful I was, how "striking" or "exotic," but what I see in the photographs is a run-of-the-mill light-skinned black girl. I was lucky, really, to get so much mileage out of average looks.

In my twenties, I connected for the first time with my seven siblings on my father's side. They all had the same mother, the woman our father had left my mother for, and they all wanted to know me and embrace me into the fold without reservation. I looked just like our grandmother Ida, they told me. They'd thought of me their whole lives. Some of them were old enough to remember the one time we'd met in our childhood, on a dark, rainy night in an Omelette Shoppe parking lot in Princeton, when they were driving north from Florida in a station wagon. I'd been eight years old. Amani was six, Aquil was four, Abebe was two, and Qari was a baby and had vomited in the car. Their mother held the sick baby and smiled kindly at me, asking how I was. The smell of vomit filled my nose as I sat in the back seat while our parents talked outside on the wet pavement. Then we got out of the car and Aquil and Abebe, in matching blue-and-green plaid shirts (which made me think, *Black kids must tend to wear plaid*), leaned against the restaurant's plate glass window. I stood next to my stepfather and father, eavesdropping on their conversation. My stepfather was asking my father if he hated all white people. I wished they would talk about me instead. Then it was time to leave and my father gathered me up for a hug and whispered in my ear, "I love you, baby." That was forty years ago, and I haven't seen him since.

I have talked with him a handful of times on the phone, most recently when I was at my brother Jamil's house over Thanksgiving. On the phone with him, I always speak in a monotone and offer almost no information, no succor. I know it's mean of me, but I can't break myself of it. This time our father was calling from a halfway house, and my siblings remarked later how odd he'd sounded, how the cadence of his voice reminded them of other addicts they'd heard. I don't usually tell my mother these kinds of anecdotes because it is too embarrassing, for both of us. How perfect that my Muslim-convert black father, her college lover, ended up so low. Instead, I brag to her about my siblings, who are universally brilliant and good-looking.

Recently, one of my relatives on the white side of my family called to tell me about a lunch she'd had with several black women. "They have this whole culture and way of being that I know nothing about!" she said to me. "Yes," I replied, half angry at her cluelessness and also half amused. "Are you just figuring this out now?"

I recently returned to Stuart Hall for a visit. My old friend and classmate Reynolds and I walked slowly down the hallway that starts at the auditorium doors and leads past a stairwell to the dorms and down to the subterranean dining room. Outside the auditorium, there were folding tables set up, topped with student history projects featuring marshmallow Peeps set into elaborate cardboard models of historically significant scenes—a concentration camp, Tiananmen Square, and I can't remember what else. The concentration camp scene in particular is seared into my brain with its little red swastikas—painted in what, red nail polish?—and the blue marshmallow Peeps lying on cots made of toothpicks, rounded up in a line facing a firing squad, piled up in a corner . . .

"Reynolds," I said, "isn't this in sort of bad taste?"

"Oh gawd," she said, rolling her eyes at the little scenes. I took some photos with my iPhone and thought of what I'd say if a school administrator rounded the corner and caught me documenting the tone-deaf homework assignment. "It's so great your students are studying the important things," I could hear myself saying in an extra-thick southern accent. And what will the students themselves say in ten years, or twenty, if my photographs surface? Will someone tell them they were not woke?

Thanks to social media, and the fact that we get together every few years, I know how everyone turned out. I know who died from weight-loss surgery complications, who married rich men, who never married at all, whose daughter died of cancer at age seven, who became a mystic, who voted for Trump in 2016, who wasted their talent, and who blossomed late, outshining all expectations.

Andrzej died walking his dog on a deserted corner of West Virginia University's campus. It was a heart attack, I think. The dog jogged to the nearest gas station and waited to be rescued. Kirk, my first boyfriend, married a Latina woman, judging by her name, and their house narrowly escaped destruction by wildfire in California. I know this from Facebook. Tim became a college football coach. Donna is a high school English teacher in Tennessee. Brannon died in her thirties. Emma Dare runs a shelter for battered women and children. Robin now wears her hair sleek and straight and is one of the leading decorative painters in the country. She always has some rich person's kitchen cabinets in the back of her big white SUV, ready to be glazed. Reynolds founded a free private school for homeless children in Atlanta. Jenny competes nationally as an amateur golfer and tennis player. There's no more Slave Day at Stuart Hall.

That day in the courthouse, sunlight streamed into the basement through a small window. I wondered if the ladies knew my granddaddy, whom most people in town referred to as "Lawyer Sanders." I held myself back from dropping his name. This whole "mulatto" thing felt very in line with my polyester white wedding dress, which was waiting for me in an upstairs closet at my grandparents' house. Our wedding theme was shaping up to be something you might title "Unassuming and Sweet 50s Nuptials on the Cheap," which I was settling for not only because we were seriously broke but also because it would make me a dutiful daughter. Yes, part of me longed for a midnight-blue silk gown and dangling earrings, for a wedding in Manhattan, where we lived, and maybe a moonlit reception in a restaurant garden in the East Village, but who did I think I was, and anyway I was five months pregnant, leaving me no time to save up money. So there we were in the place I'd called home the longest, and my wedding bouquet was washed-out green hydrangeas in a white plastic holder. The wedding would be in the Baptist church my great-grandmother had attended. My beloved uncle David, a judge, would officiate, and our reception would be walking distance away, up the long gravel driveway, in my grandparents' stately house. It was April, but it snowed half a foot the night before the wedding. My bridesmaids shivered on the front porch for the portrait after the ceremony, snowflakes swirling onto their bare arms. "Suck it up!" I told them.

Why didn't we invite my Stuart Hall girlfriends, or any of my Jannah brothers and sisters? It would have been hard to fit everyone under one roof, but I would have loved to have Reynolds meet Aquil, and Amira meet Uncle Henry and Cousin Becca, and Grandmama see that the black side of my family is beautiful and dignified too. I would have loved to have my nieces and nephews slide down the banister, and my sister Amani, wearing her headscarf or with her braids showing and dyed bright red, as she has them now, sit in my grandparents' library looking at the books

I'd read alone by the fire when I was a child. Nobody would have been harmed and nobody would have felt objectified or miscast or nervous or defensive or disappointed. Even if we'd hoarded delectable details for retelling later, all would have been well, as long as we loved each other.

That day, with the snow outside and eighty-seven of our friends and relatives crowding the downstairs rooms and hallway of my grandparents' house while we waited to sit down for dinner, I noticed the olive-green taper candles in the wall sconces. They'd been there since I could remember, never lit. The sconces flanked a large oil painting of a sailing ship being tossed by high waves. With a strike-anywhere match that I pulled from a little cardboard box I'd found in a drawer, I lit the wicks and enjoyed the glow of the flames, which wobbled and gained strength behind the glass shades. Why have them, I thought, if you're not going to burn them for light someday?

FAT

JENNIFER WEINER

Almost twenty years ago, as a way to haul myself out of the hole in which a bruising breakup had left me, I wrote a novel.

I didn't have an agent, or an editor, or a publishing deal. What I had was the Mac Classic that my father, in one of his occasional reappearances in my life, had bought me just prior to my last year of college, and a spare bedroom, and, thanks to the aforementioned breakup, a lot of free time.

I wrote with the freedom that only first-time novelists ever enjoy, without a single editor or reader or critic looking over my shoulder. I wrote without thinking about how my book would be packaged or into which genre it might fall. I gave my heroine all of my heartache, and a version of my own dysfunctional family, and my plus-size/curvy/plump/fluffy/sturdy body. My fat body. Which was easy to do when there was a good chance that no one besides me would ever read the book, and that, if they did, all they would know of its author was a half-dollar-size, extremely flattering headshot on the jacket.

I finished the book and sent out twenty-five query letters. I got twenty-four rejections, and one request for the first three chapters. That agent, the only one who asked to see the book, finally agreed to represent me. Not only was she confident that she could sell the book, but she also hoped she might get a film deal too. There was just one hitch. "The heroine of this novel is fat," she pronounced. She was on the phone, but I could imagine her thin, lipsticked lips pursing in distaste. "And nobody wants to see a movie about a sad, lonely fat girl."

And there it was. *Fat.* The other F word. The label I'd spent most of my life fighting against and running from. The word that had sentenced me to a decade of medically supervised dieting and Weight Watchers meetings, where I'd sit under flickering fluorescent lights and get weighed in and then preached at, in a secular version of the old familiar sin-and-salvation narrative. I once was lost but now am found. *I once wore a size twenty-two, and now I'm a size eight. I couldn't wear normal clothes or attract guys or fit on amusement park rides or into restaurant booths, and look at me now.* We, the congregants, lapped it up, like so many servings of the zero-point chicken-and-vegetable broth that the program recommended to stave off hunger pangs. There was not even a whiff of a notion that maybe the problem wasn't us, that maybe what needed changing was the fashion industry, or the booths, or the rides, or the men. We, our appetites, our shameful bodies, were the problem. We were what had to change.

When the literary agent told me that she had suggestions, I said, "Of course!" with unseemly eagerness. I desperately wanted my book to be published, for the story to exist somewhere besides my spare bedroom. "Anything," I told the agent when the conversation began. "I'll do anything." Except, it turned out, I didn't want to do that. Not when the heroine's body, and her eventual acceptance of her body, was the meat—no pun intended—of the story. Not when it was a message that I'd hardly ever seen in the world. Maybe I couldn't accept myself the way I was, but I could write a character who could, and if that character existed, if that possibility had been made manifest on the page, maybe someday there was hope. Hope for me, and hope for all the girls and women, and the ones who'd come after we were gone.

I spent a weekend agonizing. On Monday, I told the agent I didn't want to work with her. "We have different visions of this project," I said. Eventually I found another agent, and that agent found me a publisher and, a few weeks after my thirtieth birthday, in a size-eighteen pantsuit, the same brand Rosie O'Donnell used to wear on *The View*, I found myself in a publisher's office being interviewed by the publicity and marketing team. "Are you okay with talking about your own connections to the character?" they asked. The phrasing was as graceful and as delicate as could be, but I knew what they were really asking: *Are you prepared to be a fat woman in public?*

In my spare bedroom in Philadelphia, it had all felt like a fantasy, but there, on the thirteenth floor of a New York City highrise, it felt very real, and I was very scared. *They're going to know,* I thought. Everyone's going to know.

Which was ridiculous, insofar as, if there is anything that's ineluctably, unalterably true, it is this: fat people know we're fat.

Yes. It's true. It's not a secret. It's not something we haven't noticed; it isn't something that we're ever allowed to ignore. We know.

We know every time we walk down the aisle of an airplane, moving oh-so-carefully to keep our hips from bumping the armrests, and we see the looks of fear in the eyes of the seated passengers as we approach and the looks of relief as we pass. It's there in the annoyed sighs of whoever eventually does wind up in the seat beside ours, in the skepticism of whoever's teaching the barre class, in the faces of the other people at the grocery store taking a look inside our cart and thinking, *Bread? Ice cream? Full-fat yogurt? What does she expect?*

We learn it when we're little girls from the playground taunts, from insults shouted out of school buses or car windows. We learn it from the concerned pediatrician or the school nurse who gives us a letter to take home the day that all the kids get weighed and measured. We see our own mothers walk by the mirrors and sigh, or pull on dresses and frown, or sip SlimFast when the rest of the family's eating dinner. We learn it, if we're straight, when men's eyes skip right over us, as if we're a blank space, the place on a gallery wall where a painting might someday hang, or when we're scrolling through Instagram and we click on an ad for a cute dress and learn that the sizes end before we start. We know, we know, we know . . . and yet, every day, in every way, the world finds ways to remind us, to tell us, once again, that we are fat, and that fat is the worst thing that anyone can be. Why? Because, presumably, the fat person could choose to stop being fat.

It's not like being ugly. Plastic surgery aside, most of us are more or less stuck with the faces God gave us.

It's not like being stupid. That, too, is largely innate.

But fat? Fat people *could* change—at least, so goes the logic. We could put down the Twinkies. We could, as one memorable keyboard warrior once suggested to me, "step away from the blog and go for a jog." We could stop being couch potatoes, we could quit digging our graves with a fork, we could stop being a drain on the system with the diabetes that we're surely on our way to having. We could keto, or Paleo, or South Beach or Atkins or Pritikin or Zone or Weight Watch our way to freedom. We could eat less and exercise more.

If you're fat, not only are you physically unappealing, but you're also lazy; you lack determination and drive. You're out of control, you're run by your gluttony, enslaved by your appetites. Think of the words fat goes with: *Fat and lazy. Fat and stupid. Fat bitch. Fat cunt. Fat whore.* (That one always confused me: You're telling me that I'm sexually unappealing, and that I am also trading sex for money? Does that sound like a workable business model?)

Fat is the amplifier, hitched to whatever other poor quality the critic means to highlight—*lazy, stupid, ugly, slutty, slatternly, dumb*—to make it much, much worse. Witness "Mar-a-Lardass," a hashtag originated by Democratic Coalition chairman Jon Cooper, meant to draw attention to President Trump's body.

First people laughed and gleefully piled on, posting photoshopped pictures of the presidential posterior, his love handles or double chins or gut.

Then some progressives spoke up and said the same thing we always say, whether it's Chris Christie or Kim Jong-un being mocked: Can we make fun of his politics or the stupid things he says or the cruel policies he supports or the fact that, I don't know, he had his own half brother killed, and not just his body?

Finally came the revealing backlash: Okay, yes, *technically* we're using the word *lardass*, or posting shots of him eating burgers, but really what we're mocking is his laziness. His narcissism and his entitlement. His incompetence and his sloth.

"To me, #MarALardass isn't about his weight. It's about his obese ego, enormous narcissism and his inflated lifestyle," wrote actress Kristin Johnson.

"It made me think of his laziness/incompetence, i.e., he drags ass . . . chillin at his golf club after saying there's a national emergency," another Twitter user responded.

So *fat* gets turned into shorthand, a three-letter catchall that contains a multitude of sins, and that's before you add in gender. Because even the lardass-iest of men can be successful, financially, politically, romantically, in a larger body. Yes, maybe they'll get mocked, but they can do it. It doesn't typically work that way for women. Statistically, larger women's salaries decrease as their weight increases. We are more likely to be single, to suffer from depression, to not receive raises or promotions, to not see our careers advance, and ultimately, to die younger than our thinner peers.

Moving through the world in a fat body means that you're constantly battling assumptions that you're lazy, or slovenly, or physically unfit. It means that you live with the belief that you're sexually undesirable, that men don't want you, and that there's something suspect about any man who does. It's swallowing the gospel of your own inferiority with every mouthful of food, every breath of air. It's spending your life with your body contorted into a constant cringe of apology, shying away from mirrors or your own reflection, pressing yourself up against the unyielding wall of the airplane with your arms tucked against your sides, cramming yourself into constricting shapewear, trying to keep your unruly wobbles and bulges from imposing on the world; trying to make yourself small.

Men, meanwhile, take up space shamelessly. Once the phrase *manspreading* became popular, I started noticing how men and women, large and small, occupy space in public. On buses and trains, subways and planes, men sit with their feet planted, legs spread wide. Women cross their legs, they fold their arms, they hunch their shoulders and tuck their chins, as if they're playing a game: Simon says make yourself as tiny as possible. Simon says try to be invisible. Simon says, *No, you're still there.*

This is the truth of my big fat life: I've written novels. I've won prizes. I've gotten great jobs and raises and promotions. I've been married (twice!), I've traveled the world, I've completed sprint-distance triathlons and 10K races and biked a hundred miles in a day, I've published op-eds and written books where big girls got happy endings. I've been happy and successful, I have lived my life as fully as I could, as happily as I could, and still, I can tell you that if you want to hurt me, cut me to the quick, shut me up and shut me down, the way to do it is to call me fat.

And I can tell you, too, that when I gave birth to my daughters, after I'd counted their fingers and toes and caressed the soft tops of their downy heads, and cuddled their pearlescent-skinned little bodies close to mine, I thought, *I hope they'll take more after their father's side of the family than mine. I hope they won't be as hungry as I was, all the time. I hope they won't spend their lives battling their weight. I hope they won't be fat.*

I wish it were different. I wish I were different. And I think that my books, going all the way back to that first one, are road maps leading toward a better future where that three-letter word loses its power, where there's no need for euphemisms like *plus-size* or *curvy* or *zaftig* or *Rubenesque*, where we can peel away the stigma until *fat* is just another adjective like *tall* or *brown-haired* or *freckled*, and fat girls are just as deserving of happy endings as thin ones. I hope girls and women have read those books and followed the path I laid out. I hope, someday, to walk it myself.

FEISTY

KATHA POLLITT

Betty Friedan, Danny DeVito, Spike Lee, Bernie Sanders, Maxine Waters, Alexandria Ocasio-Cortez, Larry David, Sarah Silverman, Joan Rivers, Norman Mailer, Lewis Black, Katharine Hepburn, Spencer Tracy, Gore Vidal, St. Catherine of Siena: probably anyone who has ever shown signs of life has been called feisty at some point.

I've been called feisty more times than I can count, and trust me, while no demographic has a monopoly on the adjective, the word is most often applied to Jews, Italians, people of color, fat people, old people, short people, and, of course, women. Especially feminist women and women in politics. Bella Abzug— female, older, plump, Jewish, feminist, politician—was the queen of feist. Even her famous floppy hats announced, *Here I am. Wanna make something of it?*

My friend Lynn thinks *feisty* is a compliment. "It means energetic and passionate," she says. *Feisty* also implies pugnacity, an eagerness for combat, a short fuse. But there's something faintly ridiculous about the word. *Feisty* is incompatible with heroism, nobility, grandeur, and tragedy. It belongs to comedy. Achilles was certainly energetic, passionate, and pugnacious—the very first line of *The Iliad* announces that its subject is the "wrath" of Achilles and its terrible consequences. But *feisty* was never going to be his Homeric epithet. King Lear isn't feisty. While he's vain and hot-tempered and crazy, he's still "every inch a king." And no one would call Ernest Hemingway or Anthony Bourdain feisty, despite their tireless adventuring, pugnacity, and passionate pursuits.

To call someone feisty is a slight in the guise of a compliment. It's a cover word, like *adorable*. That should mean worthy of being adored, like, say, Jesus. Instead, we call kittens and bouquets adorable. Feistiness takes the unpredictable, dangerous energy of anger and renders it funny and harmless. To call someone feisty is to imply they are in the one-down position. It's the one-word version of "You're so cute when you're mad."

Think of *Fearless Girl*, that statue of a little girl facing down the Wall Street bull. The statue was commissioned by an index fund focused on companies with women in senior management. Why a child and not a grown woman, then, like the ones whose skills and triumphs made their companies fund-worthy? Because a grown woman facing the Wall Street bull would look too threatening. She might be confronting the actual situation of women on Wall Street: job discrimination, sexual harassment, lawsuits. She would remind the male brokers and bankers dashing by of their wives. Worse, their ex-wives. But a little girl is a daughter, full of hope and daddy love. *Fearless Girl* tells us that equality is for the next generation. Or maybe the one after that. When women are as feisty as children.

My husband tells me that earlier in our relationship, I admonished him when he called me feisty. "You said it was a putdown. I thought, 'Wow, I'd better watch out!'" (And yes, he did watch out.) More usually, though, once you've been labeled feisty, you're stuck with it. To protest only proves how cute and funny and how feisty you are. Stick with your anger, and you'll be labeled grumpy and humorless. Feminists, of course, are always being called humorless. In fact, women—and feminists—are plenty funny, but until quite recently, their humor had to be carefully calibrated: nothing too shocking, dirty, obnoxious, angry, or, god forbid, man-hating.

For a brief moment, at the end of the 1960s and beginning of the 1970s, second-wave feminists were allowed to speak the serious language of outrage. Then that wrath, for which I was ten or fifteen years too young, was replaced by postfeminism. Remember postfeminism? Angry women, with their endless complaints about child support and low pay and being dumped for women half their age, were out. Instead, there was charm, humor, the gentle domesticity of the style page—or, as editors used to call it, "writing from home": "Why I Bought My Daughter a Barbie," "Top Ten Ways to Get Your Husband to Pick Up His Socks."

I see traces of this even in my own writing. As I mentioned before, I've been called feisty many times. Yet I've spent so much time and energy toning myself down! Smiling at sexists, going for a quip instead of a growl, engaging in conversations the unstated premise of which was that I needed to prove I was worth taking seriously. When I was introduced at a campus lecture by a woman professor who characterized me as "very, very angry," I reassured the audience, "Oh, really, I'm not as angry as all that." She had meant it as a compliment—she was pretty angry herself.

But I was a political writer who wanted to persuade those open to persuasion—those nice liberal men, for example, who thought there'd be no need for abortion if women would just use birth control. Long before *mansplaining* was a word, I noticed that men—poets!—who knew no more than what they'd read in the *New York Times* that morning felt some strange need to instruct me about politics, a subject upon which I've been writing for decades. I listened politely, drew them out, put in my two cents. Sometimes I asked a pointed question—feistily but gently; I didn't want to frighten them—but mostly it seemed easier to smile and raise my eyebrows in a vaguely encouraging way while I let my mind wander until I could excuse myself to get another glass of wine. In my heart, though, I seethed.

Feisty is the flicker of fury that escapes from self-suppression, like the corona that flares around the black disk of a solar eclipse. It's anger minus the energy women expend reassuring men that we like them, that we mean no harm, that more power for us doesn't mean less for them—even though sometimes it does— that, of course, we realize they're good guys. (After all, maybe they are!) Feisty is attractive too. Nobody really wants a doormat. A feisty woman is a bigger prize. You can turn her into a doormat later, when the children come.

Feisty is all those women who manage to accomplish something in the world while also doing whatever else men (and plenty of women) thought women should be doing. It's that 1960s classic, *The I Hate to Cook Book*, in which an amusingly grumpy Peg Bracken satirizes domesticity while also accepting that the wife is chief cook and bottle washer. (Her book, which was rejected by fifteen male editors before a woman bought it, sold three million copies.) It's Elizabeth Carter, the eighteenth-century writer about whom Dr. Johnson harrumphed that a man "is in general better pleased when he has a good dinner upon the table than when his wife talks Greek. My old friend, Mrs. Carter, could make a pudding as well as translate Epictetus." I'll bet Elizabeth Carter, translator and pudding-maker, would have loved *The I Hate to Cook Book*.

I've kept the derivation of the word for last because it really is the last word needed on the subject. *Feisty*, it turns out is derived from a Middle English word meaning "fart." By the early nineteenth century, *feist* had come to mean "small dog." The connection? Ladies, especially old ones, kept lapdogs, upon whom they conveniently blamed their own breaking of wind. So basically, *feisty* means "resembling a small dog, especially one blamed for the farts of old women."

Think about that the next time you are tempted to call someone feisty. Perhaps you should choose a different word, one that does not call to mind annoying, yipping-yapping ankle-biters. Like *passionate* or *energetic* or *persistent*. Or *brave*.

APPENDIX

WORDS YOU SHOULDN'T CALL WOMEN
A Definitive Glossary

angry
Also: abrasive, aggressive, combative

Men aren't angry. They can *get* angry at something or someone: traffic, spilled coffee, a slow line at the bagel store. But for women, anger is adjectival: it's a character flaw, not a passing state. *She's such an angry woman.* An angry woman faces the world entirely from that position. Like a tempest, her anger leaves chaos in its wake: ruined jobs, relationships, family. *Such an angry woman.* An angry woman isn't angry at injustice—her anger is unjust. An angry woman doesn't right wrongs. She is the wrong.

bimbo
Also: airhead, arm candy, ditz, dumb blonde

The beauty of a bimbo is that she's not slutty or swept away by passion. It's just that she was naturally built for sex—and that's lucky for her, because as a ditz, she's too dumb a blonde to do anything else. Thank God there are old, rich men around to allow her to fulfill her destiny as arm candy.

bossy
Also: pushy, overbearing, domineering

Make these verbs and give them to men, and they're awesome. You boss. You push. You dominate. You bear stuff. And that makes sense. A boss, by his very nature, bosses. Ditto someone pushing you—a coach, a teacher, a dude helping you get your car out of the mud. Someone who dominates has already achieved first place. But once you make those words adjectives, they become a rank perhaps someone hasn't quite earned. She's bossy, but who said she's the boss? She's pushy, but who said she could push? She's domineering, but does that mean she's supposed to dominate? Listen—*this* person doing this thing? Does not compute.

catty
Also: bitchy, bitter, cunty

There are so many good things *catty* could mean. It could mean "kills vermin" or "self-cleaning." It could mean "lies on your head" or "Eartha Kitt in a spangly catsuit." But instead, *catty* just means the most absurd thing of all: two women trying to fight with each other. Women should only fight for other people's amusement, in bikinis and in mud. Otherwise, it's just silly, like when they're kickboxing, or voting, or trying to add numbers. They try to scale the wall of being angry but slip down to bitchy. Nothing's really wrong—they're just bitter. All they do is complain, because they're cunts. No, wait. They're just cunty.

difficult

Also: demanding, high maintenance, ball-breaker, battle-ax

Let's save everyone some time and just call *difficult* "in my way." Because for all other situations, difficult is a worthy challenge— something to accomplish, to transcend, to achieve. A champion skier doesn't look down a slope, say, "That looks pretty difficult," and get back on the chairlift. A mathematics professor doesn't watch a student solve a difficult proof and say, "I'm so sorry you had to deal with that bitch." A gamer isn't outraged when he reaches the next level. But no one is happy to reach the apex of a woman's difficulty. A woman's requirements—needing to speak, or wear pants, or control her reproductive system—make her difficult in an entirely different way from a ski slope. A difficult woman is needlessly obstructive, cause for commiseration, can't work with others. She might *break your balls*. But don't worry: it's bad to be easy too.

frigid

Also: prissy, ice queen, cold fish

You're not supposed to be a slut, but you're still supposed to let a man do it. Here are some things you can be: Eager. Willing.

Compliant. Yielding. Agreeable. Out cold. (No, not *cold*. We already discussed that one.) If you refuse to have sex, it's not because you are sleepy, or have to study for a test, or think he should brush his teeth. No, it's because you are so glacial that you can actually make balls blue and dicks cold. That's probably why it's so small right now.

gold digger
Also: lolita, vixen, seductress, siren

If you want sex, you're a slut. If you don't want sex, you're frigid. If you accept that your sole purpose is sex, you're a bimbo. And if you tempt men into sex to get something for yourself—money, power, a decent apartment—you are a gold digger. Note: to think a woman is a gold digger, a man has to think of himself as a gold mine, but this is not difficult for them.

hysterical
Also: hormonal, dramatic, emotional

Another way everything you say can be dismissed is that you did it because Feelings. That means that everything a woman should rationally decide is already off the rails. Women are too emotional to vote. Women are dramatic about "what happened." Nothing is actually wrong—that lady's just hormonal. She has blood coming out of her eyes, her ears, her whatever. Freud, who coined *hysteria* from the Greek word for "uterus," thus made anarchic emotion by default a condition only a woman could have.

Though he did discount the Greeks' theory that hysteria was caused by the "wandering womb," this theory of a roving uterus persisted well into the nineteenth century. Then, physicians theorized it could be returned to its rightful position by childbearing or vigorous sex—as could the woman who owned it.

irrational
Also: illogical, confused, unreasonable

There is no better way to win an argument than to say someone doesn't understand how to think. So woman are not "wrong," or "mistaken," or "misinformed." They don't even get to be liars. No. Women are unskilled at the very act of cogitating, and this is clear simply by what they assert and how they do it. (Stridently, probably.) This whole project is doomed from the start. A man is going to have to explain what your argument should be before he will even argue with you in the first place. But don't worry: you're wrong.

needy
Also: manipulative, psycho, stalker

In a just world, we would replace *needy* with "has standards," *manipulative* with "requires standards to be held up consistently," *psycho* with "objects to repeated failure to meet standards," and *stalker* with "trying to get stuff back." Unfortunately, we live in this one.

slut

Also: slattern, easy, whore, fast, hussy, harlot, loose, jezebel . . .

Wait, you let him do it? Slut. Also, did you know that *hussy* derives from *housewife*, both *slattern* and *slut* originally meant "a slovenly woman," and that an archaic name for dust bunnies is "slut's wool"? That is why an unclean woman is literally an unclean woman. So go have sex. Slut! Now clean the floor.

smart

Also: competent, driven, capable

There's only one response to someone telling you you're smart: "Did I say I wasn't?" Because, while being brilliant or submental or even *super*-smart is cause for comment, the only reason you'd call someone smart is if your default expectation was that she'd be dumb. She is so smart. She's competent. Capable, even. Why isn't she eating fake fruit from the centerpiece, like the other girls?

spunky

Also: spark plug, spitfire, tough cookie, pistol

Wait—women can be angry! At least when it's cute. Look at that spunky gal, being all mad and spirited! What a pistol—she has opinions! Okay, she's a cookie, but she's tough. Of course, to find all this power so touching, you have to believe that women are actually cookies: inherently sweet and crumbly and built to be consumed. That their spunk is ultimately a fruitless project, like a toddler trying to drive a car. But it's hilarious nonetheless. Get out the phone! Honey, be a spitfire! It's *adorable*.

strident

Also: opinionated, judgmental, outspoken

We all have opinions. We all judge. We all speak. But when women state their views, they're somehow intrinsically overdoing it—which means their views can't be trusted. Is a judgment impartial when it's by Judgy McJudgington? Can an opinion be for real if someone just hands them out like candy? That person speaking—they're like Boy, Crying Wolf. And why are they so *strident*? That hurts my throat even to say.

talkative

Also: bubbly, chatterbox, yenta

So many words about women describe a mouth doing what a mouth was not, seemingly, designed to do! While a man who talks a lot is knowledgeable, witty, expansive, a woman who speaks does it *just to speak*. In fact, this is so notable she can be defined entirely by this term *talkative*. Instead of being a noted wit, a good person to have at your dinner party, a talk show host or his straight man, a chatterbox is just chatty. She even has a place to talk that's all hers: a coffee klatch. (Do I need to tell you *klatch* is derived from *klatsch*, the German word for "gossip"? Did I tell you *yenta* also means "gossip"? No. You were with me.)

If you don't like talking over coffee, you can have a ladies' tea, which frees up regular drinking tea for men. Or you can have a hen party, so regular parties are not corrupted. You can also have ladies' or girls' or moms' night out. It's almost like you have to devalue events where women meet and talk, or something.

unlikable

Also: unappealing, cold, unemotional (a.k.a. the Female Candidate Playbook)

As support staff, women are eminently likable. Nurse. Mom. Barista. They fit an approved profile—nurturing, empathetic, getting you your drink. But a woman who wants to be in control of the staff—a.k.a. a boss—has to toss that empathetic shit out the window. Rise to the top, and you give up what we like to think of as your "womanity": being a caring, feeling, loving person. A man doesn't have to be likable to be the boss. He doesn't even need to be likable to be a human. But a woman can't be a boss without suddenly becoming unlikable. And unfortunately, to do *anything*, a woman has to be—you guessed it!—likable.

virago

Also: gorgon, fury, fishwife

Virago originally meant a female warrior. The Furies were three Greek goddesses who dispensed vengeance and retribution toward misbehaving men. *Fishwife* originally meant an attractive, competent businesswoman—collecting cockles one minute, shouting loudly to sell them the next. The Gorgons were three sisters with snakes for hair and the power to turn anyone to stone.

We're taking these back.

ACKNOWLEDGMENTS

First and foremost, I would like to thank the mom pods of Jersey City, who offered crucial encouragement, cover advice, opinions on titles, much-needed childcare, playground brainstorming, and, in at least two cases, essays for this book. Next up is my agent and forever aunt Victoria Skurnick, who stuck with this book through eighty-seven iterations and at least as many unforced errors. Contributors: you delivered fiery and wondrous works beyond my greatest expectations. Facebook commentariat, where would I be without you? Laura Mazer and everybody at Seal— thanks so much for being as enthused about word choice as I am. Many thanks to my family, including Francine Skurnick, Gene Skurnick, Blanche Skurnick, David Skurnick, Felicia Noth, and Miriam Skurnick for their support and hospitality. Thank you to all my friends near and far, who fed me, housed me, spitballed with me, went swimming with me, traveled with me, watched my kid, shot the shit, let me sleep, and generally were the best. And most of all, thanks to my son, Javier, who always, *always* wants to know what that means.

CONTRIBUTORS

Tanzila "Taz" Ahmed is an activist, storyteller, and politico based in Los Angeles. She currently is a campaign strategist at the Asian American new media organizing group 18MillionRising. Taz was honored in 2016 as a White House Champion of Change for AAPI Art and Storytelling. She is cohost of the *#GoodMuslimBadMuslim* podcast. Her third poetry chapbook, *Emdash and Ellipses*, was published in early 2016. Taz curates Desi music at Mishthi Music, where she coproduced *Voices of Our Vote: My #AAPIVote Album* (2016) and *Beats for Bangladesh* (2013). She also makes disruptive art annually with #MuslimVDay cards.

Julianna Baggott has published more than twenty books, including *Harriet Wolf's Seventh Book of Wonders* and *Pure*, both of which were *New York Times* Notable Books of the Year. There are over one hundred foreign editions of Julianna's novels published or forthcoming overseas. Baggott's work has appeared in the *New York Times* Book Review, the *New York Times* Modern Love column, the *Washington Post*, the *Boston Globe*, *Glamour*, and *Best American Poetry* and has been read on NPR's *Here and Now*, *Talk of the Nation*, and *All Things Considered*. She teaches screenwriting at the Florida State University film school.

Stephanie Burt is a professor of English at Harvard and the author of several books of poetry and literary criticism, most recently *Don't Read Poetry: A Book About How to Read Poems* (Basic) and *Advice from the Lights* (Graywolf). She likes comic books about spaceships and mutants.

Carina Chocano is the author of *You Play the Girl: On Playboy Bunnies, Stepford Wives, Train Wrecks, and Other Mixed Messages*, which won the National Book Critics Circle Award for Criticism. She is a contributing writer to the *New York Times Magazine* and has written for *Elle*, *Vogue*, *Rolling Stone*, and many other publications. She lives in Los Angeles.

Amy S. Choi is the cofounder and editorial director of the Mash-Up Americans, a publisher and creative studio that amplifies marginalized voices and celebrates life across cultures. She is a longtime journalist and editor based in Brooklyn, where she lives with her husband and two kids. She specializes in getting people to tell stories they never expected to share, and, lately, SHOUTYCAPS.

Raquel D'Apice has written for *Last Week Tonight with John Oliver*, is the author/illustrator of the parenting guide *Welcome to the Club*, and is the creator of the blog *The Ugly Volvo*. She lives in Jersey City.

Dagmara Domińczyk was born in Poland and emigrated to the United States at the age of seven, when her father, a founding member of the workers' union Solidarity, was granted political asylum. She majored in drama at Carnegie Mellon University and for the past twenty years has starred in films, television, and on and off Broadway. In 2013 her first novel, *The Lullaby of Polish Girls* (Random House), made its debut and was described by the *New York Times* as "a coming of age tale . . . brimming with teary epiphanies, betrayal, and love, as well as the grit of New York City and Kielce." She is currently finishing her second novel. Dominczyk lives in Montclair, New Jersey, with her husband and two sons.

Kate Harding is the author of *Asking for It: The Alarming Rise of Rape Culture* and coeditor of *Nasty Women: Feminism, Resistance, and Revolution in Trump's America.*

Afua Hirsch is a writer, journalist, broadcaster, and former barrister. She is a columnist for the *Guardian* and regularly presents debate and documentaries on the BBC, Sky News, and CNN. *Brit(ish)* is her first book and was awarded a Royal Society of Literature Jerwood Prize for Non-Fiction.

Emily Sanders Hopkins is a writer, artist, and cartoonist. Her cartoons have appeared in the *New Yorker* and elsewhere. She served on active duty in the US Army as an interrogator and Russian linguist from 1989 to 1992 and graduated from West Virginia University before earning a master's in fiction writing from the Writing Seminars at Johns Hopkins University. She has also worked as a magazine publisher, magazine editor, marketing writer, online editorial director, and book ghostwriter. Emily lives in upstate New York with her husband and daughter.

Laura Lippman is the *New York Times* bestselling author of more than twenty crime novels. Her latest is *Lady in the Lake.*

Dahlia Lithwick is a senior editor at Slate. Her work has appeared in the *New York Times*, *Harper's*, the *New Yorker*, the *Washington Post*, the *New Republic*, and *Commentary*, among other places. She is host of *Amicus*, Slate's award-winning biweekly podcast about the law and the Supreme Court. Lithwick won a 2013 National Magazine Award for her columns on the Affordable Care Act. She has been twice awarded an Online

Journalism Award for her legal commentary. She was inducted into the American Academy of Arts and Sciences in October 2018.

Glynnis MacNicol is the author of the memoir *No One Tells You This* and cofounder of TheLi.st. Her work has appeared in the *New York Times*, the *Guardian*, *Forbes*, The Cut, *New York Daily News*, W, and *Town & Country*, among others. She lives in New York City.

Jillian Medoff is the acclaimed author of four novels. Her latest, *This Could Hurt*, an "absorbing workplace drama with heart" (NPR), landed on many 2018 best-of/must-read lists. She also wrote the much-lauded national bestseller *I Couldn't Love You More* and *Hunger Point*, which became an original cable movie starring Christina Hendricks. Along with writing novels, Jillian has had a long and successful career in management consulting. She's worked for a range of employers, including Deloitte and Aon. Now, as a senior consultant with the Segal Group, she advises clients on communication strategies for all aspects of the employee experience.

Winter Miller is an award-winning playwright. Her play *In Darfur* premiered in a sold-out run at the Public Theater and toured nationally. *The Penetration Play*, *Look at Us*, the musical *Amandine*, and what the *New Yorker* called a "quasi comic abortion drama," *Spare Rib*, are among a dozen of her plays. Winter is a founding member of the Obie-winning 13Playwrights. A former journalist, she wrote dozens of articles for the *New York Times*. Eartha Kitt once held her hand for five minutes. Winter lives in Brooklyn and travels when she has the chance. She dedicates this essay to her beloved cat, Gato.

Tova Mirvis is the author of the memoir *The Book of Separation*, which was a *New York Times* Book Review Editor's Choice and was excerpted in the *New York Times* Modern Love column. She has also written three novels, *Visible City*, *The Outside World*, and *The Ladies Auxiliary*, which was a national bestseller. Her essays have appeared in the *Boston Globe Magazine*, the *Washington Post*, *Real Simple*, and *Psychology Today*, and her fiction has been broadcast on National Public Radio. She lives in Newton, Massachusetts, with her family.

Lihle Z. Mtshali is a South African writer and editor who swapped a big African city for a bigger American one, where she freelances for various international publications. She has pivoted from a career as a financial journalist and business editor to writing a column about living in America. Now, after endless sleepless nights, temper tantrums, and foreign objects fished out of tiny mouths, she thinks she has earned enough stripes to be a parenting writer. She spends her days researching how to raise well-balanced children. Lihle lives in the New York City area with her husband and three children and attempts to cook them cookbook-worthy vegan meals every night.

Beth Bich Minh Nguyen is the author of the memoir *Stealing Buddha's Dinner*, the novel *Short Girls*, and the novel *Pioneer Girl*. Her work has received an American Book Award and a PEN/Jerard Fund Award, among other honors, and has been featured in numerous anthologies and university and community reads programs. Nguyen was born in Saigon and grew up in Michigan, where her refugee family was resettled. She is a professor in the MFA in Writing Program at the University of San Francisco, where she teaches fiction and creative nonfiction.

Katha Pollitt is a poet and essayist and a columnist for the *Nation*. She has won many awards and prizes, including a Guggenheim Fellowship, a Whiting Award, and two National Magazine Awards. Her most recent books are *The Mind-Body Problem*, a collection of poems, and *Pro: Reclaiming Abortion Rights*.

Mary Pols is a journalist and the author of a memoir, *Accidentally on Purpose: The True Tale of a Happy Single Mother* (Ecco/Harper Collins). A recipient of a Knight Fellowship, she has been a staff writer at the *Los Angeles Times*, *Seattle Times*, and *Contra Costa Times*. Formerly a movie critic for *Time* and other outlets, she is the editor of *Maine Women Magazine*. Her book criticism appears regularly in *People* magazine and the *New York Times*. She's working on a collection of short stories set on the coast of Maine.

Irina Reyn is the author of three novels, *Mother Country*, *The Imperial Wife*, and *What Happened to Anna K*. Her work has appeared in *Ploughshares*, *One Story*, *Tin House*, *Poets and Writers*, *Town & Country Travel*, and many other publications.

Elizabeth Spiers is the founder of the Insurrection, a political digital messaging firm. She was previously the editor in chief of the *New York Observer* and the founding editor of Gawker. She lives in Brooklyn.

Rebecca Traister is a writer at large for *New York* magazine and a contributing editor at *Elle*. A National Magazine Award finalist, she has written about women in politics, media, and entertainment from a feminist perspective for the *New Republic* and Salon and has also contributed to the *Nation*, the *New York Observer*, the *New York Times*, the *Washington Post*, *Vogue*, *Glamour*, and *Marie Claire*. She is the author of *All the Single Ladies* and the award-winning *Big Girls Don't Cry*. She lives in New York with her family.

Monique Truong was born in the former South Vietnam and came to the United States as a refugee in 1975. Her novels are *The Sweetest Fruits* (Viking, 2019), *Bitter in the Mouth* (Random House, 2010), and *The Book of Salt* (Houghton Mifflin, 2003). She is also an essayist and a librettist. A Guggenheim Fellow, US-Japan Creative Artists Fellow, Visiting Writer at the Helsinki Collegium for Advanced Studies, and Princeton University's Hodder Fellow, Truong was the Sidney Harman Writer-in-Residence at Baruch College in 2016. Truong received her BA in literature from Yale University and her JD from Columbia Law School.

Adaora Udoji's career began at ABC News after she graduated from the UCLA School of Law and the University of Michigan. She reported from Boston to London to Baghdad for ABC, CNN, and public radio. She won numerous awards, including recognition from the National Academy of Television Arts and Sciences and the Alfred I. duPont–Columbia University Award for reporting on the Afghan war and Hurricane Katrina, respectively. She's on the board of NEW INC and advises SXSW Pitch, the VR/AR Association, and the Guggenheim Museum Global Innovation Council. She supports women founders and entrepreneurs—Pipeline Angels, the Helm, and SheEO Radical Generosity—and is an adjunct professor at New York University. She holds dual American and Irish citizenship.

Jennifer Weiner is the number one *New York Times* bestselling author of sixteen books, including *Good in Bed*, *In Her Shoes*, and her memoir, *Hungry Heart: Adventures in Life, Love, and Writing*. A graduate of Princeton University and contributor to the *New York Times* opinion section, Jennifer lives with her family in Philadelphia.

Meg Wolitzer is a novelist whose works include *The Female Persuasion*, *The Interestings*, and *The Wife*, among others. In addition, she is the author of books for young readers, including, most recently, the middle-grade novel *To Night Owl from Dogfish*, which she cowrote with Holly Goldberg Sloan. Wolitzer was the guest editor of *The Best American Short Stories 2017* and is a member of the MFA faculty of Stony Brook Southampton. She lives in New York City.

Credit: Raquel D'Apice

Lizzie Skurnick is the author of *Shelf Discovery: The Teen Classics We Never Stopped Reading* and *That Should Be a Word*, based on the *New York Times* column of the same name. She's the founding editor of Lizzie Skurnick Books, an imprint releasing classic YA fiction, and a contributor to Jezebel, NPR, Topic, *Elle*, the *New York Times*, and many other publications. She teaches at New York University and lives in Jersey City with her son, Javier.